THE STEAL

ALSO BY RACHEL SHTEIR

Gypsy: The Art of the Tease

Striptease: The Untold History of the Girlie Show

THE STEAL

A Cultural History of Shoplifting

RACHEL SHTEIR

THE PENGUIN PRESS   *New York*   2011

THE PENGUIN PRESS
Published by the Penguin Group
Penguin Group (USA) Inc., 375 Hudson Street, New York, New York 10014, U.S.A. • Penguin
Group (Canada), 90 Eglinton Avenue East, Suite 700, Toronto, Ontario, Canada M4P 2Y3
(a division of Pearson Penguin Canada Inc.) • Penguin Books Ltd, 80 Strand, London WC2R 0RL,
England • Penguin Ireland, 25 St Stephen's Green, Dublin 2, Ireland (a division of Penguin Books
Ltd) • Penguin Books Australia Ltd, 250 Camberwell Road, Camberwell, Victoria 3124, Australia
(a division of Pearson Australia Group Pty Ltd) • Penguin Books India Pvt Ltd, 11 Community
Centre, Panchsheel Park, New Delhi – 110 017, India • Penguin Group (NZ), 67 Apollo Drive,
Rosedale, Auckland 0632, New Zealand (a division of Pearson New Zealand Ltd) • Penguin Books
(South Africa) (Pty) Ltd, 24 Sturdee Avenue, Rosebank, Johannesburg 2196, South Africa

Penguin Books Ltd, Registered Offices: 80 Strand, London WC2R 0RL, England

First published in 2011 by The Penguin Press, a member of Penguin Group (USA) Inc.

Grateful acknowledgment is made for permission to reprint excerpts from the following copyrighted
works:
The Adventures of Augie March by Saul Bellow. Copyright Saul Bellow, 1949, 1951, 1952, 1953. Copy-
right renewed Saul Bellow, 1977, 1979, 1980, 1981. Used by permission of Viking Penguin, a member
of Penguin Group (USA) Inc. and The Wylie Agency LLC.
On the Road by Jack Kerouac. Copyright © Jack Kerouac, 1955, 1957. Copyright renewed Stella Ker-
ouac, 1983. Copyright renewed Stella Kerouac and Jan Kerouac, 1985. Used by permission of Viking
Penguin, a member of Penguin Group (USA) Inc.
American Pastoral by Philip Roth. Copyright © 1997 by Philip Roth. Used by permission of Houghton
Miflin Harcourt Publishing Company and The Wylie Agency LLC. All rights reserved.

Shteir, Rachel, 1964–
The steal : a cultural history of shoplifting / Rachel Shteir
p. cm.
Includes bibliographical references.
ISBN 978-1-59420-297-1
1. Shoplifting—History. I. Title.

HV6648.S58 2011   2010047842
364.16'23209—dc22

Printed in the United States of America
1   3   5   7   9   10   8   6   4   2

DESIGNED BY NICOLE LAROCHE

For MK, and for RR

They were not thieves by heredity; they were made. And the manufacture goes on every day. The street and the jail are the factories.

—Jacob Riis, *The Making of an American*

CONTENTS

In fiction the recourse of the powerless is murder. In real life it is petty theft.

—Earl Shorris

Dere's little stealin' like you does, and dere's big stealin' like I does. For de little stealin', dey gits you in jail soon or late. For de big stealin' dey makes you Emperor and puts you in de Hall o' Fame when you croaks.

—Eugene O'Neill, *The Emperor Jones*

INTRODUCTION

It is 4:19 p.m. on December 12, 2001. In the socks and hose area on the first floor of this posh department store, a slight, dark-haired woman wearing a beige three-quarter coat with a tab collar, a black skirt, and boots is struggling under the weight of her shopping bags. Her hair is swept back in a loose ponytail. She has sharp features, and in the creases of her deep-set eyes, you can make out shadows that look like her eyelashes. She is carrying many bags. There is a bulky, dark garment bag, either navy blue or black, which looks like it is stuffed with clothing, and a red, rectangular shopping bag. The woman is also carrying a tote bag and two purses, a white one and a turquoise one. Her thin face might register trouble—fear or guilt or sadness—it is difficult to tell because the surveillance video does not have good resolution.

The backdrop is more clearly visible: She is walking among mirrored pillars and display cases, crystal chandeliers, and caramel-colored wood paneling. All around are socks and stockings made of silk, cashmere, and fine wool. This is not the kind of store that caters to basic needs.

Indeed, in 1938, the architect designed this store to resemble a movie star's home. The first black-and-white photos show sinuously curved walls, elegant Regency furniture, and subdued lighting. There is a sense of spaciousness in these photos. This store was also one of the first ones in the United States to be divided into individual boutiques so that customers would feel as though they had just stumbled out of bed, surrounded by even more fabulous clothes than the ones hanging in their closets. Each boutique conjured a specific destination: Swimwear looked like a tropical resort.

Perhaps it is the harsh color or the low-quality image of the surveillance video, or the metal fixtures or the number of products piled on the shelves, but the store today is cold and uninviting, crowded, devoid of its original elegance. Three handbags the size of small dogs crouch on a wooden end table. The woman is between the hat boutique and the hose boutique of the accessories department when the amount of stuff she is carrying overpowers her. She drops something and squats on the floor to pick it up. She begins messing about in the garment bag and the shopping bag. After a few minutes of shuffling (there is a digital clock in the upper-right-hand corner of the screen and you can see time passing), she crams one or two pairs of socks and some hair bands into the crown of a hat, which she plops on top of the clothing and bags. She hoists herself off the floor and wanders back to the hat section. From a wooden shelf, she takes a floppy black hat and sets it on her head. The tag hangs in front of her ear. She takes off that hat and tries one whose brim hides more of her face.

The woman moves past the cosmetics counters to the up escalator. On the second floor, the hat, the socks, and the headbands are no longer visible. A little while later, a camera picks her up again on the third floor at the Gucci boutique. She is still wearing the second hat, but you cannot see its price tag. She peels a white, strappy dress and some other items from their hangers and piles them on top of her bags. She visits Marc Jacobs, Yves Saint Laurent, Jil Sander, and Chanel and chooses clothing from these boutiques. It is 5:19. She brushes up against a rack of Chanel coats. A camera lingers on her back as she sets foot on the down escalator. Two naked alabaster mannequins recede behind her as she adjusts the garment bag over her shoulder.

The woman is now heading toward the exit. A camera zooms in. She cuts through the shoe department. She glides to the plate-glass doors. Another camera zooms in, this time on her back. Another picks her up from the front and another from her side. She passes a cash register. Her reflection looms in the glass doors as she walks toward them, and just before she pushes past the shoes, she tosses the garment bag once more over her shoulder. She is outside.

Like windup toys set in motion by the department-store Oz, two security guards—a stocky man and a woman in a long, dark skirt—walk stiffly after the woman into the parking lot. You can just make out a confrontation in the shadows. A third guard joins the group. The woman tilts her head, listening. She doesn't resist. It is not as if anyone is a criminal here. When she comes back inside the store, she is flanked by two of the guards. The trio walks back down the marble aisle. The guards have divvied up her bags. There is no tension among them. They appear to be exchanging pleasantries as they stroll to the down escalator. They vanish, their destination the holding room in the basement, where the woman will be interviewed, and where she will be turned over to the police. The screen goes fuzzy. It's 5:37 p.m. in Saks Fifth Avenue, Beverly Hills. Winona Ryder is about to join that notorious category—the celebrity shoplifter.

I watched the videos tracking Ryder in a conference room behind the Beverly Hills courthouse in the summer of 2007. But I first became fascinated by the movie star four years earlier, after I read excerpts from the Court TV transcripts of her trial and studied the few clips of surveillance camera footage posted on the Internet. Along with millions of Americans, I wondered why a Hollywood star would shoplift.

At first I resisted writing about the subject but soon came to realize that there was more to my fascination than prurience or schadenfreude. I am inveterately curious about the boundaries cultures establish: the lines we draw between civilization and barbarism, madness and sanity, the appropriate and the inappropriate. We live by these boundaries. And yet the line we draw for shoplifting is murky: Is it a serious crime worthy of criminal prosecution, or what André Gide would call an *acte gratuit*— an impulsive, unpredictable act, childish, but deserving of forgiveness? Is it a disease or a symbol of greed? How has our response to shoplifting changed over time? Who are the outliers and who are the scapegoats? What does it mean that more and more white-collar shoplifters are caught committing the crime? How is shoplifting connected to the economy and to consumption? Do shoplifters grow up to rob banks and embezzle multinationals?

I wrote this book because, unlike gambling, which has a history, a medicine, and a literature, shoplifting remains unwritten. I met shoplifters by placing ads on Craigslist and by joining listservs for those suffering from obsessive-compulsive disorder. Some shoplifters I literally met at dinner parties or while interviewing people at Starbucks. Psychiatrists and mental health counselors asked their patients if they would talk to me. A handful of probation and police officers, security personnel, and not-for-profit groups serving shoplifters helped, as did a few scholars.

Of the shoplifters in this book, a surprising number of them agreed to talk freely, although many did not want to use their names. But not everyone. "This ends here," a lawyer screamed several times before she hung up on me, even though the story of how she resold the household appliances she shoplifted from a big-box store had gone viral and she had been disbarred. At first when this sort of thing happened—and it happened a lot—I felt ashamed, as though I had stumbled onto an episode of *Candid Camera*. A challenge of this book was to explain, in an era of diminishing privacy, the superheated responses to the crime. Another was to write about shoplifting without collapsing the subject into a "he did it" tabloid headline.

I also looked to the history of the crime, beginning in sixteenth-century London, as urbanization and consumerism made the city into Europe's busiest mercantile capital. In this era, anyone who shoplifted an item worth more than five shillings could be hanged. Shoplifting reappeared in a new guise after the Industrial Revolution in Paris—a cynosure of the alluring retail palace. Treating the style-crazed lifters who frequented the city's new department stores, psychiatrists made the first diagnoses of kleptomania. Although shoplifting emerged in America as early as colonial times, the crime became a symbol here in the 1970s, when the yippies politicized shoplifting into "liberating" and Abbie Hoffman wrote *Steal This Book*, turning the crime into an antiestablishment act. In response, modern antishoplifting technologies were developed, as were modern methods of studying shoplifters. The number of shoplifters skyrocketed. Instances of racial profiling of shoplifters began to be recorded.

Today we see all three interpretations of shoplifting—crime, disease, protest. Increased prison sentences, shame punishments, and over-the-top surveillance techniques have all been employed to curb the crime. Alcoholics Anonymous–inspired shoplifting rehabilitation programs have cropped up all over the country. A new, more ironic international generation of political shoplifters has come into view. More savvy professional shoplifters steal greater quantities and use violence more frequently.

One of this book's projects is to bust myths and preconceived ideas about who is shoplifting now and why it is done. Another is to overturn common wisdom about what is being shoplifted, surveying so-called hot products—the everyday household items and luxury goods most frequently stolen. Besides tracing the various narratives the crime has produced, this book also examines the complex and often contradictory things shoplifting stands for.

Shoplifting today is understudied, but the best analyses show that the crime is everywhere. According to the 2008 Department of Justice annual survey, the Uniform Crime Reports (UCR), over a million shoplifting offenses were committed. As one expert noted, the dollar amount lost to shoplifting is almost more than "the losses suffered by all individual victims of property crimes combined." (In 2008, around 800,000 people were arrested for charges involving marijuana.)

But even the UCR cannot present a full picture of the extent of shoplifting. Critics say that the survey undercounts shoplifting more than other crimes because it is so easy to miss: Video cameras do not always catch the shoplifter. Stores do not always keep good records. Because contributing data to the UCR is voluntary, because many police departments lump all theft crimes together or focus on thefts of large amounts of money or violent robberies, the UCR documents only a partial account of shoplifting. Many states don't have a specific crime called shoplifting on the books. Some stores use euphemisms, calling shoplifting "external theft," to contrast it with "internal theft" (employees stealing), or "customer theft"; others just lump all stealing together.

Despite its shortcomings, the UCR offers one of the more complete pictures of shoplifting. It tells us not only which periods in history have seen shoplifting spikes—more than 150 percent between 1960 and 1970—but that shoplifting sometimes ebbs and flows independent of trends in crime overall. Between 2000 and 2004, even as other property crime including pickpocketing and bicycle theft dropped, shoplifting grew 11.7 percent. The number of people shoplifting also climbed slightly between 2004 and 2008. Year after year, the shoplifting rates of many American cities show substantial upticks: In 2008, shoplifting rose 13.2 percent in Cape Coral, Florida; 18.7 percent in Long Beach, California; 40.6 percent in L.A.; 9.9 percent in San Francisco; and 27.3 percent in Las Vegas. In 2009, shoplifting rose almost 8 percent.

According to the National Association for Shoplifting Prevention (NASP), the number of American shoplifters is 27 million, or 9 percent of the total population. But a massive study of 40,093 Americans—the 2001 National Epidemiologic Survey on Alcohol and Related Conditions (NESARC)—found that 10 percent had a "lifetime prevalence" for it and 11 percent had shoplifted. Ten percent is higher than the percentage of American teenagers who have tried cocaine or used methamphetamines. Ten percent is often cited as the number of Americans estimated to be suffering from depression.

And shoplifting may be even more common. A NASP report estimated that store security catches a person shoplifting one in forty-eight times and informs the police of the incident one in fifty times.

If one obstacle to seeing shoplifting as an epidemic is the dearth of good numbers about the subject, another is the media, which trivialize the crime. News stories about shoplifting usually blame its rise on simple economic downturns and its fall on increased security measures. A 2008 *USA Today* story, "More Consumers, Workers Shoplift as the Economy Slows," like many such stories, relied heavily on the retail industry's assertions: "Retail experts agree that they've seen an increase in shoplifting." The story quotes a National Retail Council study saying that 74 percent of retailers "believed" shoplifting was rising. Retailers "felt" that the economy was forcing people to steal.

What's new about shoplifting today is that it has become a cultural phenomenon—a silent epidemic, driven by pretty much everything, in our era. Some scholars connect it to traditional families' disintegration, the American love of shopping, the downshifting of the middle class, global capitalism, immigration, the replacement of independent stores with big chains, and the lessening of faith's hold on conduct. Shoplifting gets tangled up in American cycles of spending and saving, and boom and bust, and enacts the tension between the rage to consume conspicuously and the intention to live thriftily. The most recent suspects include the Great Recession, the increasing economic divide between rich and poor, and an ineffectual response to the shamelessness of white-collar fraudsters: the shoplifter as the poor man's Bernard Madoff.

Yet many shoplifters see themselves as escape artists, stealing out of inscrutable cravings and unexamined desires. Having lost their old solaces, people shoplift as an anodyne against grief or to avenge themselves against uncontrollable forces or as an act of social aggression, to hurl themselves away from their identities as almost-have-nots. Whatever form shoplifting takes, it is as difficult to stamp out as oil spills or alcoholism.

Shoplifting is further misunderstood because the line between crime and disease has blurred. Although most estimates put the number of kleptomaniacs among shoplifters at between 0 and 8 percent, some experts believe that the disease is far more prevalent. Others contend that so-called shoplifting addiction has replaced kleptomania altogether.

In fact, what we don't know about shoplifting does hurt us. Shoplifting continues to dent retailers' profits. In 2009, the University of Florida National Retail Security Survey (NRSS), the most reliable survey measuring American shrink (goods lost to theft and error), totaled shoplifting for that year at $11.69 billion annually, or about 35 percent of all shrink. According to *Consumer Reports*, the shoplifting "crime tax"—the extra amount that families spend on household products each year when stores raise prices due to loss from the theft—is $450. Stores measure shoplifting—indeed, all shrink—as a percentage of profits, and if that percentage balloons much above 2 percent (the industry average for that year was 1.44 percent), it can lead to layoffs or even to bankruptcy. Profit margins can be thin: Supermarkets operate on margins between 1 and 5 percent, which means that the theft of one $5 heirloom tomato from Whole Foods can require sales of up to $500 to break even.

Richard Hollinger, the criminologist who directs the NRSS, believes that we significantly underestimate shoplifting and its impact. Scholars from other disciplines concur. In 2004, Timothy Jones, a professor of anthropology at the University of Arizona in Tucson, found that shrink in convenience stores represented 24 percent of the profits. According to the 2009 *Global Retail Theft Barometer*, the only international survey of the crime, "There has been a dramatic rise in customer shoplifting related to the recession . . ." in America, and stopping shrink costs Americans more per household than it does any other country. America's multibillion-dollar private security industry—whose bread and butter is store detectives—has been growing at about 5 percent a year.

Just as experts can't agree on why people shoplift, they can't agree on how to stop it. There are behavioral schools of thought. Others put their faith in psychoanalysis, pharmaceuticals, or voodoo. Some, like a judge we will meet in Tennessee, believe in shame. Stores stockpile surveillance and antitheft devices, ensuring that going to the mall will soon resemble enduring TSA procedures at the airport. Many theft prevention techniques recall the repertoire of Buster Keaton, like the one requiring shoppers to leave a shoe at the register. Not everything is vaudeville, though. Chasing shoplifters, store detectives—some of whom have no more than a few days of training—have killed them.

In hyperconsumerist America, where shopping is part of the lifeblood of the economy and the culture, shoplifting takes many shapes and represents many things, some of which cancel each other out. It sits on one side of the struggle over a key aspect of the American identity—in the tension between "getting something for nothing" and "working hard to achieve the American Dream." Shoplifting, like gambling, offers immediate gratification, an apparently effortless (though illegal) way to get ahead. In boom times, much shoplifting, like much shopping, is aspirational. Encouraged to covet what the superrich possess, those who can't afford, go a step further and steal. Yet shoplifting can also be cast as a desperate theft that the little guy commits to rail against big corruption. In the wake of financial frauds perpetrated at the top, such as the prime mortgage bust, which has been justified in the name of necessary risk taking, it is easy to imagine a shoplifter thinking his crime is irrelevant, or should be. In fact, while working on this book, I heard many shoplifters say exactly that. Finally, in our tough economic decade, the crime is also regarded as proof of the failure of the so-called New Thrift—by this depressing logic, frugality alone cannot counter the recession's woes: Americans must shoplift to survive.

Defying easy categorizing, the shoplifting going on—committed by blacks and whites, immigrants and native-borns, men and women, young and old, rich and poor, religious people and nonbelievers—is unsettling, funny, and sad. But the different sentences meted out to rich and poor and black and white reveals the tenacity of prejudice.

Even in our loquacious age, shoplifting produces squirming. Stores dislike talking about it. Retail security experts are reticent about their techniques for various reasons, including "giving the secrets to bad guys," although most secrets can be gleaned from the Internet. One magazine that had assigned me a story on luxury shoplifting decided in the end that publishing it would alienate advertisers. An Orthodox rabbi declined to talk about what shoplifting, if any, existed in his congregation, since doing so, he reckoned, would be "bad for the Jews." Shoplifters were unreliable narrators and "badly brought up," I was told. Philosophers explained to me that the crime was not evil and was therefore not worthy of study. A doctor claimed to be "fearful" that the public would "misunderstand" his research to "cure" kleptomania. But the wisest psychiatrists and psychologists that I encountered understood that any "cure" for shoplifting would require refashioning both social arrangements and the human psyche.

Shoplifting has been a sin, a crime, a confession of sexual repression, a howl of grief, a political yelp, a sign of depression, a badge of identity, and a back door to the American Dream. The act mirrors our collective identity, reflects our shifting moral code, and demonstrates the power that consumption holds over our psyches. The techniques shoplifters use may change; how stores catch the crime and how the law punishes it may change. But shoplifting, whether we find it creepy, or sinister, or even exhilarating, will always ripple through our culture to torment and attract us. Inside stores, these thefts appear when we least expect it.

PART ONE

SHOPLIFTING IN HISTORY

I didn't mean to settle down to a career of stealing.

—Saul Bellow, *Augie March*

1. | THEFT AND PUNISHMENT

There are no malls in the animal kingdom, so there is no shoplifting. Hyenas, grackles, crows, ravens, and other birds and mammals steal from one another, which is determined in part by the species, in part by evolution, and in part by scarcity of food. Some birds filch brightly colored string and lightbulbs to decorate their nests: avian kleptomaniacs. All nonhuman stealing is adaptive, John Marzluff, a professor of biology at the University of Washington in Seattle, and an expert on crows, explains: If you steal, you can provide better, more quickly, and in a greater variety of ways for your offspring and you can spend more time doing things that advance your family, like mating and building your nest. The only difference between bird and human theft, Marzluff says, is that "we're the only [species] who determines whether stealing is good or bad culturally."

Where shoplifting begins depends on where you think the crime falls on that spectrum. Eve was the first shoplifter, a security expert once quipped, adding that being banned from the Garden of Eden and cursed with mortality was not too severe a punishment for a petty thief. Certainly every ancient culture was preoccupied with thieves and how to stop the crime. Around 2500 BC, the laws of Hammurabi, the first set of recorded directives guiding how a society should work, ruled that the penalty for stealing from a rich man should be harsher than that for stealing from a poor one.

In the Iron Age, at the dawn of the eighth century BC, the Greeks invented myths in which clever heroes steal in order to create; sometimes they endure terrible fates, sometimes they escape discipline. Prometheus takes fire from Zeus and gives it to mankind; birds pick at his liver. Hermes, the god of thieves and shepherds, steals cattle from Apollo and presents human beings with milk; Zeus does not punish him at all.

Greek legislators tackled the ethics of theft. In the sixth century BC, Draco—the word "draconian" comes from his name—advocated death for any amount stolen, no matter how small. It took a hundred years for Athenian thinkers to begin to distinguish between the small theft, which society punished, and the large, abstract one committed by a despot, which, defined as tyranny, often went unpunished. These philosophers searched not just to explore whether petty theft merits a lesser punishment, but to understand the sources of different-size and differently ordered thefts, the connections among them, and how who steals matters.

In *The Republic*, Plato asks whether thieves are made or born. His strikingly modern answer is that theft is the fault of both society and the individual. He also connects theft, earning, and hoarding.

Socrates asks, "Then he who is a good keeper of anything is also a good thief?"

Polemachus: "That, I suppose, is to be inferred."

Socrates: "Then if the just man is good at keeping money, he is good at stealing it."

Musing about theft's causes, Aristotle, anticipating the Enlightenment and the 1960s, concluded that thieves reflect a sick social body. The Stoics were less meditative. Once, while beating a slave who said, "It was fated that I steal," Zeno quipped, "And that you should be beaten."

Saint Augustine believed that petty theft was as tantalizing as sex. He begins book 2 of *The Confessions* by nodding to divine law's condemnation of the crime. Recalling Eve's temptation, he describes stealing's sensuous allure and his theft at age sixteen of pears from an orchard with a group of friends: "Yet I lusted to thieve, and did it, compelled by no hunger, nor poverty, but through a cloyedness of well-doing, and a pamperedness of iniquity. . . . Nor cared I to enjoy what I stole, but joyed in the theft and sin itself." Augustine and his friends never even tasted the pears. They fed them to the hogs.

To put an end to this sort of chicanery, the Byzantine emperor Justinian amplified the amount of restitution required, concluding that thieves caught red-handed should pay four times as much as the object's worth, whereas those caught later on without the object should merely pay double. Justinian also made the first observation about the crime's clandestine nature. In "Concerning Theft," a chapter in *The Justinian Institute*, his legal textbook on the subject, he attributes the Latin word for theft, *furtum*, to the jurist Marcus Antistius Labeo, who connected it to *furvus*, the word for black, since theft mostly happens secretly at night.

After the Inquisition, English judges began sentencing thieves to be branded on the thumb instead of the face, since the latter, it was acknowledged, condemned criminals to a life of crime. In France, the brand was in the shape of a V, for *voleur*.

Christian thinkers in this era sought to soften the law's severe sentences for petty theft when it arose out of necessity. On stealing to satisfy hunger, Saint Thomas Aquinas wrote, "It is not theft, properly speaking, to take secretly and use another's property in a case of extreme need: Because that which he takes for the support of his life becomes his own property by reason of that need."

Aquinas also examined the relationship between theft and shame. He concluded that theft was sometimes synonymous with shame; it could sometimes arise out of shame, and sometimes cause shame. He perceived, in other words, the complex web between shame and stealing that still haunts and confounds. Distinguishing between theft and robbery, Aquinas noted that guileful theft is considered more serious because thieves steal at night—a concrete manifestation of their shame. He went on to observe that robbery, which happens during the daytime, is punished more severely.

Aquinas was not the only Christian writer to object to the law's punishing petty theft by death. Responding to the regular hanging of thieves caught in the act, Thomas More asks in *Utopia*, "Be we then so hasty to kill a man for taking a little money?"

For the next three centuries, the answer was yes.

THE LIFTING LAW

In Elizabethan London, milliners, mercers, pawnbrokers, booksellers, opticians, cheese mongers, bird sellers, curriers, serge makers, soap boilers, sailcloth makers, and linen weavers opened beautiful stores with glass windows to display their wares, inviting theft. The first shoplifters, called "lifters," were roving bands of men. In 1591, the year that Shakespeare began the Henriad, the history plays in which "thieves and robbers range abroad unseen," a privately printed pamphlet, *The Second Part of Cony Catching*, described the lifters—and the act itself—the "lift."

The Second Part of Cony Catching (the title refers to a con artist "catching" a dupe) was written by Robert Greene, a rake, playwright, journalist, and friend of Shakespeare and Marlowe who died the following year at age thirty-four. In the chapter "The Discovery of the Lifting Law," Greene, under the pretense of being shocked by this vile crime, instructed would-be "shoplifters"—lifts—how to carry it off.

"Attired in the form of a civil country gentleman," the lift should stride into the store, wearing only hose and doublet (cloakless, he would avoid suspicion), and call to the merchant, "Sirrah, reach me that piece of velvet or satin or that jewel chain or that piece of plate."

The lift should continue to ask the merchant to pile more and more goods on the counter, and eventually, while the merchant's back was turned, a second thief should creep into the store, grab some of it— "garbage" in the trade—and pass it out the window, where a third thief, whom the second pretends to engage in conversation, is strolling by.

"Sir, a word with you. I have a message to do unto you from a very friend of yours, and the errand is of some importance."

If caught, Greene advised, the three thieves should swear innocence and "call for revenge" against those who accused them.

Although these lifters were men, Greene anticipated centuries of women dominating the theft when, in yet another pamphlet, he wrote, "Women are more subtile than the cunningest . . . lift." If "starring the glaze"—slang for breaking glass shop windows with a diamond, nail, or knife—was men's work, lifting was a female crime. Lifting suggested illicit sex and the shame that it incited. "So young and so old a lifter," Cressida jokes about Troilus, punning on "limb-lifter," slang for having sex with a prostitute against a wall.

The word "shoplift" first appeared in the tsunami of pulpy biographies, novels, and guides to criminal haunts printed at the end of the seventeenth century. One picaresque tale depicted the underworld setting that shoplifters prowled through. "Towards Night these Houses are throng'd with People of all sorts and qualities . . . Lifters, Foilers, Bulkers"—the reader is dragged on an anthropological tour of the city's nightspots. *The Ladies Dictionary*, in addition to providing tips on losing weight and fixing hair, described the female shoplifter who might "go into a mercer's shop and there pretend to lay out a great deal of Money; Whereas her whole intent is to convey into her nap a piece of some silk or satin that she may the better facilitate her purpose." Another manual to the criminal element helpfully portrayed this shoplifter as "commonly well clad."

Beneath the shoplifters' fancy clothes lay prostitutes, bounders, con artists, female pimps, and actresses. Mary Frith, aka Moll Cut-Purse, procured, shoplifted, and picked pockets. An anonymously written pamphlet attributed *her* stealing to her "being born under Mercury." But *The Newgate Calendar*, a short, weekly biographical pamphlet about the lives of executed criminals, offered another explanation: Moll stole because she "was so ugly in any dress as never to be wooed nor solicited by any man." Nor, *The Newgate Calendar* added, did this androgyne ever have her period or fall in love. Another Moll, sometime prostitute Moll King, shoplifted to dress better, or maybe to attract better clients. She stole a red petticoat (part of the prostitute's uniform), Flanders lace, and a hair fringe, the front piece of one of the enormous powdered wigs that conferred status on men and women.

Lady shoplifters, sometimes called Amazons or roaring girls, wore pants to pass as men in the underworld and to more easily rob the drunks and scoundrels whose rooms they shared at notorious lodging houses. Diarist Samuel Pepys dwelled for several entries on Maria Carlston. Also called the German Princess, or Mary or Maria Carleton, Carlston performed in a play about her own larcenous adventures. As Mary Blacke, she shoplifted before she was executed.

In the century since Robert Greene's guide was printed, London had doubled in size, becoming the largest and wealthiest city in the world. Londoners scrutinized clothes; the luxury-goods business exploded. A partial inventory of a mercer's shop might include silks and brocades, cloth of silver and gold, Genevan and English velvet, satin, mohairs, and crepes. Such shops were crowded—sometimes as many as sixty customers vied for one salesperson's attention. The shops also established credit, extending the possibilities of what people could buy—if not up front, then by paying usurious interest. Whatever the reasons for the rise in shoplifters, they crimped merchants' profits.

By 1699, under William III, Parliament passed a group of laws increasing punishment for theft. The Shoplifting Act was one of over 150 laws pertaining to theft passed between 1688 and 1800, creating what historians call the Bloody Code—capital punishment for petty crimes. The Shoplifting Act decreed that shoplifting an item worth more than five shillings could get you hanged. (An alternative since 1660, shoplifters' transportation to the North American colonies or to Botany Bay was becoming less practical, as those places were increasingly reluctant to accept England's convicts.) Another part of the law spared those who turned in shoplifters to the police from the duties of serving in public office. William also eliminated "benefit of clergy" for some crimes, including shoplifting items valued over five shillings. (From the fourteenth century, any criminal who could read verse 1 of Psalm 51—the so-called neck verse—from the Bible had escaped with branding on the "meat" of the thumb or, for a few years, on the cheek near the nose instead of transportation or death.)

The Shoplifting Act did not stop shoplifting. Although the murder rate remained low, shoplifting flared, as did theft generally in London, where most historians agree that it comprised the majority of all crimes. Shoplifting was the third most prevalent offense among transported women.

Found guilty, a shoplifter might be rushed to Newgate Prison, where, if she could pay the weekly half-crown rent for the "Master's Side," she could also fill her apartment with comfortable furniture, carpets, books, wine, and even, in one case, servants. There, while waiting to be tried, hanged, or transported, shoplifters and other well-to-do criminals consorted with radicals such as Lord George Gordon, after whom the 1780 Gordon Riots were named. Sentenced to death, the shoplifter might go to the Tyburn Tree, a gallows built in the Middle Ages on the site of what is now Marble Arch in Hyde Park—today one of London's busiest shopping areas. The Tyburn Tree was shaped like a long triangle and supported by three legs, so that the cart from Newgate could be backed directly up to the gallows and groups of criminals could be hanged at once. Thousands of people watched. During the eighteenth century, two-thirds of all executions were for property crimes. Not every shoplifter did the "Tyburn jig," and some merchants protested the Shoplifting Act's severity. By the 1720s, when London's population was 700,000, by one estimate, 10,000 thieves called the city home.

Among the first printed books were biographies of thieves. In these books and in eighteenth-century court records, shoplifters were young, unmarried women fleeing villages and towns (although at least one, Mary Robinson, was a senior citizen) for London. They were anonymous, desirable, available. They also shoplifted differently from men. Whereas men wore cloaks (or went without and used teams), women depended on the pocket, a recent innovation initially designed to protect female shoppers against "purse cutting," a form of pickpocketing. Since the pocket hung freely under the skirt and on top of the hoop, and could be reached through slits in the cloak, shoplifters used it to stash rolls of "Holland," as linen was called. When women were caught shoplifting, they fainted, or tried to sell the merchant stolen fabric, or as a last resort, staged a fight.

Yet for all her popularity, the shoplifter might never have become illustrative of the era if Daniel Defoe had not made her the heroine of the first modern English novel. Published in 1722, *The Fortunes and Misfortunes of the Famous Moll Flanders*, supposedly set forty years earlier, traces the rise of Moll, beginning with her mother, who began *her* life of thievery thanks to "the devil, who began, by the help of an irresistible poverty" as she described it, "even when my necessities were not so great." Written from Moll's point of view at age seventy, *Moll Flanders* is supposedly based on the life of Moll King. The book follows the heroine as she becomes a prostitute, marries, and loses her husband and her income. To support her children, Moll gets drawn into shoplifting.

I pass'd by an apothecary's shop in Leadenhall-street, where I saw lye on a stool just before the compter a little bundle wrapt in a white Cloth; beyond it stood a Maid Servant with her Back to it, looking up towards the top of the Shop, where the Apothecary's Apprentice, as I suppose, was standing upon the compter, with his Back also to the door, and a Candle in his Hand, looking and reaching up to the upper Shelf for something he wanted, so that both were engag'd and no Body else in the Shop.

Moll snatches the bundle. A professional shoplifter trains her to steal a plate, brocaded silk, ribbons, and other expensive items. She catches on. Three days later:

I venturid into a house, where I saw the Doors open, and furnishid myself as I thought verily without being perceivid with two Peices of flowerid Silks, such as they call Brocaded silk, very rich. . . . I was attack'd by two Wenches that came open mouth'd at me just as I was going out at the Door . . . that I had neither broken anything to get in, nor carried anything out, the justice was enclin'd to have releas'd me: but the first saucy Jade that stop'd me, affirming that I was going out with the Goods, but that she stop'd me and pull'd me back as I was upon the Threshold, the Justice upon that point committed me, and I was carried to *Newgate*. . . .

Moll's confession to the court is either ironic or sincere, depending on how seriously you take the book as a cautionary tale. Instead of being hanged, she is transported to America, to riches, respectability, and romantic happiness. Defoe tells his heroine's biography in comic as well as moral language: "I grew as impudent a thief and as dexterous as ever Moll Cutpurse was," she brags.

It is no accident that Defoe, the first modern writer to make a living from his craft, chose a shoplifter as his heroine. Nor that he picked Moll Flanders, a character born from mingling fiction with interviews and newspaper articles who inspired a debate about her real identity. Then, as now, no one knows exactly what happens when a shoplifter steals or why she is doing it. Like espionage or a love affair, the details have to be imagined or conjured.

If the first female shoplifters stole to get ahead, the first so-called thief catchers—organizers of shoplifting gangs who doubled as snitches— walked the thin line between consuming and stealing. These thief catchers were always men. Of all of them, Jonathan Wild—who also "helped" victims recover the objects shoplifters had stolen for a fee—is the most fascinating. Wild was a precursor of Charles Dickens's Fagin, the sinister abuser of shoplifting kids. But in the eighteenth century, Wild's mash-up of buying and stealing and shoplifting and catching shoplifters made him celebrated and defamed.

The man who organized and caught shoplifters was brought down by the crime. In 1725, Wild was tried for shoplifting fifty yards of lace from the shop of Catherine Streham. The judge acquitted him, since it could not be proved that he was on the scene, although he most likely set up the crime. The transcript from his trial reveals how Wild's thieves planned to shoplift or "speak with"—another euphemism—lace from Streham's shop by impersonating demanding customers.

After Wild was hanged, a shoplifting craze hit London, inspiring some merchants to appeal to King George I to establish a large reward for catching shoplifters. This resulted in a wave of executions and in the institutionalizing of the thief catcher, the half shoplifter–half snitch role Wild introduced. But neither of these measures halted the shoplifting spike, which some observers attributed to an underworld protest over Wild's death and others believed was a delayed reaction to the bursting of the South Sea Bubble, a financial catastrophe to rival the great Wall Street crash of 2008. In the rise of small thefts, some saw a revolt against big larceny among the nobility.

Wild became a hero, first commemorated in another semifactual account, possibly also by Daniel Defoe, *The True and Accurate Account of the Life of Jonathan Wild*. Wild then appeared as Peachum in John Gay's satiric play *The Beggar's Opera*, which unfavorably compared merchants, police, and politicians to shoplifters, prostitutes, and fences. Gay's point of view was that everyone was corrupt: The shoplifter was at one with the world. In a conversation among several shoplifting prostitutes, one boasts about the technique of holding the shopkeeper's gaze while she snatches trinkets and another complains about competition.

In *The Life and Death of Jonathan Wild*, Henry Fielding, the satirist, lawyer, and crime-fighting pioneer, writes that one synonym for the crime is "buttock and file," slang for a prostitute. Another is "sneaking budge." But although Fielding founded the first private police force, his explanations for the crime were less those of a crime stopper than a social critic. His manifesto, *An Enquiry into the Causes of the Late Increase of Robbers*, blamed shoplifting on "the increase in luxury among the lower orders of the people" and on consumers' greed: "Indeed, could not the Thief find a Market for his Goods, there would be an absolute End of . . . Shoplifting." Still, in his novel *Tom Jones*, exploring *theatrum mundi*—the idea that the world is a stage—Fielding proposed an even more radical cause of theft. On the stage of London, where what you wore determined status, shoplifting might provide the costumes and props necessary to escape the role you were destined to play.

A handkerchief-shoplifting drama captured international interest by pitting a foreigner against the country he was protecting. In 1756, Christopher William Schroeder, a Hanoverian soldier stationed in England, allegedly shoplifted two silk handkerchiefs from a store in Maidstone, a town about thirty miles from London. (The Hanoverian forces were defending England from France.) Harris, the merchant whose handkerchiefs Schroeder allegedly stole, reported the crime. The press seized on the incident, which became known as the Maidstone Affair, as proof of British corruption and foreign decadence. One question was whether Schroeder should be punished according to local laws, which might hang him, or more benevolent military ones, as his general recommended. After he threatened to withdraw his troops, the general prevailed. That Schroeder was, according to some sources, sentenced to run three times through a gauntlet of three hundred men, each of whom whipped him, did not pacify British nationalists. Nor that the Hanoverian troops withdrew ahead of schedule. The handkerchief shoplifting stood for England's shameful dependence on a foreign power and for the luxury-loving soldiers protecting the nation that invented the Bloody Code.

REVOLUTIONS

In 1778, the satirist John Collett painted a marvelous scene, *Shop-Lifter Detected*. The shoplifter stands in the foreground, dressed in a fashionable yellow-and-pink gown and a white stomacher. She gathers her skirts around her legs, while a boy kneels on the floor in front of her and pulls a lace ribbon from beneath her petticoats, where she had stashed it. He is looking up her skirt. A scandalized older female customer watches. A few rolls of lace and ribbon lie on the floor near the shoplifter's feet. Another man—perhaps the shopkeeper—stands behind her, grasping her upper arms. He appears to be pulling fabric out of her décolletage. The shoplifter is turning her head to look at him, and in a moment, he might embrace her. Through the open door, a peace officer (a precursor of a policeman) bursts, intending to take the shoplifter to Newgate. A small dog is barking. In the corner of the room, on a shelf near the ceiling, sits a statue of Hermes, or Mercury, the god of thieves.

Collett painted *Shop-Lifter Detected* as British soldiers were returning home and taking back the menial jobs women had held during wartime, thus creating a new generation of female shoplifters. The most famous, Elizabeth Barnsley, a real-life Moll Flanders, played the part of an upwardly mobile Londoner. When a Bond Street merchant confronted the twenty-nine-year-old Barnsley and her partner Ann Wheeler as they tried to shoplift eighteen yards of muslin and some Irish cloth, the women denied it. Friends of Lady Spencer, the Duchess of Devonshire, frequent shoppers, and servant owners would never "tumble" cloth, as shoplifting was then called. Those excuses did not prevent the thieves from being arrested, although in court, the bailiff referred to them (perhaps ironically) as "ladies." Barnsley was sentenced to transportation. On the voyage to Botany Bay, she demanded to wear her own clothes, as opposed to the dull uniform of the guilty. But she underwent a conversion onboard. Even before she had arrived in the penal colony, she graduated to midwifery.

The American Revolution inspired all manner of rebellion, including theft. English literature at the end of the eighteenth century abounds with Robin Hoods of both genders. William Godwin's novel *Caleb Williams, or Things as They Are*, gives the leader of the thieves, Captain Raymond, these lines: "We, who are thieves without a licence, are at open war with another set of men who are thieves according to law."

But in England a long half century passed between the end of the American Revolution and the end of hanging shoplifters. Attempts to stop began in 1771, when Mary Jones, an indigent woman whose husband had been impressed by the navy, was hanged for shoplifting a piece of linen to clothe her baby. The Whig orator and politician Sir William Meredith protested, "I do not believe a fouler murder was ever committed against the law, than of this woman by law." In his famous speech, "On Frequent Executions," Meredith pleaded that not only was Jones "young" and "most remarkably handsome"—as if her looks should have prevented her from shoplifting—she was penniless and in debt because her husband had gone off to fight for his country. But even using the word "stolen" to describe the young soldier's impressment failed to convince the House of Commons that hanging a shoplifter was wrong.

In France, a great thinker, Jean-Jacques Rousseau, was remaking petty theft from a sin into a political act committed by citizens to even the score against the aristocracy and the monarchy. Published in 1787, two years before French peasants stormed the Bastille, Rousseau's *Confessions* admits to masturbation, *ménage à trois*, masochism, child abandonment, and petty theft. The volume recounts how, years earlier, while apprenticed to an engraver in Geneva, to help a friend make some money on the side, Rousseau steals asparagus from his master's garden. He steals apples from the cellar. He steals his master's "talent" by using his tools secretly. Then Rousseau gets caught, and the penalty for stealing and the pleasure of doing it become intertwined. "I was convinced that to rob and be punished were inseparable," he writes. "A kind of traffic, in which, if I perform my part of the bargain my master would not be deficient in performing his."

Two years later, at age sixteen, Rousseau graduates to women's trinkets. He has worked as an apprentice in the household of the comtesse de Vercellis for only a few months before her death. From the comtesse's possessions, he steals a pink-and-silver ribbon. When the theft is discovered, Rousseau lies: Marion, a pretty, young cook whom he believed was infatuated with him, gave it to him. In the *Confessions*, he describes how, as the rest of the household staff looks on, he professes his innocence and lays blame on an innocent woman. "I accuse her boldly: she remains confused and speechless, casting a look on me that would have disarmed a demon." Marion apparently ventured her own accusation: "Ah, Rousseau! I believed you were a good fellow! You are making me very unhappy and yet I wouldn't want to be in your place." Both servants were let go.

Though apparently shameless enough in the moment of being accused of the theft, Rousseau was sufficiently responsible to social norms to feel guilty about Marion's fate. He never revealed the details of the incident until writing the *Confessions*. It may have been one of the reasons—the only reason—for his writing them. Yet the childhood thefts and Rousseau's attitude toward stealing also provided the root for some of the most intriguing material in his philosophical treatises, specifically his ideas about forging a new self separate from the one determined by social injustices.

Rousseau ultimately insists that society—not sin—makes us steal. He did not consider thieving to be part of his authentic self. For example, he wondered whether, if he had been questioned in private—as opposed to being publicly shamed—he would have confessed instead of blaming Marion. "Thus I learned to covet, dissemble, lie, and, at length, to steal, a propensity I never felt the least idea of before, though since that time I have never been able entirely to divest myself of it. Desire and inability united naturally led to this vice, which is the reason pilfering is so common among footmen and apprentices."

Echoing Saint Augustine, Rousseau confesses that he stole out of "complaisance," as well, observing "it was not so terrible to thieve as I had imagined" and writing, "I applied myself to thieving with great tranquility."

After the French Revolution, a revolutionary tribunal apparently decided that pregnant women could shoplift with impunity. The Marquis de Sade endorsed theft as a prescription for freedom. In the pamphlet he inserted in his 1795 erotic novel, *Philosophy in the Bedroom*, "Frenchmen! One More Effort If You Wish to Be Republicans!" he writes:

If we glance at the history of ancient times, we will see theft permitted, nay recompensed, in all the Greek republics . . . stealing nourishes courage, strength, skill, tact, in a word, all the virtues useful to a republican system and consequently to our own. Lay partiality aside, and answer me: is theft, whose effect is to distribute wealth more evenly, to be branded as a wrong in our day, under our government, which aims at equality?

Two hundred years later, the French philosopher Michel Foucault describes how the last years of the eighteenth century realized a key "shift from a criminality of blood to a criminality of fraud." Driven by the birth of capitalism, a renewed hunger for material goods, and an escalation in the number of people able to afford such goods, the shift incited theft, a surge in police activities, as well as penalties for the crime—15 percent of people who stole food were executed in the 1790s, as opposed to 5 percent before the Revolution. Ultimately, bourgeois society—not political upheaval, Foucault writes—redoubles theft and its punishment.

"NOTHING WAS VALUED BY ME UNLESS I HAD SUCCEEDED IN PILFERING IT"

According to Alexis de Tocqueville, who on his trip to America transcribed the remarks of Sam Houston, the governor of Tennessee, theft was unknown before the Europeans arrived. "Since then it has been necessary to make laws to prevent theft. Among the Creeks who are beginning to get civilized and have a written penal code, theft is punished by strokes of the whip."

Lacking the tradition of a king as well as England's volume of luxury goods and rigid class system, shoplifting did not immediately catch on in the colonies. Some transported shoplifters continued to practice their crime here, of course. But although the first colonial Americans occasionally hanged thieves and printed their confessions in chapbooks for all to read, many colonies, establishing their own laws, preferred shame punishment. Pennsylvania required restitution be four times the amount of the stolen item. New Englanders favored the ducking stool, the stocks, and the pillory for theft. Overall, Americans reserved hanging for witch-craft, sodomy, espionage, and adultery.

Shoplifting by slaves in colonial America was often treated by the courts as a precursor to flight or other rebellion and was punished severely regardless of the amount stolen. Hannah, an eighteen-year-old mulatto slave who stole "as much Bristol stuff as would make her a Gown and Pettycoat," as well as a handkerchief and a small piece of calico fabric, because her mistress left her naked in the North, would have been fined, branded, or sold to meet a debt. In some states in the South, she might have been hanged.

Men of the Enlightenment, the Founding Fathers opposed capital punishment for theft. Thomas Jefferson proposed its abolition as early as 1776. But when the House of Delegates voted on his proposal nine years later, it was defeated. (Outrage over horse thieves killed it.) "Crimes against property; the punishment in most countries immensely dispro-portionate to the crime," Jefferson wrote in 1792, by which time the majority of states had replaced capital punishment for minor property crimes with public labor and imprisonment.

American writing about theft in general and shoplifting in particu-lar evolved from cautionary tales to Barnumesque bragging. Published in 1803, the first American thief's memoir, more mocking and prurient than redemptive and contrite, casts off shame more dramatically than any British confessions that preceded it. Seth Wyman's *The Life and Adventures of Seth Wyman* not only anticipates our criminal tell-alls today but also presents a new kind of shoplifter.

Wyman is no roaring girl or queen of thieves, as shoplifters were sometimes called. He is a thieving Davy Crockett who crows about his meanness and his quick fingers as skills necessary to survive in the New World. He is a rugged individualist who makes his living by shoplifting. He was born in 1784, in Goffstown, New Hampshire, to a prosperous farmer, another Seth Wyman who fought in the Battle of Bunker Hill, and "a kind, noble-hearted" mother. He writes, "Nothing was valued by me unless I had succeeded in pilfering it . . . and the more value I was obliged to take in stealing an article, the higher I valued it." Wyman began as a toddler stealing shiny silver coins. At thirteen, he stole "a loaf of sugar" from some soldiers. Later, fortified with brandy, he graduated to shoplifting, stealing guns from gunsmiths, gingerbread cakes from bakeries, and cloth from dry-goods stores. He bought a cloak "capacious enough to hold a small family and a pig" and stole mink furs and seven pairs of gloves from an English dry-goods store. Later, after he seduced a tailoress, he had her sew shoplifted cloth into garments. Wyman shoplifted both for his own pleasure and to impress "the fair sex." Imprisoned several times in Massachusetts, he redoubled his larceny when released, only slowing down after marrying a widow who bore him six children.

A thief practically from the cradle, Wyman is yet a representative figure. At times, Americans have celebrated shoplifting's most confessional, violent, and liberational aspects, and at other times have excessively punished the crime. The roots of our forays into shoplifting as a revolutionary act, an aspirational transaction, and a reimagining of the self lie in the first decades of the nineteenth century.

2. KLEPTOS AND REFORMERS

When the first trial of a shoplifter who was not a prostitute or a professional took place in England in the spring of 1800, it turned on the question of whether she really stole or whether she was a victim of dishonest shopkeepers. The trial is notorious because this alleged shoplifter belonged to literary royalty: Jane Leigh Perrot was Jane Austen's aunt. Nine months earlier, she was fifty-four years old and living with her husband in an estate outside Bath and in a house in town. Childless, she suffered from many infirmities, as did her husband.

On the afternoon of August 8, 1799, Leigh Perrot traveled from her country estate to Bath for the day and bought a card of black lace from the milliner's at the south end of Bath Street. The clerk wrapped it up for her. Leigh Perrot left the shop to meet her husband, and they strolled together through the streets. As they passed the milliner's, one of the shopkeepers, a Miss Gregory, ran out to meet them and demanded that Leigh Perrot unwrap her parcel. When Leigh Perrot complied, Gregory found, in addition to the black lace, a card of unpaid-for white lace. Leigh Perrot said that Gregory must have mistakenly rolled it in with the black lace, but right there on the street the woman accused her of shoplifting. According to a pamphlet published at her trial, Leigh Perrot "trembled very much . . . and coloured as red as scarlet."

Gregory and her colleagues waited to formally complain to the mayor, who was occupied with a phalanx of soldiers heading through town. Three days after the alleged shoplifting took place, Leigh Perrot received an anonymous note threatening to tell her friends that she was a thief. Two days later, the mayor and the magistrates arrived at Leigh Perrot's house to arrest her, and though they "lamented their being obliged to commit me . . . to prison I was sent."

Had she been poor, Leigh Perrot would have spent the next seven months in Ilchester Gaol, a day's journey from Bath. Instead, she bribed the warden to stay in his home while she awaited trial. Her husband accompanied her. Although Leigh Perrot could wear her own clothes, she had to eat the greasy toast served by the warden's wife. While at the warden's, Mr. Leigh Perrot received another anonymous letter, this one maintaining that her blackmailer was the shop owner, Mr. Gye. Writing to her cousin Montague Cholmeley in September of that year, Mrs. Leigh Perrot explains the plot as she understands it thus far: Gye, with Miss Gregory's help, framed her for shoplifting, hoping to get paid off for keeping quiet about it. In league with pawnbrokers and fences, he had already tried the same trick on several other unsuspecting shoppers. In October, London judges denied Leigh Perrot's request to be released on bail.

That trial began on the morning of Saturday, March 29, 1800, seven months after Leigh Perrot's arrest, in the Great Castle Hall in Somerset, the site of the 1685 Bloody Assizes, when the notorious Judge Jeffreys sentenced 139 people to death for treason. (Thirty-eight were eventually hanged.) Measuring eighty by twenty feet, the hall could hold two thousand people. That day it was so full that "hundreds" were nearly "pressed to death" and "suffocated," a magazine covering the trial reported.

Three pamphlets about the trial were later printed. One contained a diagram of the shop interior laying out for readers how Leigh Perrot might have shoplifted the lace while the clerk turned her back. In court, Leigh Perrot's friends wept. The accused wore a hat adorned with black lace trim and looked "pale and emaciated." A supposedly neutral eyewitness testified that she saw the alleged shoplifter tuck the lace into her cloak that day in the store. (Leigh Perrot would later object, saying she had not been wearing a cloak.) Mary Kent swore that, having purchased four pairs of gloves at Gye's store, she discovered, upon arriving home, that the package contained five pairs.

One of Leigh Perrot's lawyers, a Mr. Jekyll, delivered what has now become a standard defense for wealthy shoplifters: the absurdity of a woman of Leigh Perrot's stature shoplifting. On this point, Leigh Perrot dictated a statement to Jekyll, who read it in court: "Placed in a situation the most eligible that any woman could desire, with supplies so ample that I was left rich after every wish was gratified; blessed in the affections of the most generous man as a husband, what could induce me to commit such a crime?"

After seven hours of testimony, the jurors—local tradesmen and a schoolteacher—acquitted Leigh Perrot in fifteen minutes. The audience applauded when the verdict was read. But some of Leigh Perrot's enemies were unappeased. They discussed distributing a caricature of her husband's crest with a parrot holding a piece of lace in its beak. The week after the trial, Leigh Perrot complained to her cousins: "That these wretches had marked <u>me</u> for somebody timid enough to be Scared and <u>Rich</u> enough to pay handsomely rather than go through the terrible Proceedings of a public Trial nobody doubts; and by timing it when I had only my Husband with me they were sure that I could have no Evidence against them."

Publicly vindicated, she lived to the age of ninety-two.

Not so fast. In the 1980s, Austen scholars began to unearth new material concluding that Leigh Perrot was a kleptomaniac *avant la lettre*. One recent literary study dredges up an observation from 1832: Thirty years after the trial, her lawyer Joseph Jekyll "considered Mrs. L.P. was a kleptomaniac." A university acquaintance of a distant descendent of Leigh Perrot had it on his authority (according to annotations in a manuscript copy of *Northanger Abbey* in the Victoria and Albert Museum in London) that Leigh Perrot enjoyed stealing. One of her contemporaries reported that Leigh Perrot stole a plant from a nursery four years after the shoplifting charge. Another contemporary, a vicar of a nearby parish, accused Leigh Perrot of buying off the prosecutor. The fate of Jane Austen's aunt invites comparison to our celebrity shoplifting trials today, except that in our ravenously aspirational, democratic world, a jury would likely find her guilty.

Whereas Leigh Perrot's story has been told and retold, the story of Whig Party members fighting to end the Shoplifting Act remains less known. The loudest voice was that of Sir Samuel Romilly, distinguished lawyer, abolitionist, uncle of Peter Roget (creator of *Roget's Thesaurus*), and friend of prison reformer Jeremy Bentham. After the French Revolution, Romilly spent time in Paris, where he was impressed by the work of Denis Diderot and other Enlightenment figures, especially by Cesare Beccaria's 1764 essay, "On Crimes and Punishments," which argued that the certainty of punishment—not its severity—deterred crime. But Romilly's crusade against the Shoplifting Act met strong and unique opposition, unlike capital punishment for pickpocketing, which he succeeded in abolishing immediately.

In 1810, Romilly failed to get the Shoplifting Act repealed in the House of Lords, despite presenting anecdotes and statistics showing that hanging shoplifters did not deter stealing. One of Romilly's opponents, Mr. Windham, asked, "Had not the French Revolution begun with the abolition of capital punishments in every case?" Romilly's most committed adversary, Lord Ellenborough, warned, "I trust your lordships will pause before you assent to an experiment pregnant with danger." Asked whether he considered disemboweling to be a suitable form of punishment, Ellenborough sided with those who supported barbaric ancient sentences. Without hanging, he declared, all that was left was transportation, which criminals viewed as "a summer airing by an easy migration to a milder climate." Those who voted against Romilly's proposition in 1810 included the archbishop of Canterbury and a number of bishops, who contended that overturning capital punishment against pickpocketing several years prior had led to an explosion of that crime, an assertion Romilly disputed, arguing that these divines had conflated more prosecutions with more crime.

Romilly brought up the Shoplifting Act again in 1811, and yet again in 1813, when the vote tilted more to his side—seventy-two yeas as opposed to eleven in 1810—and thirty-four nays. His proposal again failed in the House of Lords. Three years later, not even Romilly's poignant story of a ten-year-old boy awaiting death in Newgate Prison for shoplifting could sway the Lords. In his memoir, Romilly accused his opponents of wanting to "make an example" of the boy. In 1818, the *Morning Chronicle* printed an eloquent speech Romilly made in the House of Commons on what would be his last attempt to overturn the Shoplifting Act. Later that year, Romilly killed himself over grief at his beloved wife Catherine's death.

By the time Romilly's friend, the Scottish legal reformer and lawyer James Mackintosh, took up the cause of repealing the Shoplifting Act two years later, Tory zeal for maintaining it had evaporated. Mackintosh managed to raise the hanging threshold on the monetary amount of the item shoplifted from five to ten shillings. Still, in 1821, sixteen people were hanged for shoplifting. But the following year, the reformers prevailed: The last shoplifter was hanged. In 1832, the House of Lords declassified shoplifting as a capital crime and ended transportation of shoplifters in the bargain.

These legal shifts were due less to Mackintosh's advocacy than a general embracing in England of Enlightenment ideas about crime and punishment. The appointment of the reformer Sir Robert Peel as Home Secretary in 1822 helped. Interested in reforming criminal law, Peel worked to make all of the Bloody Code, including the Shoplifting Act, obsolete. To compensate, he replaced the plainclothes thief catcher with a modern, uniformed British policeman—the bobby—to arrest shoplifters and other petty criminals. Thus Peel turned catching shoplifters into a legitimate occupation, if not a vocation.

Once the Shoplifting Act was decapitalized, British writers repudiated it. Living in Bath as a child, Thomas De Quincey must have been inspired to base his novella *The Household Wreck* on Leigh Perrot's misfortune. But he added a gothic twist. In the 1838 novella, Mr. Barrett, upon being romantically spurned, frames the saintly (and married) Agnes for having "that morning secreted in her muff, and feloniously carried away, a valuable piece of Mechlin lace." Agnes dies in jail. Narrated from the point of view of Agnes's bereaved husband, *The Household Wreck* is a cautionary tale about petty theft transforming an ordinary individual—the husband—into a wreck. But it also depicts a nineteenth-century crowd's transformation at witnessing the hanging of a wealthy shoplifter. "By that time all the world was agitated with the case . . . the nation was convulsed and divided." First published in serial form in 1841, *Barnaby Rudge*, Charles Dickens's novel about the Gordon Riots, uses the furor that erupted over Mary Jones's shoplifting to arraign Victorian attitudes toward the crime. Dickens's hangman, Ned Dennis, wonders how future generations will judge a nation that killed a starving woman for shoplifting.

AN IRRESISTIBLE IMPULSE TO STEAL

The earliest mentions of a stealing disease occur shortly after Leigh Perrot's trial in the now-discredited science of phrenology, which held that you could understand a person's character by measuring his or her skull. In 1801, German phrenology's founder, Franz Joseph Gall, and his colleague, Johann Gaspar Spurzheim, were kicked out of Austria for their theories, which were considered anticlerical. The two men began a multi-year lecture tour across Europe. They wound up in Paris, where they were mostly celebrated. Along the way, they studied the brains of murderers and robbers as well as those of ordinary people. Gall suggested that people steal because of the size of the "organ of the propensity to covet," and ultimately concluded that they also did so out of a "propensity to acquire." Unlike the propensity to murder, which was on top of the head, the one to steal was on the side.

The first parts of Gall and Spurzheim's major work, *The Physiognomical*

System, were published in France in 1810. The volumes include a study of not only plebian thieves but also numerous members of the gentry and royalty who stole. Gall preserves some of their subjects' anonymity, like the man who became a Capuchin monk to escape the possible fatal consequences of his crimes (which continued after he joined the monastery) and "the Countess M***." But he named other petty thieves of note, such as Henry IV of France, the wife of the famous German physician and chemist Hieronymus David Gaubius, and Victor Amadeus II, king of Sardinia, who from 1720 to 1730 "pilfered everywhere objects of little importance." (It is not clear what Gall based these diagnoses on, although Victor Amadeus was known for his penchant for conquering other nation-states.) But Gall revived Defoe and Fielding's view, ventured a century earlier, that society punishes poor thieves more harshly than rich ones. "Petty larcenies are overlooked by the world when they are committed by the rich and polished members of society."

In an era that betrayed the French Revolution's promise, this charge packed more force. If Gall seems almost gleeful outing members of royalty in the shadow of the French Revolution, the alienists—the next generation of scientists, working mostly in France in the 1820s—turned the study of the passions in a less overtly political direction. Though the alienists were interested in pyromania, nymphomania, and trichotillomania (hair-pulling), none of these manias presented as dramatic a legal and moral challenge as kleptomania.

Other roots of the idea of stealing as a disease appear in Philippe Pinel's 1806 *Treatise on Insanity*. Pinel, Napoleon's personal physician, the founder of modern psychology, unchained inmates, originated a more systematic method of diagnosing mental illness, and taught these methods to other physicians at the Salpêtrière Hospital in Paris. In 1816, André Matthey, a Swiss protégé of Pinel, coined the word "klopemania," borrowing from the Greek words *kleptein* (stealing) and *mania* (insanity). He called this type of shoplifting *penchant au vol* and *vol sans necessité*— "desire for theft" and "theft without need," and listed several people "of character" who had committed it. Matthey believed that klopemaniacs' desire to steal was "permanent but is hardly accompanied by mental alienation. Reason is conserved and resists this secret impulse, but the penchant to steal subjugates the will." These theories resulted in courtroom acquittals.

If early medical ideas about klopemania betray the romantic movement's influence on the connection between insanity and crime, Théodore Géricault was one painter who turned to realism to depict mental illness. In 1820, Géricault visited England, where capital punishment for shoplifting was being abolished. Two years later, upon returning to Paris, at age thirty-three, he began to paint portraits of the insane at the request of a friend, a young doctor at the Salpêtrière Hospital. This series of ten portraits, of which only five survive, are melancholy, somber—less case studies than ordinary people. *The Kleptomaniac of Ghent* is neither a madman nor a prosperous burgher. His shabby attire fades beneath his cold, pinched gaze. His indifference to the painter—to anyone who would judge him—implies that he is in the grip of irrational forces of some kind, that the Industrial Revolution as well as an inner revolution have taken their toll. Shame is not a factor; no social reproof can stop him. Nothing in his face reveals remorse.

Another medical advance occurred in 1838, when Pinel's protégés, Jean-Étienne-Dominique Esquirol and C.C.H. Marc, the physician of King Louis-Philippe of France, began work on the disease. Marc renamed it kleptomania and formulated ideas about how conscious those who did it were of their action. He was also the first to use the phrase "the instinctive, irresistible propensity to steal." Esquirol distinguished between those afflicted with this propensity and the criminals who impersonated them. He also discriminated between mental deficiency and insanity, and speculated that a reasonable person could commit an unreasonable act—like kleptomania. His book, *Mental Maladies: A Treatise on Insanity*, linked insanity of all forms, including kleptomania, to melancholy (later known as depression) and showed how it could manifest itself in one particular type of unreasonable act, like shoplifting. He and Marc describe one shoplifter confessing she would have stolen even if the store had been a church. Esquirol also was among the first scientists to notice that kleptomania, which he believed to be the consequence of "moral insanity"—a respectable woman (or man) risking her social status by stealing—is accompanied by dread.

The political writer Pierre-Joseph Proudhon's 1840 book, *What Is Property?*, indirectly proposed a philosophical corollary to artistic and medical summations of why middle-class people were stealing. Despite his famous epigram "Property is theft," Proudhon does not advocate the crime. Eight years before *The Communist Manifesto* was published, though, Proudhon does list the outrages "the inalienable right of property" perpetuates—"the reign of libidinous pleasure," a "hypocritical bourgeois morality," and rents for the ruling class—and argues that the unequal distribution of property is society's leading problem. *What Is Property?* not only shocked and angered many Frenchmen but also angered the July Monarchy, which banned the book.

The construction of Parisian department stores with glittering displays did much to turn kleptomania into a female disease. These stores seemed to persuade middle-class and wealthy women to shoplift and reinforced the idea that the crime *was* shopping's dark side. To lure female customers, stores installed mirrors and adorned enormous display windows with Chinese and Japanese objects and fashions or reproductions of stage sets from popular ballets, operas, or variety shows. Women who a decade earlier would never have left home spent hours in these temples of commerce. But if the dazzle of the modern department store helped to gender kleptomania, so did fashion. As the crinoline became chic, the "kick," "a short overskirt covering an ordinary dress skirt and stitched so that the lining and the skirt made a bag around the body from the waist to the heels," replaced the pocket as a receptacle. Kleptomaniacs tucked handkerchiefs, gloves, lace, candies, scarves, needles, combs, and other trinkets and accessories inside.

The French psychiatrist Ernest-Charles Lasègue, who identified other modern conditions like anorexia and *folie à deux*, was the first to scientifically link kleptomania—now understood to be a women's disease—to

the rise of the department store. Lasègue's colleague M. Letulle introduced several phrases charting the cultural anxiety about middle-class
and wealthy kleptomaniacs—one was "honest thief." Another was "the
madwoman in the store" whom modernity, by multiplying temptation,
was "forcing" to shoplift.

In the crowded, late-nineteenth-century world of French novels with
female kleptomaniacs as heroines, one stands out: Madame de Boves
in Émile Zola's 1883 novel *The Ladies' Paradise*. Consumerism crushes
beautiful, impoverished, forty-year-old Madame de Boves, whereas her
counterpoint, Denise, resisting both material and carnal temptation,
marries the store owner. Set in the eponymous Parisian department
store, *The Ladies' Paradise* depicts de Boves's shoplifting as though her
life depended on it. Gone is the Rousseauian/Proudhonian protest of
shopping's new ideology and the redistribution of the wealth. De Boves
shoplifts to compensate for her husband's affair as her daughter watches,
horrified. When the detective searches de Boves in the back room of the
store, he finds

> flounces of Alençon lace, twelve meters at a thousand francs, which
> were hidden in the depths of her sleeve . . . in her bodice, flat and
> warm, a handkerchief, a fan, a tie, in all about fourteen thousand
> francs worth of lace . . . Madame de Boves had been stealing for
> a year ravaged by furious, imperious needs. The fits got worse,
> increasing until they became a sensual pleasure necessary to her
> existence, causing her to cast aside all prudent considerations, sat-
> isfying her with a pleasure that was all the more eager because she
> risked, under the eyes of a crowd, her name, her pride, and her
> husband's high position. . . . She stole for the pleasure of stealing,
> as one loves for the pleasure of loving, goaded on by desire.

The detective forces de Boves to sign a confession. "Women were
capable of anything when they get carried away by their passion for
clothes," he muses. Yet, like Moll Flanders, de Boves is not unsympa-

thetic. Nor are the real-life female kleptomaniacs whom French news-papers and case studies often described more as children or overexcitable women than hardened criminals. When a kleptomaniac told one foren-sic investigator that she preferred shoplifting to "the father of her chil-dren," the crime was trivialized into the petulant protest of a little girl and glamorized as the longing of an amorous woman, at least in France.

In Victorian England, the more women kleptomania afflicted, the more physicians regarded the disease with disbelief. But this kleptoma-nia seemed to reveal anxiety about the genetic feebleness of monarchs as much as women. Here is an excerpt from the winner of a contest, titled "Prize Essay on Kleptomania, with a View to Determine Whether Klep-tomaniacs Should Be Held Disqualified for Employments of Trust and Authority under the Crown," written by one Henry Allen.

> The personal appearance of kleptomaniacs is easily recognized by many distinct marks. . . . They are commonly tall and stoutly built, but clumsy and badly knit. Their carriage is very noticeable. They walk with a nimble step, carrying the leg rigid from the hip downward and especially stiff at the knee . . . the eyes never look straight. They shift easily from side to side, the glance is habitually aslant. They are of neutral colour, which frequently changes its predominant tint; green when dejected, red when furious.

Somehow, though the monstrous kleptomaniac minister of state was as noticeable as the hunchback of Notre Dame, he was never unmasked. The "prize essay" turned out to be a political treatise rather than a medi-cal one, concluding, "Only in a country of hereditary legislators could it be needful to inquire whether a kleptomaniac is fit for public offices of trust and authority yet as statistics attest, our hereditary legislators are particularly subject to mental derangement."

In 1880, even the eminent British doctor and advocate for mental health, John Charles Bucknill, criticized the ease with which judges—and the public at large—allowed kleptomaniacs to dupe them: "In the slang of the day, a burglar has become a kleptomaniac and a prison a kleptomaniac hospital." As Bucknill knew, the number of middle-class British women pleading the "irresistible impulse" defense for shoplifting had spiked so sharply that laws punishing the crime had to be tightened.

In its condemnation of kleptomania as a euphemism for the shoplifting of the well-to-do, America followed England. More attention was paid to the crime and how to stop it than to the disease and how to cure it. Founded in 1850 as a private security company, the Pinkerton National Detective Agency established a division to catch shoplifters after the Civil War and most of the major department stores took advantage of it. Pinkerton detectives pursued shoplifters, while socialists, transcendentalists, and humorists lampooned kleptomaniacs as proof of democracy's failure. In his 1888 essay "A New Crime," Mark Twain writes, "In these days, too, if a person of good family and high social standing steals anything, they call it KLEPTOMANIA, and send him to the lunatic asylum." Twain was not the only Gilded Age American to lampoon the disease. A lifelong advocate for free speech, suffragism, and a classless society, the anarchist Emma Goldman derided kleptomania. In a speech she gave in 1896 in Pittsburgh, she denounced it as yet another strategy the wealthy enacted to steal from the poor:

Moses, when he came down from Mt. Sinai, brought us ten laws one of which was "Thou Shalt not Steal." This law has come to be applied only to a certain class. For example, a poor starving wretch, dying from hunger and cold, steals bread or clothing or money. Brought before a judge it is demanded of him if he did not know of the Divine prohibition of theft. Then he is given a so-called trial and imprisoned. If the man of wealth steals whole estates, whole factories, entire railroads or immense fortunes on change he is called a "shrewd man" and honored with rank and title [*applause*]. If a rich woman is caught shoplifting the wealthy court has a new word for her and says she is afflicted with "kleptomania" and pities her [*applause and laughter*].

Ida B. Wells, civil rights activist and journalist, was critical of how differently the law punished African Americans and whites for petty theft. The majority of African Americans being lynched were not rapists, but those accused of small offenses such as shoplifting, she complained. And: "Negroes are sent to the workhouse, jail, or penitentiary for stealing five cents of bread whereas white men are rewarded for stealing thousands." Wells also told how, in Philadelphia, a white kleptomaniac accused a young black man of raping her to cover up her shoplifting.

As the historian Elaine S. Abelson points out in her book *When Ladies Go A-Thieving*, the advent of moving pictures provided a new popular forum for skewering the disease as a rich woman's euphemism for shoplifting even as it titillated audiences with scenes of shoplifters getting caught. She describes how, in the 1905 Edison film, *The Kleptomaniac*, the eponymous title character emerges from her brownstone one snowy day and takes her horse-drawn carriage to Macy's, Herald Square. There, pretending to browse, she stashes gloves and scarves in her muff. A second sequence of shots follows, and a second character: An impoverished, single mother departs from her barren flat and her beloved children to grab a loaf of day-old bread the baker has left on the doorstep. Both women are arrested and appear in court. The police let the rich kleptomaniac go and imprison the indigent mother.

Headline-making American kleptomaniacs included a countess, a nurse, and Lizzie Borden, who shoplifted two porcelain paintings four years after allegedly slaughtering her father and stepmother with an axe. Mrs. Ella Castle, a wealthy San Franciscan, filched a fur muff while on vacation in London. Yet these celebrity shoplifters were the exception in that their names were revealed in newspapers. Jane Doe, Maria Miller, Mary Brown, and Mary Smith were aliases who wore thick veils to their court dates to protect their families from the shame of shoplifting. Husbands, though often shocked to receive requests to bail their wives out, complied. If the kleptomaniacs were wealthy, the stores rarely pressed charges. Today's kleptomaniac is tomorrow's big spender.

As European social scientists moved from classifying kleptomania as a biological imperative to classifying it as a new type of social and emotional expression for women, they linked the disease more explicitly to new theories about female sexuality. The pioneering sociologist Emile Durkheim attributed the disease to the temptations bewitching women to deviant acts; for him kleptomaniacs' inability to resist beautiful objects in department stores was about modern life's expansion of what women felt they needed. Although in his 1886 encyclopedia, *Psychopathia Sexualis*, Richard von Krafft-Ebing eschews the word "kleptomania," the sexologist counts some stealing as a fetish, which he defines as a charged interest in an otherwise ordinary body part or activity. He writes that the unfortunate creatures who steal "are the subjects of a deep mental taint," especially those individuals prone to shoplifting handkerchiefs, shoes, and aprons.

The birth of criminal anthropology codified scientists' ideas that kleptomaniacs, mostly women, were born to steal. In *The Female Offender* (1893) Cesare Lombroso wrote: "Shoplifting, which has become so fashionable since the establishment of huge department stores, is a form of occasional crime in which women specialize. The temptation stems from the immense number of articles on display. . . . We saw that fine things are not articles of luxury for women but articles of necessity since they equip them for conquest." This, according to Lombroso, resulted in "women's organic inability to resist stealing."

The idea that kleptomania arises out of female sexual repression was made popular around 1906 by Freud's disciples, who attached the Oedipal myth to the disease, attributing it to infantile revenge fantasies and the castration complex, and sometimes equated shoplifting with sex. Best known as a charismatic anarchist, free-love advocate, and cocaine addict who influenced expressionism and Franz Kafka, Otto Gross was the first psychoanalyst to champian kleptomania as sexual release. Published in 1907, Gross's major work, *The Freudian Moment of Ideogenity and Its Meaning in Kraepelin's Manic Depressive Psychosis*, explores "Case #33," a female kleptomaniac he treated at Emil Kraepelin's visionary clinic in Munich.

Gross portrayed Case #33 more like a lover than a patient, writing that she shoplifted from a desire to "take hold of something forbidden, secretly." In his second book, published two years later, he added: "This broad motive plays a tremendous role in the soul of women, especially of the women belonging to the better classes—not, of course, with regard to property, but in the realm of the erotic." The next Freudian to tackle the disease, Karl Abraham, proposed that kleptomaniacs shoplifted to take revenge on their parents: "So-called kleptomania is often traceable to the fact that a child feels injured or neglected in respect of proofs of love—which we have equated with gifts—or in some way is disturbed in the gratification of its libido. It procures a substitute pleasure for the lost pleasure, and at the same time takes revenge on those who have caused it the supposed injustice."

The most notorious exporter of Freud's theories about kleptomania to America was Wilhelm Stekel, whom the master himself described as "wayward." As early as 1906, Stekel was reading French case studies on department store kleptomania for a paper he was working on about the subject. In one study, a former seamstress becomes sexually aroused stealing silk blouses and is unable to remember what she does with the silk at home. Another silkaholic who was also an ether addict described the "amazing and voluptuous spasm" shoplifting the fabric gave her and ended this confession with a "shiver."

In 1910, Stekel's essay "Sexual Root of Kleptomania" married Gross's theories to those of Abraham and the French studies, proposing that kleptomania, whether it substitutes for a primal sexual urge or expresses an infantile desire for revenge, is all about the repressed id. "The root" of kleptomania is "ungratified sexual instinct," he wrote in one of his most provocative sentences. In 1911, when Mae West had yet to swagger across our stages, Stekel's essay, translated into English, annotated, and published in the *Journal of American Criminal Law and Criminology*, shocked American sensibilities. Harry W. Crane, an esteemed professor at the University of Michigan, bristled in his response: "Doubtless there may be something of sexual symbolism in some of the abnormal acts of some of the psychoses, but to go to the extremes to which the writer in question goes seems absurd."

Once America entered World War I, psychoanalysts on both sides of the Atlantic retreated from the sexual roots of kleptomania and moved toward theories explaining all stealing—including shoplifting—as the behavior of traumatized groups. The massive social and cultural upheaval made Victorian-era ideas about sex appear trivial. When the war ended, Stekel combined psychoanalytic theories with those of mass trauma; he theorized that the carve-up of the Austro-Hungarian and Ottoman empires into nation-states and allied protectorates at the Paris Peace Conference made it difficult to distinguish stealing from winning. In *Peculiarities of Behavior*, he writes: "It is not enough to discover the symbolic meaning of the stolen article. The act in itself has its significant stolen value; it stands for some other act which is a part of the subject's past and it amounts to a game; it is a compulsive repetition."

As psychiatry replaced psychoanalysis, the shift dealt the sexual roots of kleptomania another blow. In 1952, the American Psychiatric Association, in the first edition of the *Diagnostic and Statistical Manual of Mental Disorders (DSM)*, did not mention sexual repression—or even define kleptomania at all. By the 1970s, the rise of pharmacology and the sexual revolution made attributing kleptomania to repression obsolete. Shedding its sexual reputation, shoplifting was reborn as a political action.

3. ABBIE HOFFMAN MEETS THE CHINESE HANDCUFFS

Shoplifting came of age in America in 1965, when the FBI reported that it had jumped 93 percent in the previous five years and was "the nation's fastest-growing form of larceny." The crime was part of President Johnson's Commission on Law Enforcement (the Katzenbach Commission or the Crime Commission); his "Special Message to Congress on Crime and Law Enforcement in the U.S." marked the first time a president ever mentioned shoplifting. The shoplifting spike also inspired three men in different parts of the country to launch the modern antishoplifting technology industry, which in the past half century has claimed multibillion-dollar profits, evoking both rags-to-riches tales and a morality play about the costs of trying to suppress the crime.

Arthur John Minasy was born in 1925 to a Hungarian mother and a Greek father who had settled in America only three years earlier. The family opened a teahouse, Leon's, on Thirty-fourth Street in Manhattan. As Minasy told the *Washington Post* in 1991, growing up on Queens Boulevard, he was not thinking about stopping shoplifting as a career. In fact, he and his friends used to "get marbles and erasers and pencils and tennis balls and kind of drop them in our knickers."

During World War II, Minasy met Jayne Leary on a train from New York to her hometown, St. Louis. He was in uniform. In 1946, the couple married, moved to Woodbury, Long Island, and had their first child. Minasy liked family life, but he was restless. He got his BS in administrative engineering at New York University in 1949 and did graduate work at the Case Institute of Technology in Ohio. After that, he worked as an assistant general manager at the Bulova Watch Company. By the late 1950s, although a consultant at Booz Allen Hamilton, he had tired of inventing things for other people.

In 1962, while a vice president at Belock Instrument Corporation, Minasy worked on a project that interested him more: He helped NASA develop a gyroscope that could run on a spaceship. When his youngest daughter, Kathy, was in sixth grade, she wanted her ears pierced, and he made her clip-on earrings with magnets for clasps. He invented a napkin with a buttonhole at the top so airline diners would not spill soup on their clothes.

Minasy began to hang around the New York City Police Department, where he devised a facial recognition device he called Vaicom (variable image compositor). Noticing that the police hardly arrested any shoplifters, Minasy came up with the idea for what he dubbed "Chinese handcuffs," after the novelty toy that traps your index fingers in a snare. The "handcuffs" would attach a sensitized tag to a piece of clothing and use a radio-wave frequency system to sound an alarm when the shoplifter passed two pedestals at the store exit. If the shoplifter tried to remove the tags, the garments were rendered unwearable.

Minasy's tags changed shoplifter catching. Until this moment, the act was much the same as it had been since the time of Moll Flanders. A few things had been added in the nineteenth century—some stores now hired off-duty cops, called floorwalkers, to protect the merchandise. Their techniques resembled a game of hide-and-seek: Detectives stood for hours inside Trojan horses, or "observation perches"—hollowed-out pillars—peering through one-way mirrors watching for shoplifters. Other stores installed rudimentary pinhole cameras behind mannequins' eyes. But in general, when a store employee found garment tags on the dressing room floor, she would let the shoplifter go rather than arrest "the wrong person," which might incur false-arrest lawsuits and alienate customers.

Analog waves, the technology that allowed Minasy to create the Chinese handcuffs, had existed since Scottish physicist Sir Robert Alexander Watson-Watt developed radar in 1935. Minasy began to build prototypes of tags and pedestals that could "read" analog waves and set off alarms. He dragged pieces of the prototype from his basement workshop into the living room. While he was at the office, Jayne checked the needle gauge. If the prototype system shivered when a car drove by, anything might set off a false alarm in the store.

Minasy applied for his first patent for an electronic article surveillance (EAS) tag in 1966, a year after the FBI announced the shoplifting spike. His inaugural theft protection device was a white plastic rectangular tag or wafer that a salesclerk could clip on a piece of clothing. The pedestal at the door would screech if a shoplifter tried to leave the store. The second version, a round dome with a nipple in the middle, looked like a diaphragm.

Minasy named his company Knogo and set up headquarters in Hicksville, Long Island, not far from his home. Shortly afterward, EAS made Minasy rich. The family moved to an eleven-room house in a swanky part of town. Minasy bought his *first* Rolls-Royce. But his dreams of persuading other industries to adapt EAS foundered. Although he convinced one old-age home to try it to prevent Alzheimer's patients from wandering off, and he hoped hospitals would use it to protect newborns from kidnapping, neither of these applications ever gained traction. Minasy's bread and butter remained retail shoplifting.

In 1977, the company went public. Minasy received a letter from Richard Nixon offering him a job in security. (He turned it down.) Stevie Wonder's people called to ask if he could design something to prevent Stevie from falling off the stage during concerts. (He couldn't.) With many American retailers increasingly concerned about customer lawsuits triggered by EAS, Minasy expanded into Europe. Soon that business generated 75 percent of sales.

Minasy became an industry hero. The *Congressional Record* honored him at the Library of Congress in 1984, a year when Knogo was making about $6 million in profits. Never shy about his accomplishments, Minasy compared his invention to Fulton's steamboat. In 1991, the Smithsonian Institution placed Minasy's tag in the National Museum of American History.

Ronald Assaf, who would supersede Minasy as a businessman, did not meet his rival until 1968, when Knogo's EAS system was already installed in stores. But two years earlier, just as Minasy was applying for his first patent, Assaf was working on his own antishoplifting device. Of Lebanese and Irish origin, Assaf had attended the University of Akron for three years, then dropped out to manage a half dozen supermarkets in Ohio for the Kroger Company, a midwestern chain. All the stores had shoplifting problems, but the Case Avenue store in downtown Akron, which Assaf described as a "mixed" neighborhood, was the worst.

The store had already fired three managers. Assaf tried all the security methods then in vogue: mirrors, detectives, TV cameras. He moved the cigarette rack into the clerk's line of vision; he stopped selling shoes, which shoplifters could wear out of the store, and hosiery, which they tucked into their pockets. He placed mannequins above the meat department so detectives could look down through their eyes and catch shoplifters stealing tenderloin.

Nothing worked. Then Assaf's cousin, Jack Welsch, an amateur inventor who, according to Assaf, had designed a novel pizza cutter, began to experiment with a device similar to Minasy's—an antishoplifting gizmo with a sensitized label that could be attached to products and that pedestals placed at store exits would detect. One day, a big, burly guy came into Assaf's Kroger store, picked up two bottles of wine, looked Assaf in the eye, and walked out. Assaf chased the thief to the railroad tracks but lost him. Fifteen minutes later, Jack Welsch came in to cash a check, and Assaf said, "Jack, if we can invent something to stop shoplifting, we're gonna make a lot of money."

The team hired two University of Michigan engineers to help. In

1966, they borrowed $10,000 and formed JKR—named after Welsch's three children: Jack, Karen, and Randy. But like Minasy, Assaf couldn't get financing at first. So he developed a franchise program to sell the marketing rights in each state; his salesmen formed the lab prototype into handmade units. Assaf's first tag was a piece of paper and an aluminum antenna. The second, a small diode hand-soldered onto the antenna, cost a dollar.

Assaf paid Stephanie's, a small retail clothing store in Akron, $400 a month to pilot the tag. In 1967, JKR produced and installed twenty-five pairs of pedestals on a free trial basis in Akron, Cleveland, and other midwestern cities. Assaf said, "Even more than today, there was no accurate way of calculating shrink; stores generally did inventory twice a year and couldn't measure how much missing stuff had been shoplifted and how much just lost via other means. It was difficult to come up with numbers that could show the product's effectiveness."

Gradually stores began to install the systems. In 1969, now called Sensormatic, Assaf's company went public and raised $12 million. Like Minasy's, Assaf's tags modernized stores' methods of catching shoplifters. Before, the store detective had to see a person shoplifting with his own eyes. Once stores installed tags, catching shoplifters became more objective. Or that was the theory. The detectives were able to rush to the door after the alarm went off when the shoplifter was attempting to leave with the stolen goods. But she could still defend herself by saying that she had forgotten to pay. As more and more stores relied on tags and pedestals, the number of false-arrest lawsuits for shoplifting skyrocketed. Thus Sensormatic and state retail lobby associations worked to broaden existing retail laws or pass new ones allowing stores to stop people if they had probable cause.

Assaf's first tags operated on microwave frequency—as opposed to Knogo's radio frequency tag—and could be detected at a greater distance. Thus, they worked better in the new malls with wide entrances for each store. Called "alligator tags" because of their big "jaws," these tags are removed from garments with a tool resembling a giant nutcracker.

Some retailers acknowledged that shoplifting comprised a significant part of inventory losses, but many others remained skeptical that Assaf's product would help. The decadelong shoplifting spike and the computer revolution (stores used them for inventory) finally helped push Sensormatic into profitability. "Stores began to let salespeople go and shoplifting skyrocketed. Almost out of desperation, stores decided to give EAS an opportunity," Assaf said, adding that his first client, Macy's, installed the tags in the fur department, but years passed before the store used them on designer and ready-to-wear clothing.

Of the other basement inventors, garage engineers, and Saturday-afternoon entrepreneurs who created the antishoplifting technology industry, Peter Stern is typical. While Assaf and Minasy were tinkering with their tags, Stern, an engineer living outside Philadelphia who served as president of a branch of the local public library, asked the director about his problems. The director said: book stealers.

Stern designed his own antishoplifting device—a refined metal detector that picked up signals from small slips of paper lined with a laminate of lightweight conductive metals such as aluminum. These were pasted on books' flyleaves. Libraries at New York University, Yale, and the University of Pennsylvania used this system.

Albert "Ted" Wolf, a prominent local family's scion who worked with Stern, became CEO of a new company founded by Stern dedicated to this technology, later called Checkpoint. Wolf set up headquarters in Barrington, New Jersey, and later, a little farther to the west in Thorofare. In 1974, the two men decided that the library market was too dull and switched to retail and to radio frequency tags. Soon Korvette's, CVS, Walgreens, Urban Outfitters, and the U.S. Postal Service installed the tags Checkpoint manufactured.

EAS drove shoplifters to find new ways to steal, such as using booster bags—shopping bags lined with metal to deflect the electronic technology. In one of the scaremongering articles about the shoplifting surge in this decade, *Kiplinger's Personal Finance* announced, "Strengthened security and crackdowns don't seem to help much."

WHEN "STEALING THIS BOOK" WAS COOL

Just when the technology began to boom, the counterculture introduced a new motive for shoplifting: the revolution. In 1970, a new generation of euphemisms for the crime came into vogue: "Five-finger discount," "liberating," and "ripping off." The same year, two books endorsed the crime as one that belonged to the people: *Do It: Scenarios of the Revolution* and *The Anarchist Cookbook*. Jerry Rubin, a thirty-two-year-old yippie and hero at the trial of the Chicago Seven, wrote *Do It*. William Powell, nineteen, was responsible for the cookbook. Chapter 22 of *Do It*, titled "Money Is Shit—Burning Money, Looting and Shoplifting Can Get You High," is not so much a how-to as a crude celebration of theft. The famous line comes after Rubin tells the story of destroying dollar bills with Abbie Hoffman at the New York Stock Exchange. But even that commemoration of American outlaw cheek fails to prepare readers for Rubin's out-and-out endorsement of shoplifting as an exhilarating, revolutionary act: "All money represents theft . . . shoplifting gets you high. Don't buy. Steal. If you act like it's yours, no one will ask you to pay for it." In "shoplifting gets you high," the yippies found an anthem.

In a chapter on electronics, sabotage, and surveillance, Powell lumps shoplifting in with other pranks such as tapping phones, squirting glue in keyholes at the Stock Exchange, and hot-wiring cars. Like Rubin, Powell makes out liberators to be more discriminating than common thieves: "The revolutionary will steal from large corporations and the common thief will steal from anyone. If you can ever get over the Protestant ethic you will see what I mean." But where Rubin provides epigrams, Powell gives readers "commonsense tactics" in the form of an eleven-point list. Two of the items instruct the would-be revolutionary (shoplifter) how to disguise herself as a civilian: "Operate in pairs with one person holding the employee's attention, the other stealing him blind," and "If caught for shoplifting or robbery never admit to being part of the movement. It will get you more time in jail."

These handbooks of the counterculture mark the first time that any American had argued for shoplifting as a revolutionary act. While Elizabethan pamphlets noted that shoplifters wore silk to disguise themselves as nobility, and Enlightenment memoirs blamed stealing on class inequity, yippie books and articles advised liberators to gear up as establishment squares to steal for politics' sake. In the underground feminist newspaper *Rat*, "Lizzie Liftwell" and "Pearl Paperhanger," reportedly the pen names of Sharon Krebs, later a Weatherwoman, wrote one column, "Rip Off," instructing the would-be shoplifter, who perhaps prior to becoming a revolutionary enjoyed the op-ed page on the commuter train from Connecticut: "If you read a *New York Times*, buy one before you go to the A&P."

The figure most responsible for pushing the shoplifting-as-revolution meme into the mainstream, Abbie Hoffman, was not content with dressing up as the Man. In January 1971, after more than two dozen New York publishers rejected his manuscript, Hoffman scrounged $15,000 from friends and set up Pirate Editions to put out *Steal This Book*. Grove Press distributed the book, which endorsed Hoffman's stealing from rage at bourgeois America's materialism. Barney Rosset, Grove's publisher, wrote me, "We chained the books to the counter (in other words, buy the book, don't steal it)."

Reading *Steal This Book* today gives a sense of how innocent the world used to be: Scamming free plane rides simply by boarding without a ticket is unimaginable in our post-9/11 world. Even some of Hoffman's notes on stealing are a bit dated. "Ripping off . . . is an act of revolutionary love," he writes. A section on free food, invoking Robin Hood, offers a slightly more up-to-date line: "We have been shoplifting from supermarkets on a regular basis without raising the slightest suspicion, ever since they began. . . . We are not alone and the fact that so much stealing goes on and the supermarkets still bring in huge profits shows exactly how much overcharging occurs in the first place." Hoffman includes helpful hints, photos with funny captions, and a bibliography. He also advises that "the food tastes better" shoplifted.

At his best, Hoffman elaborates on how-to: "Sew a plastic bag onto your tee shirt or belt and wear a loose fitting jacket or coat to cover any noticeable bulge," he writes. "Fried chicken is the best and easiest to pocket, or should we say bag." Other tips Hoffman incorporates: Work with a partner to distract security; slide sandwiches between your thighs; cart stolen goods into the ladies' room and rewrap them in the stalls. "Specialized uniforms, such as nun and priest garb, can be most helpful."

In four months, *Steal This Book* sold upward of 100,000 copies. No newspaper would review it. Few radio stations would advertise it. Many states banned it. In Ohio, stores wrapped the state shoplifting law on a brown paper band around the book. Canada seized copies at the border; Doubleday bookstores refused to stock it, blaming the title. Some authors might have seen this as failure; not Hoffman. He set up a table outside the Doubleday store on Fifth Avenue and Fifty-seventh Street and sold books there.

Thirteen New York bookstores declined to sell the book. Only the *San Francisco Chronicle* ran ads. The New Left political journal *Ramparts* published an excerpt as well as an advertisement containing hints on how to steal *Steal This Book* from the nine stores in America carrying it. In Boston at BookMart, "second aisle on the left is the best bet."

A June memo from the FBI's New York office to the Washington office revealed that the government regarded *Steal This Book* as "a man-uel [*sic*] for revolutionary extremists . . . foisted on the reading public by Grove Press." And "In view of the contents of *Steal This Book*, Internal Security Division of Department being queried for an opinion as to whether authorship, distribution, and/or publication constitutes a violation of Federal Law."

Regardless of its legality, *Steal This Book* incited controversy and censorship everywhere. In Coldwater, Michigan, a librarian resigned after the board objected to, among other things, his adding copies of *Steal This Book* to an exhibit about the Chicago Seven, as the mayor put it, "where a ten-year-old could see them." No more than midwestern libraries, the American literary establishment was not ready for *Steal This Book*. In July, *Esquire* writer Dotson Rader convinced John Leonard, then *New*

York Times Book Review editor, to let him review the book. Rader called the book "a hip Boy Scout handbook," used its phobic reception to condemn the timidity of the publishing industry, and described Hoffman as a countercultural Thoreau. "It reads as if Hoffman decided it was time to sit down and advise his children on what to avoid and what was worth having in America." *Steal This Book* "possesses its own peculiarly righteous morality."

Basking in his one positive review, Hoffman descended on Boston, where, accompanied by a reporter, he shoplifted a Currier and Ives coffee table book, giving the clerk at the downtown bookstore the finger after learning that it did not carry *Steal This Book*. In Cambridge, he visited the Harvard Coop, where he demanded that the manager move *Steal This Book* from his office to a display in the front of the store: "Where the f—— do you keep it—in the safe?"

In the wake of *Steal This Book*, Hoffman became a celebrity. He also seemed to have stimulated a shoplifting craze. A Sunday *New York Times Magazine* article, "Ripping Off: The New Lifestyle," led with the lyrics from the Jefferson Airplane song "We Can Be Together": "In order to survive we steal cheat lie" was one lyric, followed by "We are obscene lawless hideous dangerous dirty violent and young." The article then jumped to a scene in which a Harvard Divinity School dropout smokes pot and extols shoplifting's virtues. "Ripping off—stealing, to the uninitiated—is as rapidly becoming part of the counterculture as drugs and rock music," it warned.

The article pits Harvard sociologist Seymour Martin Lipset ("Stealing is stealing even if you call it revolution") against Hoffman's passionate contention that any crime the individual "liberator" commits will never add up to the volume of stealing the big corporations are doing: "Saying that shoplifting accounts for high prices is like saying that people using colored toilet paper are responsible for the ecological mess. All our rip-offs together don't equal one price fixing scheme by General Electric."

That fall, two yippies claimed that Hoffman stole ideas and research for *Steal This Book* from them. One of the malcontents wrote an article for *Rolling Stone* about how the über-ripper-offer ripped him off. *Time* and the *New York Times* covered the kerfuffle and the tribunal Hoffman held in Manhattan to air the charges against himself.

"OUR SO-CALLED SHOPLIFTING CASE"

While Hoffman was a media creation, protected by publicity, reveling in it, and talking about shoplifting as a revolutionary act, in the real world, at the exact same time, an ordinary human being was chewed up for allegedly having committed the crime and by the publicity surrounding it. Being in the spotlight cost him his job, defamed him, and affixed a stigma to him that nothing could erase. Far from seeking to steal to make a political point, what happened that day is barely known. But that this man was victimized by the event shows the reality of shoplifting in the lives of those who have been accused of committing the crime. What Hoffman treated as a joke is grim and earnest. The shame and burden of being exposed as a shoplifter cannot be erased.

In Louisville, Kentucky, the same year Hoffman was promoting *Steal This Book*, a young black photojournalist, Edward Charles Davis, was launching a legal battle over whether a police flyer showing photos of people who had been accused—but not convicted of—shoplifting violated their civil rights. The battle would eventually reach the Supreme Court.

Born in Louisville, Davis began shooting pictures at an early age. His father was an army photographer, and his mother, a social worker, "took pictures as a hobby." The family lived in West End, an African American neighborhood scorched by looting in the riots after Martin Luther King Jr.'s assassination in 1968. Davis attended a local community college and then took to the street to document street protests and young people all over his city.

On June 14, 1971, Davis was detained for allegedly shoplifting several eight-track tapes from Consolidated Sales, a five-and-dime store in the neighborhood. Years later, he said, "I don't remember what happened." Nineteen years old at the time of the alleged shoplifting, Davis was the only black photographer working for the *Louisville Courier-Journal* and the *Louisville Times*. Consolidated Sales declined to prosecute, and the police dismissed the charge. Eighteen months after Davis was detained, though, in November 1972, the police in Louisville and the Tri-Cities, which also comprises Bloomfield and Lafayette, Indiana, printed a flyer with the names and photos of ninety people identified as "subjects known to be active in the criminal field of shoplifting." There was nothing unusual about this. Both police departments had been distributing such flyers for years. Edgar Paul, the police chief in Louisville, and his colleague in the nearby Tri-Cities distributed over a thousand copies of the flyer to local merchants. It did not distinguish between those who had been convicted of shoplifting and those merely detained by stores.

The "active shoplifters" on the flyer are all races, ages; there are slightly more women than men. On every page the logo "active shoplifters" brands them even though their "activeness" did not necessarily lead to a conviction.

When the flyer was circulated, Davis recalled, "my supervisor called me into my office and basically said, 'You need to do something about this.'" Davis hired Daniel T. Taylor III, a lawyer whose specialty was—as an action against him brought before the Kentucky State Bar a few years earlier described it—"civil liberties, civil rights activists, the poor, the disadvantaged."

By the time Eddie Davis appeared in his office, Taylor had defended a number of civil rights cases and sixty-eight capital ones. He had become a pariah to some of the local judges, who tried to disbar him, in part for his connection to radicals like the man he called "the great William Kunstler" and in part for his contrarian temperament. In 1969, one such judge, a conservative who wore a pistol in court, tried to force Taylor's disbarment for *his* theatrical outbursts. (Taylor admitted that "it was possible" that he was "antagonistic," reciting *Spoon River Anthology* in his closing remarks, or staging an associate's entrance with a briefcase with the word "Antics" written on it. He denied, however calling the judge "a dirty son of a bitch.")

In October 1971, a second conservative judge, hearing a case in which Taylor was defending a black man accused of murdering a white police officer, reprimanded the lawyer nine times for contempt. The judge eventually sentenced Taylor to four and a half years. As Taylor liked to joke, William Kunstler had only been sentenced to four years, three months for that offense. He sent Kunstler a telegram: "We try harder."

One description of the trial described Taylor as "the star performer in the center ring of a three-ring circus." The judge settled for calling the star performer flippant and saying that he badgered some witnesses, interrupted others, and was in general disrespectful. Taylor demanded the right to go to trial over the contempt charges, which he was denied. But when the case arrived in the U.S. Supreme Court in the spring of 1974, Taylor was vindicated 8–1. The majority ruled that he had been denied due process and that the Louisville judge, personally embroiled in Taylor's fate, was biased.

Taylor and Davis never discussed whether the photographer had shoplifted or not. The attorney immediately moved the case from the local court, where it had languished, to the Western District Court of Kentucky. Since the flyer depicted alleged criminals and Davis had not been tried in a court of law, it constituted punishment without due process, was unconstitutional, and violated his civil rights, Taylor argued. By then, Davis had quit the paper. "The case made it difficult to get assignments," he said.

The district court dismissed Davis's case. "[T]he facts alleged in this case do not establish that plaintiff has been deprived of any right secured to him by the Constitution of the United States." Taylor appealed. In 1974, the Court of Appeals for the Sixth Circuit ruled in Davis's favor after Taylor attacked the flyer as an "indiscriminate lumping of the innocent and guilty alike." The police chiefs appealed and the case was bumped up to the Supreme Court. Taylor sought to sustain the Sixth Circuit decision. When *Paul v. Davis* was heard at the Supreme Court on November 4, 1975, Eddie Davis was living on food stamps.

In Washington, Davis sat in the front row in the gallery with what

Taylor called his "gang," a group of people who worked on civil rights cases pro bono. Most had traveled from Kentucky and were staying with a Catholic priest in Silver Springs. Although he had been a defendant, Taylor had never argued a case at the Supreme Court.

Carson Porter, the attorney for the police chiefs began by explaining the lower courts' dismissal of Davis's case and by saying that it should never have made it to the Supreme Court. At most, *Paul v. Davis* should have constituted an allegation of defamation; he rejected the argument that the flyer violated "(a) deprivation of constitutional right of privacy or (b) a denial of due process."

In the years prior to *Paul v. Davis*, the court had favored the individual over the state in some rulings on privacy cases. In 1973, *Roe v. Wade* had guaranteed privacy in the matter of abortion. Porter argued that shoplifting was hardly a fundamental right like abortion and that since Davis had not experienced "proof of any type of grievous injury," his civil rights had not been violated. He quoted Albert C. Allen, Davis's boss at the paper: "I have taken no action against this gentleman."

Porter next argued against the precedent that influenced the Sixth Circuit Court of Appeals to rule in Davis's favor. This was based on a 1970 case called *Wisconsin v. Constantineau* in which the police chief of Hartford, Wisconsin, had posted pictures of heavy drinkers in liquor stores and bars and allowed these establishments to decline to serve those pictured for one year. The Supreme Court ruled this DIY Al-Anon to be an abuse of due process.

Justice William Brennan, then the court's most liberal member, objected that the flyer was circulated "without the slightest regard for due process."

Porter replied that because the shoplifter flyer had limited circulation, the chiefs' abuse of Davis's civil rights was less egregious than that of *Constantineau*, which dragged in the whole community. Brennan snapped that accusing someone of shoplifting is more serious than not serving someone a drink. "These fellows have to go through the rest of their lives with what is the apparently untrue label of active shoplifter."

Daniel Taylor, Davis's attorney, spoke at the lectern. In his thick Kentucky accent, he re-presented the flyer and the testimony of Davis's boss at the newspaper, Albert C. Allen, whom he quoted: "Our photographers must be accepted as reasonably honorable and truthful men . . . wherever they go. I felt that in view of this flyer's circulation to members of the community I could not for example assign Mr. Davis in anything in a mercantile assignment."

Taylor's point was that although Allen did not fire Davis, he infringed on his civil rights. Taylor also sought to correct Porter's assertion that the flyer was difficult to get hold of. And he noted that alcoholism was more socially acceptable than shoplifting: "As for *Constantineau*," he drawled, "I couldn't help reflect . . . I would rather be reprobated as a drunk than a thief."

Taylor protested that Davis had never been convicted and yet the police chiefs "characterized him as active in his field." The question of Davis's guilt hung in the air. Porter pointed to Davis's failure to challenge the dismissal of the case years earlier as proving his guilt.

The court overturned the Sixth Circuit's ruling by a vote of 5–3. Justice William Rehnquist wrote the majority opinion, and Justices Warren Burger, Potter Stewart, Harry Blackmun, and Lewis Powell supported him. Brennan filed the dissenting opinion, supported by Justice Thurgood Marshall and Justice Byron White in part. (Justice John Paul Stevens did not participate.) The majority opinion ruled that the police's choice to put Davis on the flyer violated neither his civil nor his constitutional rights. "While we have in a number of our prior cases pointed out the frequently drastic effect of the 'stigma' which may result from defamation by the government in a variety of contexts, this line of cases does not establish the proposition that reputation alone, apart from some more tangible interests such as employment, is either 'liberty' or 'property' by itself sufficient to invoke the procedural protection of the due process clause."

In the dissent, Brennan worried that "the potential of today's decision is frightening for a free people. . . . The court today invites and condones such lawless action by those who wish to inflict punishment without compliance with the procedural safeguards constitutionally required of the criminal justice system."

Legal scholars characterized the decision as defining the Burger court's narrowing of the Fourteenth Amendment and broadening of states' power. The *New York Times* scolded that it meant that "government officials may, in bad faith, defame the innocent." No one paid attention to the question of whether Davis had shoplifted or not, or to how the crime's very stigma influenced Rehnquist's ruling. In his private notes, Blackmun called *Paul v. Davis* "our so-called shoplifting case" to submit that the crime was a trivial matter, not the real issue. One man's reputation did not merit a Supreme Court case. The injury to Davis was not worth the court's time.

Davis still lives in Louisville and still takes pictures. Some of them are archived at the University of Louisville, and others are reproduced in the free community monthly *FORsooth*. Davis photographed the 1985 mayoral campaign of Jerry Abramson; he participates in protests himself, and has over the years made two failed bids for alderman. He sees himself as carrying on the legacy of the great Harlem photographer James Van Der Zee—in showing how history collides with the present, as in the picture he took of Muhammad Ali's daughter standing on Muhammad Ali Boulevard. He views photography as an extension of his activism, serving on the board of the Kentucky Alliance Against Racism and Political Repression, a not-for-profit group devoted to combating social injustice. Some of his work was included in Documenting Dissent, a group exhibit of Louisville street protests at the Speed Art Museum in 2006.

Since the 1970s, though, Davis has never worked as a photojournalist for a mainstream newspaper, instead supporting his art at a variety of jobs: car salesman and more lately audiovisual technician. According to a 2006 article in the *Louisville Courier-Journal*, the very paper he worked for years earlier before his court case, he was "struggling" financially.

On a 2007 local television show, he did not mention the shoplifting case. "I just wish things had turned out different," he told me just before he hung up on me when I asked if he also saw shoplifting as political activism.

A new addition to retail theft laws made some progress in converting shoplifting into a civil act. Called civil restitution, these laws allowed stores to charge shoplifters fees—sometimes many times more than the shoplifted item was worth—and forgo criminal proceedings. In 1975, Washington State passed the first such law. Other states followed suit.

By that time, two out of three of the yippies who had written handbooks promoting shoplifting as a revolutionary act had recanted. After someone broke into his apartment, Rubin wrote, "In advocating stealing as a revolutionary act, I guess I didn't make clear the difference between stealing from General Motors and stealing from me." Powell become an Anglican and renounced *The Anarchist Cookbook*. As early as 1972, Abbie Hoffman had moved on to other obsessions. Shoplifting continued to flourish, albeit beneath the pop culture radar. But a few years ago, even before tough economic times returned, the American Robin Hood reemerged in a disguise that Hoffman might not have recognized.

4. ⁞ ROBIN HOODS 2.0

Like his forefathers, Robin Hood 2.0 steals from the rich and gives to the poor, to which category he might belong. This Robin Hood still shoplifts to redress otherwise uncorrectable social wrongs. But he is known by different names, the hero of generations X or Y: by the oxymoronic label "ethical shoplifter" or the apparently ironic art school locution "tactical interventionist." His influence is part Hoffman. His revived popularity is demonstrated by manifestos like *The Coming Insurrection*, written by the Invisible Committee in 2005 in France, published by Semiotext(e) in Cambridge, Massachusetts, and Los Angeles in 2009, and attacked by Glenn Beck as "evil" in 2010. There is a whiff in such polemics of the graduate school seminar as well as the streets: "'Becoming autonomous' could just as easily mean learning to fight in the street, to occupy empty houses, to cease working, to love each other madly, and to shoplift." Playing the old game of euphemism, Robin Hood 2.0 sometimes substitutes the word "taking" for "shoplifting."

"People secretly applaud those who do not play by the rules. It's a vital fantasy among the law-abiding bourgeois," says Stephen Mihm, author of *A Nation of Counterfeiters: Capitalists, Con Men, and the Making of the United States*, explaining Americans' preoccupation with such figures. Mihm adds that Americans tolerate Robin Hoods and Butch Cassidys

more in times of social tumult. "Whenever there is an economic disloca-
tion, theft rises. We often fall in love with the little thief if there is a big
one at work. The analogs of the robber barons and their rapacious greed
are the small-time thieves in the underworld."

In his popular 1969 book (revised in 2000) *Bandits*, Eric Hobsbawm,
the distinguished nonagenarian British Marxist historian, presents the
figure of the "social bandit" as an individualistic hero, a leader who
appeals to poor people and champions them even as he distances himself
from them. "They are little more than symptoms of their society," and
"the essence of the bandit myth is social redistribution and justice for the
poor." Hobsbawm also maintains that in times of economic stress, the
line between criminal theft and theft as social act blurs. "Bank robbery
might be theoretically punishable by law, like distilling moonshine or (for
most citizens in the 1980s) smuggling goods through customs or illegal
parking, but it was not a real crime. It might in fact be an approved kind
of social justice." But Hobsbawm sees shoplifting as a less communitarian
theft. "I don't think shoplifters are into social redistribution as distinct
from individual redistribution," he told me. "Most shoplifters I know
don't think they are causing their victims an obvious loss."

Adam Weissman, my first Robin Hood 2.0, a sophisticated connois-
seur of twenty-first-century media, does not think of stores as victims.
The media-savvy Weissman was until 2009 a spokesman for Freegan
.info, the website associated with the Freegans, a group most known for
Dumpster-diving—scavenging in Dumpsters for food that supermarkets
have recently tossed. He has appeared on *Life & Style*, the morning TV
show, where he illustrated Dumpster-diving for horrified host Kimora
Lee Simmons and a live audience. He has been the subject of a number
of television documentaries, including several on PBS, and he is quoted
about activism regularly. Victoria's Secret prints its catalogs on unrecy-
cled paper, he told CBS. "Those lacy panties that are advertised are coming at a cost to our planet's environment." The *New York Times* described
him as having "the air of a Latin American revolutionary."

Shoplifting first appeared on the men of Freeganism's alternatives to buying in 1998, when Warren Oakes, the former drummer for the punk rock band Against Me!, wrote an informal manifesto, "Why Freegan," and posted it on the Freegan website. Oakes defined Freeganism as "an anticonsumeristic ethic about eating," which might comprise "Dumpster diving, foraging, bartering, and shoplifting." When I tracked him down, Oakes said that he did not speak for the Freegans. But, he explained, "some Freegans consider shoplifting steaks to be a perfectly acceptable way to get free food while many (including myself) feel that the whole purpose is to use resources that would otherwise be wasted instead of just shoplifting from store shelves." He added, "Shoplifting from a locally owned place was seen as a really shitty thing to do, but shoplifting a toothbrush from Walmart was harmless at worst. Some would say shoplifting from corporations you dislike was direct action sabotage against them. I wouldn't go that far, but there was a time when I could morally defend the concept."

When I called Weissman to ask for an interview, he at first seemed reluctant to talk about shoplifting as part of Freeganism. He e-mailed me to set the terms of the conversation. "Well, I don't drink coffee and don't buy beverages/food in general, but am fine with meeting you." I said I would like to meet with him, since he was the spokesman for the website Freegan.info. Like Oakes, Weissman said that although he was a spokesperson for the website, he did not speak for the Freegans. He spoke as "an individual."

I arrived early for our rendezvous at noon in the café at the McNally Jackson bookstore in SoHo, but the tables were too close for a chat about shoplifting. So I decamped to a stoop across the street and waited. Forty-five minutes later, a disheveled Weissman appeared, apologizing. He had not known where the bookstore was, and since he didn't own a cell phone, he could not call.

Thirty-one, slight, with pale skin, Weissman, his black hair stuffed into a short ponytail, arrived at our meeting wearing a full beard, a blue coat, rumpled khakis, and a heavy, grayish sweater. He spread his dusty coat out over the hot stoop and we sat down on it. Except for Metro-Cards, Weissman has not bought more than a potato chip since he was seventeen. Spending money equals wasting it. But shoplifting is another matter. "Shoplifting is the most controversial topic in the Freegan community," he told me. "Even to have the discussion [about whether shoplifting was a legitimate Freegan act] is controversial."

The son of a pediatrician and a teacher, Weissman grew up in Woodcliff Lake, a prosperous town in Bergen County, New Jersey. He attended four high schools. In ninth grade, "private school was forced upon me," because at public school he kept getting beaten up. He didn't know why. In 1999, instead of applying to college, he began to coordinate political evenings at the Environmental Justice and Social Activist Center at Wetlands, a nightclub and forum in Tribeca. He has been doing little else since then. His parents accepted his vocation, more or less. "It's not what they would have chosen. They keep suggesting I go to law school. At my age, it's too late."

Weissman launched into the history of the Freegan attitude toward shoplifting, which he saw as part of the movement's attitude toward property, with gusto. The Freegans, he said, claim as antecedents Depression-era hoboes; the Diggers, the seventeenth-century Protestant utopians who believed that they, like the nobility, should have the right to own land; the back-to-the-land movement; and Eastern philosophy.

Were they organized? I interrupted. He looked startled. The Freegans were against organization. Their organization was an antiorganization. To ask if they were organized was to miss the point. And Weissman's "guidelines" for Freegan shoplifting could not be construed as "rules," he cautioned: Food was okay, even organic food. Fur coats and iPods were not okay, because they were luxury products. "Fur coats should be burned," Weissman said, chuckling. "Ninety percent of the stuff we buy we don't need." Reselling shoplifted merchandise was not okay. "We don't want anyone to make a profit." To the Hoffmanesque credo that it was okay to shoplift from a "corporate monolith" but not a mom-and-pop business, he added that shoplifting from thrift stores was not okay unless the owners exploited their salespeople or mislabeled the store "vintage." Coca-Cola, coffee, and chocolate could be shoplifted anytime because the companies manufacturing them exploit their workers.

Like Oakes, Weissman said that shoplifting is one "strategy"—Dumpster-diving, graffiti, and squatting are others—to finance a life free from obligation, "like Thoreau's." And like many self-described anarchists I met, Weissman not only gave these "strategies" equal weight, he proselytized for them. "We shouldn't ask, Is it ethical to shoplift? Rather we should ask, Is it ethical to buy?"

Not all Freegans agreed that this was the question. Madeline Nelson, a Freegan who in a former life had worked for Barnes & Noble, asked rhetorically, "Is shoplifting a Freegan issue? I think not."

But on the stoop, Weissman had an answer for everything. He mentioned Proudhon as an inspiration, and when I wondered aloud if Proudhon really advocated shoplifting, he turned to Peter Kropotkin, the nineteenth-century Russian anarchist and colleague of Emma Goldman who advocated the "right" to expropriation.

Could I use his real name? I interjected.

If I was going to say that he supported shoplifting philosophically, I could. But not if I was going to say he actually shoplifted.

Had he actually shoplifted?

He tilted his head to the right like a bird looking at the ground to see if a worm was there. "I don't want to say I never have."

Shoplifting, he said, posed a theoretical problem for Freegans most concerned with consuming less. "By shoplifting we are creating more demand for products. So unless you set out to shoplift or destroy a particular item because you believe it is evil, shoplifting can be seen as working counter to Freegan aims."

It was nearly 2:00 p.m. I left Adam Weissman and walked down the street to Savoy, a restaurant in a brick town house, to meet an old friend. I arrived first and settled in. The interior of Savoy looks like a well-oiled yacht. Even though it was summer, a fire burned in the fireplace behind the bar, where a well-groomed couple sat feeding each other olives with their fingers. My table was set with heavy silver cutlery. The menu arrived, printed on thick, creamy paper. Duck rillettes or Spanish mackerel?

I ordered a glass of wine. The large windows were open onto Prince

Street. Sipping my wine, I looked out at the people walking by. A few feet away, Weissman was suspended over the rim of a metal trash can. Standing on tiptoe, he stretched the upper half of his body into the can and pulled out a half-eaten Danish wrapped in wax paper. He held up the Danish, examining it. And then he took a bite. I pushed my silver fork off the table and ducked to retrieve it. I counted to ten. When I reemerged, Weissman was gone.

Weissman is hardly alone in his belief that shoplifting for survival is legitimate. *Adbusters*, a magazine from a Vancouver-based international group of socialist artists and anarchists known for its spoof advertisements, such as Buy Nothing Day, inspired a Montreal-based group to launch Steal Something Day, whose slogan, according to one website, is *"Diranger les riches dans leurs niches!"* (Knock rich people from their perches!) The American radical collective CrimethInc., whose every move is hidden from all but the most devoted followers, celebrates shoplifting from behind pseudonyms. "Good luck in your shoplifting quest," a CrimethInc.-er wrote on a piece of corrugated cardboard enclosed in the packaging of my copy of the paperback manifesto *Evasion*, which I purchased over the Internet for $12.95. Written by Anonymous, *Evasion* tracks its hero shoplifting, Dumpster-diving, and train-hopping across "Amerika." Another CrimethInc. tome, written by the CrimethInc. Ex-Workers Collective, *Days of War, Nights of Love: Crimethink for Beginners*, containing the essay "Why I Love Shoplifting from Big Corporations," has attracted even more acclaim in these circles.

Many anarchists asked if I had read it—their *Das Kapital*, apparently. Did I like it? One self-described "online organizer" and curator smiled, went to her bookshelf, tipped *Days of War, Nights of Love* from a high shelf, and pulled it down. She read the first paragraph:

Nothing compares to the feeling of elation, of burdens being lifted and constraints escaped, that I feel when I walk out of a store with their products in my pockets. In a world where everything already belongs to someone else, where I am expected to sell away my life at work in order to get the money to pay for the minimum I need to survive, where I am surrounded by forces beyond my control or comprehension that obviously are not concerned about my needs or welfare, it is a way to carve out a little piece of the world for myself—to act back upon a world that acts so much upon me.

The essay ending with the command "Shoplifters of the World, Unite!" was so admired in this community that the Canadian radical filmmaker, "media jammer," and activist Franklin Lopez adapted it into a short narrative video. Using the text as a voice-over, Lopez follows a mustached shoplifter on a spree through CVS and other stores. The video is full of comic-book effects; Lopez slaps words like "Shaazam!" on the screen as Superboy Shoplifter scrambles through the aisles, grabbing household items. But (spoiler alert) the shoplifting hero turns out to be a single mom trying to make ends meet. She removes her disguise in the car. The security guard chasing her is only doing so to give her a candy bar she dropped in the parking lot.

In May 2008, Adam Weissman posted the video on the Web. It sparked an angry conversation about whether shoplifting was a legitimate form of breaking eggs. The arguments CrimethInc., the Freegans, and other anarchists use to justify shoplifting from multinational corporations are not new. They are Industrial Revolution ideas run through the situationists and tarted up in Gen X clothing. At first, I found these ideas rhetorically and imaginatively jejune. "Why I Love Shoplifting from Big Corporations" read more like a summa of adolescent grudges than a sophisticated political treatise. As I continued to think about it, I began to reconsider. Was living outside of capitalism *really* impossible?

Weissman forwarded me an e-mail sent by Cookie Orlando, the nom de e-mail of James Trimarco, a former doctoral candidate in anthropology at the City University of New York, a student of the sociologist and political activist Stanley Aronowitz, and a writer who publishes in alternative magazines. To research an article about political shoplifting he was writing for *Fifth Estate*, an online "antiauthoritarian magazine of ideas and action," Cookie/James posted the following e-mail on anarchist academic and activist listservs.

> I am not taking a side in the debate about whether shoplifting is revolutionary or not, or whether it is good or bad. Instead, I am trying to see what role it plays in the lives of activists. Does [shoplifting] help keep a sense of direct action alive? Does it develop skills that can come in handy in other forms of political work? Does it provide a kind of "euphoria of disobedience" against private property that's not easily found elsewhere?

The post inspired another debate on the Freegan.info listserv. "My concern is that if you need to eat or feed your children, and you do not have money to pay for the items, the only moral thing to do is get the food any way you can," one poster wrote. Another exclaimed, "As far as I'm concerned there is no argument to be made that stealing from a bunch of murderers and con-artists is immoral . . . the WHOLE POINT is that they are stealing from us and we have to take back the world from them."

One of the shoplifters in Trimarco's article was an activist trying to support his family. Another was a self-described kleptomaniac-anarchist who had shoplifted $10,000 worth of food from Key Foods over the years. A third amped up his shoplifting during the Republican National Convention in New York as if to achieve through stealing what he could not through voting. But however devoted they were to their crime, these shoplifters were too ashamed to use their real names. Trimarco concluded that shoplifting arises from "a missing place in the battery of activism. There's a lust for direct action and even though this is futile, people do it."

David Graeber, an American cultural anthropologist who has taught at the University of London since 2007, defended shoplifting in even stronger terms.

> One doesn't destroy (or steal) people's personal property, in the sense of things they own to use themselves. One doesn't deprive people of their means of livelihood. Almost all anarchists I know don't feel it's morally wrong to steal from a large corporate store, but wouldn't think of stealing from a mom and pop grocer. I feel that way, though I don't think I've ever shoplifted anything myself. . . .
>
> It's really hard to imagine a scenario where we can overcome capitalism without breaking or taking anything that the law says doesn't belong to us. So then it comes down to a question of tactics: When is it helpful and when isn't it? . . . But then for me at least the question becomes: Who gets to say? Is there some central authority that can dictate what are appropriate revolutionary tactics? On what basis?

Although some ethical shoplifters use Abbie Hoffman's word "liberating," their fascination with the crime springs from seismic shifts in technology and culture in the last two decades. The phrase "ethical shoplifting" itself indicates an ironic stance toward an act that is descended from Hoffman's idea of stealing to beat the Man, yet is also quite different. Ethical shoplifting is a practical joke—a postmodern, plugged-in, hipster crime. It is a powerful moral glue holding together groups of radicals who don't believe in anything in a post-Internet age.

ART FOLLOWS LIFE

At the Point of Purchase exhibit at the Dumbo Arts Center in Brooklyn in 2006, organized by Gretchen Wagner, then a curatorial assistant in the prints department at the Museum of Modern Art, few artists were older than thirty, and like Adam Weissman, many of them regarded shoplifting as a necessary populist, intellectual, and creative protest against consumer culture.

Standing in the crowded gallery, I wondered if this was the first time in history artists had committed "fake" shoplifting. Some of the artists exhibiting here called themselves "shop-droppers"—or "reverse shoplifters." They buy an item, alter it, and return it to the store to send up consumerism or lament the absence of individuality in mass culture. Ryan Watkins-Hughes did photo collages of abandoned buildings, which he then glued onto cans of peas. The idea, he said, was to assert "the individual's rights over those of mass culture by making the peas unbuyable." Zoë Sheehan Saldaña shoplifted some candy once, but as an artist, she, like Watkins-Hughes, was into shop-dropping. For her this meant buying an article of clothing at Walmart, remaking it by hand, and sneaking the one-of-a-kind garment, complete with tags, back onto the rack. "Gen Y all watched Winona Ryder movies and they're all interested in shopping. . . . The store is my gallery," she told me.

The shop-droppers reminded me of a Dada prank. As did urban sprinting, kids miming shoplifting so that security guards would chase them for nothing. The fake thieves' most ambitious stunts borrowed from the theater.

Andrew Lynn is a slight man with an MFA in integrated electronic art from Rensselaer Polytechnic Institute, in Troy, New York. At age twenty-four, he invented Whirl-Mart, a ritual in which "shoppers"—wearing shirts emblazoned with the words "Whirl-Mart" or aprons designed to resemble salespeople's smocks—push empty shopping carts through a Walmart store in what Lynn calls "a silent protest of commercialism."

At the Point of Purchase exhibit, Lynn was embarrassed to find his Whirl-Mart photos hanging in a traditional gallery. Still photos, he said, failed to capture Whirl-Mart's dynamic radicalism, which came to life when in 2001, still a graduate student, he answered a call from *Adbusters*, asking him to create a "participatory and anticonsumerist happening" for April Fools' Day. "In Troy, there were about three Walmarts in a radius of seven to ten miles, and they put a lot of small stores out of business," Lynn said.

The first Whirl-Mart, on April Fools' Day 2001, happened during daylight saving time. Lynn forgot to set his clock. When he arrived at the Walmart, almost in tears at the thought of having missed the event that he had worked so hard to set up, a line of fifteen people snaked into the parking lot outside. They whirled "of their own accord" for two hours.

For a few years, Whirl-Marts sprang up all over the world: in Stockholm, Sweden; Finland; England; Pittsburgh, Pennsylvania; Germany; and Austin, Texas. According to an Internet rumor, a Whirl-Mart took place at the foot of the Mayan pyramids, where Walmart was improbably planning to build a store. Asked how shoplifting was connected with Whirl-Mart, Lynn said they were both on a continuum of "risky anti-consumer rituals," repeating the point of view, common in his circle, that shoplifting doesn't hurt stores financially since they are insured for less.

Store personnel missed the postmodern inflection. In 2001, Kmart chased some "Whirl-Marters" out of the Astor Place store, as did a Walmart in Latham, New York, the following year. Zoë Sheehan Saldaña approached Sam Walton's daughter to see if she was willing to buy some of the shirts to exhibit in Crystal Fields, the company art gallery at store headquarters in Bentonville, Arkansas. She never heard back. "It's not worth anything to them to touch it," she said, explaining that her shoplifting artwork was too radical for a Walmart gallery in a Southern town.

SHOPLIFTING IS YOU

If part of ethical shoplifting comes from Abbie Hoffman, part is imported. In 2004, a group of Barcelonese artists interested in social justice introduced Americans to their version of the crime: Shoplifting in Barcelona is a belated response to Franco's regime, as well as a reflection of the city's history of anarchism, an unemployment rate of 18 percent, the lack of a solid middle class, and Spain's lack of interest in what the law considers in most cases an irrelevant crime. In Spain, if you shoplift an item worth less than 400 euros ($600), you are unlikely to go to jail.

Though not exactly the mecca of anarchism, Barcelona "is not far off," explained a British expatriate and self-admitted "technical anarchist" I met while visiting the city in 2009. "During the Spanish civil war," he said, launching into a history of the movement justifying shoplifting,

> uniquely in Cataluña, anarchism had organizational structures. . . . Barcelona was full of meeting clubs and anarchist unions, fighting against the fascists. . . . Anarchism in Barcelona is best understood in relation to . . . being an anarchist rather than writing down rules or talking about it. You can find many of the components of Anarchist philosophy in the Scottish enlightenment philosophers— but when a contemporary anarcho-syndicalist like Noam Chomsky wants to illustrate a conceptual example about this form of politics with a positive historical example, there are few places to turn to other than Barcelona.

I visited Barcelona to interview members of the anarchist artist collective Yomango in person. Now I was standing at 15–17 Portal d'Angel Avenue, in front of Bershka, a popular clothing company with a branch near the Plaza de Cataluña, one of the most touristy spots in the world. Seven years earlier, Yomango staged its first shoplifting "action" at this "mall," which looks like malls everywhere.

On June 5, 2002, at five-thirty in the afternoon, Yomango, whose name is slang for "I steal" and a pun on the Spanish ready-to-wear clothing line Mango, attracted a crowd. They cordoned off a runway with tape on which they had written *"gratis/dinero"* (free/money) and which stretched from the store entrance into the street.

As a uniformed security guard watched, Yomangoites clad in revolutionary rags set up an impromptu catwalk and began to vogue. An emcee in a blue jacket with a bullhorn announced the Yomango brand and its models. A fashionista in a ratty beard wore a glitter heart on his cheek. Several men in pink minidresses and belly shirts waved blue pompoms. A man in a Rasta cap stripped to blue-and-white-striped boxers and shimmied across the cobblestones. Some "models" wore red smocks with multicolored nylon tights and Uggs, others tulle skirts, leather miniskirts, or green polyester pants. One carried a Danish butter cookies tin as a purse; another grasped a person-size fork.

A crowd gathered. The Yomangoites raided Bershka, chatted with customers and guards, and handed out flyers. An extra phalanx of guards arrived. As if on cue, the model with the Danish butter cookies tin deposited a maxi sky-blue spandex dress worth 9.50 euros inside it and left the store. Outside, she popped the lid off the tin and twirled the dress around her head. Everyone cheered. The hairy guy in the blue striped shorts put on the dress.

A guard chased them, but according to one Yomangoite whom I'll call "A," "our security convinced their security to back down." As A explained to me, "stores want to deal with this sort of business as discreetly as possible, as if resistance to shopping is something that does not exist."

Yomango displayed the "liberated" dress and showed a video of their shoplifting at the Cultural Center of Barcelona, at INn Motion, an arts festival. The police denounced Yomango as crooks, but a columnist in *El País* applauded them, summarizing the message they propagated. "Yomango accuses the market of appropriating ideas, ways of life, fashion (desired by 'cool hunters'), sexuality, already invented by society, in order to resell them as new luxury products. It believes that stealing is nothing more than reclaiming what belongs to us."

On July 8, some members of Yomango returned the shoplifted dress to the men's department of Zara, another store on Portal d'Angel Avenue. They attached to it a note explaining the dress's adventures, part of which read "The liberated dress took a walk through Barcelona and now it's back. Because Yomango does not recognize borders or security alarms."

Yomango intended the shoplifting to critique multinational companies' failure to give consumers "real" choices. And many American media sources treated them as countercultural heroes. *Wired* magazine traced Yomango's roots to Argentina, where protesters angered by the economy's collapse in 2001 looted stores. Another news article linked them to 1990s Barcelonese performance artists famous for constructing a *prêt à révolter* clothing line with pockets sized to fit guns.

But according to "Leo de Cerca," a pseudonym for one of the group's founding members, Yomango's birth occurred in 2001, after an antiglobalization demonstration against the Group of Eight meeting in Genoa. "We realized that we needed to build a protest not just for the summits but for our daily life, a political tool it [*sic*] can be useful every day," he said. "We wanted to show the false alternative that capitalism offers us." He wrote of "circulating goods," of "a million shoplifters rising," of Yomango as a meta-brand, as a synonym for ethical shoplifting and as either a noun or a verb.

In response, I fired off a simple e-mail, "Who are you?"

De Cerca replied, "We are an international network, we are a transnational brand name, as all the brand names of today we don't sell anything, we just offer a lifestile [*sic*]."

I e-mailed back: "I meant literally 'Who are you?'"

De Cerca scolded, "I told you, Yomango is an open process, no authors, no stars, no personal names, Yomango is you!"

The Yomangoite A, a fashion designer who described himself as Israeli, Barcelonese, and American, was among those leading "magic bag" workshops—magic bags are Yomango's version of booster bags—all over the world. Asked how many workshops took place, A said between dozens and hundreds of people had studied with him. A's inspiration for the bags came from magic. He had learned from magicians' card tricks and sleight of hand. "The gesture [to shoplift] has to be quick. It's an ergonomic study," he said.

To make their political points, Yomango stole not just from magic but from bourgeois rituals: The 2003 "Yomango Tango" began as Yomangoites, wearing berets and holding accordions made of tinfoil, crashed a super-market on Las Ramblas. Seven couples in costumes tangoed through the aisles. A woman in a red dress slid a bottle of champagne into her boy-friend's knapsack. One salesclerk shouted to another that the tangoers were shoplifting champagne, but a security guard just crossed his arms over his chest.

Through a bullhorn, the leader of the tangoers proclaimed Yoman-go's support of "the populist rebellion" in Argentina a year earlier as the dancers, champagned-up, waltzed past the cashiers onto the street. They bowed to the onlookers. They uncorked more champagne the next day in the lobby of a bank that supposedly supported the crackdown on the "populist rebellion."

Even more popular were dinner parties serving shoplifted gourmet food. One took place in Geneva during the World Summit on the Infor-mation Society conference, where, in Yomango's view, communications companies met to carve up the Internet. The grainy YouTube footage of the Geneva dinner began as about two hundred guests ate, drank, danced, hugged, and laughed. A girl in a ponytail and a fisherman's cap asked the camera in a German accent, "You want some free food?" And then she answered the interviewer's question: "If you want happiness, steal it" before a lecture on capitalism and how Yomango had transformed the shoplifted food into a "gastro riot" was delivered in Spanish, with subtitles.

"This is the first time I've done it in an organized fashion with a big group of people," declared a young American in an Andean cap over house music as the camera panned through the aisles of a supermarket where, in predinner madness, Yomangoites had stuck steak, wine, bottles of Moët, and Lindt chocolate bars in their socks, shoes, pants, and in shopping carts. One shopping cart after another was filled up with "liberated" products, which were then slapped with Yomango stickers. "I take the best wine, of course," the American said as he unpacked one cart.

Several diners repeated the phrase "Shoplifting builds community" as they plowed through cheese, fish, chocolate, and expensive bottles of wine, alluding to something young Americans are hungry for—a nip of luxury, a taste of possessing something out of your reach, and the possibility of creating your own rough justice.

Yomango became a darling of the American art scene in 2004, when MASS MoCA, the contemporary art museum in North Adams, Massachusetts, included them in a group show about activist artists. A booster bag was exhibited near their art. The following year, New York University invited Yomango to "The War of the Worlds," an international two-day symposium on art and activism. According to one person who was there, the group did an "action" at the Diesel store in SoHo. (Or as Bani Brufadino, one of the founders of Yomango, told me, they "changed the space.")

One evening Brufadino delivered an informal talk at the Change You Want to See Gallery in Williamsburg. About fifty people gathered there to imbibe Yomango's wisdom about shoplifting: hipsters, politically committed New Yorkers, fellow travelers, and gawkers perched on folding chairs. Many in the audience wore leather jackets or granny glasses or both. In front of a large screen displaying small avatars and brands stood Brufadino and a female accomplice.

An Italian who lived in Barcelona, Brufadino was in his twenties. Dressed in a red hoodie with an unrecognizable black logo and jeans, he began to describe shoplifting (he preferred the word "taking") as a mashup of Hoffman and Rousseau: Shoplifting was both a righting of personal wrongs and a theoretical exit ramp out of the system. "Corporations steal fashions like baggy trousers, which kids wore while their older brothers were in jail, and then they sell them back to us," he said in a thick accent, but added that he had shoplifted his jeans because "he needed trousers."

The audience peppered Brufadino with questions. One person kept interrupting, "I want to make sure I get it."

Another asked, "Is this Marxist?"

A young woman joked, "What would Jesus say?"

Laughter. Someone else yelled, "He's not for private property!"

"Let's e-mail Jesus," a third person screamed.

Asked what sort of people joined Yomango, Brufadino responded "Yomango is you."

PART TWO

DIMENSIONS

She could not help feeling the claim of each trinket and valuable upon her personally and yet she did not stop. There was nothing there which she could not have used and nothing which she did not long to own.

—Theodore Dreiser, *Sister Carrie*

5. AMONG SHOPLIFTERS

For much of its six-century history, shoplifting—whether defined as disease or crime—was considered something women did. But since the 1980s, men have caught up. While men shoplift more, there are more female kleptomaniacs. Yet when it comes to what men and women steal, some studies sound drawn from a pre–Betty Friedan world. In 2005, the Centre for Retail Research in the United Kingdom measured what men and women shoplift: Women steal cosmetics, clothes, jewelry, and perfume; men steal electronics, televisions, and handheld and power tools. Women shoplift from department and discount stores; men from home centers and hardware stores. Although 80 percent of all readers are women, the Centre discovered, most book shoplifters are men.

In the summer of 2009, I lunched at the Oxford and Cambridge Club, near Buckingham Palace, with Joshua Bamfield, a professor of management turned retail researcher who heads the Centre in Nottingham. Where the sheriff of Nottingham used to work, he joked.

As we wandered toward the club's bar, in a dark, cavernous room in the Greek Revival building, I asked him to explain the gender breakdown in his research. Bamfield, a cheerful, balding man in his sixties, leaned into the bar, ordered a pre-lunch port, and said, "A few years ago I went to the Bodleian Library, at Oxford, and I saw their new security system. So what kinds of books are being stolen here, I asked? Porn and business, right?"

"'No, it's theology,' they said."

Bamfield began to laugh. "It just goes to show you."

We moved upstairs to the dining room. Although the club has accepted female members since the 1970s, there were no women, except for a few coat-check girls hovering in the reception area.

As Bamfield and I settled in, we returned to the topic of gender. Were men stealing books for their girlfriends? What about the other gender-obvious exception in Bamfield's study? Men shoplift hair dryers. Does this suggest that men are more sensitive about their looks? Or that they are becoming more so? Or does it mean that women are shopping less and men sharing the household chores (like shopping and therefore shoplifting) more?

Bamfield laughed again and answered, "There are many different things. Some men are stealing for resale. It is easier for men to get away with stealing electronics than women's clothing. We think that men look at [the hair dryer] as an electrical device rather than beauty device. It's easy for men to sell to other males."

Bamfield was also referring to the commonly held belief among criminologists that men resell the items they shoplift, whereas women dabble, shoplifting domestic items to enhance their homes, food to sustain their children, and clothing and accessories to improve their appearance. Bamfield ordered meat and potatoes and a carafe of rosé, and I decided on a Cajun salad.

Bamfield, who introduced civil restitution to the United Kingdom in 1998, said it was important to study further how men and women shoplift differently: "The picture is complex," he said, adding that professionals of both sexes used gender-specific tools to steal. Men liked knapsacks. Women preferred strollers.

At the same time as criminologists began to express skepticism that shoplifting was exclusively—or even primarily—a woman's crime, feminist historians endeavored to overturn the idea that kleptomania is uniquely a women's disease. In her award-winning 1989 social history, *When Ladies Go A-Thieving: Middle-Class Shoplifters in the Victorian Department Store*, Elaine S. Abelson contends not just that the Victorians invented kleptomania, but that American popular culture's treatment of the disease as proof of women's omnivorous appetites echoes the misogyny with which Victorian doctors, stores, and the popular press described it.

A very different attempt to attribute kleptomania's all-girl reputation to misogyny in this era came from Louise J. Kaplan's 1990 book, *Female Perversions: The Temptations of Emma Bovary*, which was made into a feature film starring Tilda Swinton as Eve, an icy, manipulative lawyer who has forged ahead by playing a man's game, while her sister, a dysfunctional graduate student, gets arrested for shoplifting. Kaplan, a psychoanalyst, wrote the book to challenge Freudian sexism. She believes that kleptomania, a female disease, "is a response to the social order where those with penises control the source and flow of economic goods." She is one of a few writers to perceive shoplifting and kleptomania as reflections of the same excessive consumption problem.

> Very rich women just shop and then shop some more and even steal a trophy or two, now and then, whenever they might otherwise get anxious or depressed. Not-so-rich women are kleptomaniacs who replace an experience of deprivation or anxiety with an impulse to steal what they feel deprived of. And poor women merely shoplift, steal what their families need in the way of food and clothing, with an occasional extra . . . to assuage the violence of deprivation.

Kaplan almost convinces the reader that gender equality will stop women from shoplifting. But Jon Grant, a professor of psychiatry at the University of Minnesota who studies compulsive gambling and shoplifting, believes that we continue to gender kleptomania because of stereotypes. "Men tend to be criminalized and sent straight to jail whereas women get sent to doctors and get a chance to be rehabilitated."

I encountered plenty of men of all ages, races, and occupations who shoplifted. But I met far more female chronic shoplifters who shoplifted regularly over long periods of time. Of these, the majority were unemployed or underemployed women (although some were gainfully employed but underpaid, like schoolteachers). Besides that, the shoplifters did not share a particular profile: They were married with children, childless, or single; college coeds and retirees. Hardly any women shoplifting were comfortable describing themselves as kleptomaniacs, even if they had stolen from stores twice a day for ten years. Some flinched when I used the word. Others talked about shoplifting in the same hushed voices that I imagined kleptomaniacs used in Freud's era when confessing to it led to ostracism or the asylum. It disturbed and thrilled them.

Framing shoplifting as a reflection of female consumption caught on (again) in the 1990s, when psychoanalysts and research psychiatrists began to explore whether "female appetite diseases" such as body dysmorphia, anorexia, bulimia, and compulsive buying were connected to kleptomania. In a talk she gave at the Freud Museum in London, the feminist writer and psychoanalyst Susie Orbach attributed her female patients' shoplifting to consumerism. The frustration of wanting something more sustaining than a mere article of clothing and yet not being able to get it, she wrote, the disappointment left over from childhood, and the disappointment that going to the store turns out to be more of a sentence than an adventure explain why women steal.

The Belgian psychiatrist Walter Vandereycken found that kleptomania was more common in people who have bulimia—most of whom are women—than in those without it. "There's an immense gender difference between how men and women deal with psychological disorders," he told me. "Women internalize problems and men externalize them. Is it cultural? Is it biological? We don't know."

But Gail Caputo, a professor of criminology at Rutgers University, believes that more women shoplift because women are more susceptible to poverty and depression. Her 2008 book, *Out in the Storm: Drug-Addicted Women Living as Shoplifters and Sex Workers*, refrains from judging its subjects, most of whom are working-class or poor, drug-addicted women. She defines shoplifting as an illegal form of work. "[Shoplifting] is less invasive [than prostitution] and [women shoplifters] can see themselves as the caretakers of the situation," she told me, explaining that women would do anything—even steal—to protect their children.

I found the most convincing explanation for why there may be more chronic shoplifting among women in an essay by the late writer Caroline Knapp: Unable to navigate the supposed freedoms that the sexual revolution delivered, women still struggle more with consumption and identity than men. "Where are the lines between satisfaction and excess, between restraint and indulgence, between pleasure and self-destruction? And why are they so difficult to find, particularly for women?"

Age is as murky a factor as gender in predicting who will shoplift. According to Ellen Chandler, a counselor who has worked with senior criminals for over ten years at the Broward Senior Intervention and Education Program in Hollywood, Florida—one of the only programs in the country devoted to helping the elderly navigate the criminal justice system—shoplifting is the most common crime: 75 percent of her clients do it. She added that very few of them steal food. "Some of 'em have a sense of entitlement and . . . they kinda get real, real snippy. . . . But the majority of them admit it, but they don't understand why. Sometimes people really think it was purely accidental. The first case I ever had, the woman was eighty-four years old . . . went into Walgreens. She bought some items. And then for the other stuff, she walked out and got caught."

Although retail stores used to tolerate shoplifting among the elderly, some big-box stores have installed zero-tolerance policies for the crime, which has led to the arrest of more seniors for stealing everything from dentures and hearing-aid batteries to fruit. Whatever kinds of things elderly people shoplift, their crime incites more than its share of rage and suspicion.

In 2009, Ella Orko, eighty-six years old, was arrested for shoplifting at a Chicago supermarket. It was her sixty-first arrest since 1956. The police referred to her as both a "career" shoplifter and a "habitual" shoplifter. Among the items Orko shoplifted were wrinkle cream, canned salmon, instant coffee, and batteries. Over the course of her life, she had assumed at least fifty aliases, police said.

At sentencing, Orko rolled into court in a wheelchair wearing a neck brace and pleading deafness, although when arrested two days earlier, she was wheelchair- and neck-brace-free. The judge, who wore hearing aids on both ears, sentenced her to time served in light of her advanced age.

While Americans are far more comfortable regarding shoplifting as a young person's moral problem than as an old person's social or economic one, some scholars believe young people may be overrepresented in the most dramatic studies, which show that 40 percent of young people have shoplifted. The criminologist Richard Hollinger attributed high percentages of young people shoplifting to this group's availability to social scientists. "Where would we be without the sophomore survey?" he joked.

Just because children shoplift does not mean they will grow up to be—as Hollinger put it, referring to the felled Enron executive—"the next Kenneth Lay." Developmental psychologists believe that up to age nine, children shoplift to test boundaries. Tweens should have a more fully formed sense of these boundaries, and if teenagers shoplift, they may be acting out or depressed, peer-pressured into performing a rite of passage, or seeking a thrill.

The prejudices many feel toward immigrants, especially since 9/11, may inflate statistics averring that the group shoplifts more than whites. On May 1, 2006, the so-called Day Without Immigrants, when Latinos across the country boycotted stores to agitate for amnesty and legalization, an Internet rumor circulated that shoplifting decreased 67.8 percent. Watchdog websites discredited the rumor, but that it was floated in the first place testifies to prejudice's power.

The American legal system sentences noncitizens more harshly for the crime than those born here. Bill O. Hing, a lawyer and professor of Asian American studies and public policy at the University of California, Davis, tracks the government's deportation of illegal immigrants who have committed petty crimes, including shoplifting. "It's considered a felony even if the state does not consider it one," he said. In a *Washington Post* op-ed piece published during Winona Ryder's trial, Hing criticized the 1996 Illegal Immigration Reform and Immigrant Responsibility Act (IIRIRA), which allows the government to detain or deport those without green cards for crimes of moral turpitude: "Every day the United States deports lawful immigrants and refugees who have been convicted of minor offenses such as shoplifting," he writes.

Marlene Jaggernauth, a woman of Indian descent whose ancestors come from Trinidad, was deported because of an old shoplifting case. Jaggernauth's family brought her to the United States in 1977, when she was twelve years old. At first they lived in New York. In 1990, she moved to Miami, where she worked at her parents' auto parts business. She bought a house. Six years later, depressed and anxious over a divorce, suffering from postpartum depression after the birth of her twins, reeling from an abusive relationship and from losing her job, she began to shoplift. "I just got the urge to pick up stuff," she said.

Jaggernauth was arrested. "I didn't care. I kept doing it. The arrest didn't mean anything." She was arrested again and given a suspended sentence. She got counseling and stopped shoplifting. Seven years passed. She obtained her BA and began working at Florida Atlantic University. And then one night in 2003, the Immigration and Naturalization Service (INS) barged into her house and detained her for the old shoplifting charges. She was held in four different county jails—one each year—and then sent back to Trinidad, where she stayed for a fifth year.

While she was in jail, her family fell apart. She sent her children to her parents', but her daughter did not complete high school and her son dropped out and began to take drugs. In Trinidad, she knew no one. She was only able to survive thanks to her mother, who sent her money. "I would have prostituted myself if not for her," she said.

In 2004, Jaggernauth created a foundation, the Displaced Nationals in Crisis Coalition, to help immigrants like herself. She continued to fight her deportation and eventually successfully appealed it. Three years later, she returned to the United States, determined to make her case known. She began giving press conferences exposing the atrocities in the jails she stayed in and telling of the untreated mentally ill women there. She never felt "violated" when she was arrested for shoplifting. But she did by her ordeal with the INS. Today, Jaggernauth works as an advocate for the mental health court in Florida, in the courtroom of the judge who sentenced her after she shoplifted. She has never mentioned her past. "One day I will get the nerve."

The few studies gauging the connection between shoplifting and income reveal counterintuitive results. In the 1960s, one landmark paper showed that shoplifters who looked affluent were detained less frequently. than those who looked scruffy. Joshua Bamfield argues that wealthy shoplifters are statistically underrepresented. "Every few months Harrods arrests a millionaire shoplifter," he says. The study "Who Actually Steals" observed that one common shoplifter is the "primary household shopper" who "usually has gainful employment" and steals to stretch the budget. The most recent study measuring income and shoplifting ascertained that Americans with incomes of $70,000 shoplift 30 percent more than those earning up to $20,000 a year. Having some money arouses desire more than having little.

The most overrepresented groups of shoplifters are young African American and Latino men. Among the first to document the inequity was JoAnn Ray, a professor emeritus in social work at Eastern Washington University. In 1984, after Ray compared court records with a thousand questionnaires she randomly distributed at ten different shopping centers in Spokane, she found "considerable differences may exist between people who shoplift and those few who get caught." Shoplifters who answered Ray's questionnaire were overwhelmingly young and white, whereas those she pulled from court data were very old or very young Hispanic and black men.

Twenty-five years later, criminologists continue to argue that African Americans are overrepresented in store data because of profiling or "shopping while black." A pool of lawsuits brought against stores for "SWB" over the past decade exposes the tenacity of this prejudice. In one case in New York in 2005, Macy's paid the state attorney general's office $600,000 in sanctions after an investigation concluded that whereas the percentage of nonwhite shoppers in Macy's, as in most stores in most states, hovers between 10 and 12 percent, 75 percent of people detained for shoplifting were "nonwhite."

No African American shoplifter I interviewed identified herself as a kleptomaniac or a theft addict—the disease's hipper cousin. Perhaps considering shoplifting as a disease is a luxury the most frequently profiled feel they cannot afford.

On March 10, 2006, a few months after I began work on this book, I broke the story in *Slate* of the shoplifting of Claude Allen, then the highest-ranking African American men in George Bush's White House. I first heard about Allen a month earlier at the National Retail Federation (NRF) in Washington, D.C. A cop I was interviewing there told me that besides all the professional thieves he busted, there was *one* well-known white-collar shoplifter he was investigating—Allen, then a senior domestic adviser in the White House. "Maybe he has two wives," the cop joked, puzzled over why someone with money would shoplift. Particularly, he added, when the person shoplifted, as Allen did, something as insignificant as a mop.

Allen was the first government official convicted of shoplifting to be tried against the backdrop of the twenty-four-hour newsroom, and the first to confess in public. He first shoplifted the day after Scooter Libby was indicted and several weeks after Hurricane Katrina ravaged New Orleans. In the following weeks, the sharecropper's grandson, Covenant Life Church member and advocate of homeschooling, allegedly committed refund fraud—a twenty-first-century variety of shoplifting—over fifty times from Target and Hecht's.

Like price switching, wardrobing (the returning of once-worn dresses to the store) and grazing ("self-sampling," as Whole Foods warns at its salad bar in some stores, or "eating your way around the store," as one security guard put it) are new versions of shoplifting. Wardrobing is also technically legal, and stores look the other way if they decide that grazing is a prelude to buying, although some salad tasters have been detained. Refund fraud, which is illegal, also belongs in this twilight category. In the days after Allen was arrested, I found myself explaining how refund fraud works: You buy a TV set and wheel it to the car in your shopping cart. You go back to the store and put a second one, identical to the first, in a shopping bag in the cart. Using receipts from the first item, you refund the second for credit. Some chains allow you to do the refund at a different store from where you purchased the first item. Others, like Nordstrom, actually give you cash.

According to incident reports, Allen's spree began in Gaithersburg, Maryland, on October 29, 2005, with his most expensive item: a Bose stereo worth $525. Next, on Christmas Eve, was a $237 Kodak printer from the Germantown Target. According to loss prevention reports, on December 30, Allen returned a suit jacket, two pairs of slacks, and two lamp shades valued at $25 at the Rockville Target. On New Year's Day, he went back to the same store for an $88 RCA stereo. On January 2—the day that he was caught—the items he allegedly shoplifted included a scrub mop priced at $11.99, two bras priced at $9.89, and massage gloves valued at $4.99. When Pete Schomburg, then a floor detective at the Gaithersburg Target, detained him, Allen immediately confessed.

In February, Allen resigned from the White House, according to a Bush spokesperson, "to spend more time with his family." A month later, John Lalos, then the Maryland assistant state's attorney, charged Allen with a felony theft scheme—a more serious offense, signaling that the state was going to treat Allen like any other shoplifter.

In covering Allen's shoplifting, the *Washington Post* wavered between casting the crime as a character defect and blaming it on the Bush administration's hiring and promoting an incompetent, African American ideologue. When Bush had nominated Allen for a judgeship in 2004, the American Bar Association declared him partially unqualified, citing his lack of trial experience. The National Organization for Women and the NAACP lobbied against Allen for his support of abstinence as sex education and his pro-life position.

What irritated liberal commentators more than Allen's politics was the puniness of his hauls. *Post* columnist Eugene Robinson asked, "Why would a man who met several times a week with the President of the United States, and who earned $161,000 a year, risk everything to steal an $88 radio?"

The media were so at a loss to explain Allen's shoplifting that dark family secrets were hinted at. A *New York Times* story, "For Bush's Ex-Aide, Quick Fall after Long Climb," mentioned Allen's identical twin, Floyd, a security guard, who, according to his stepmother, "kept running into trouble." And a *Washington Post* reporter told NPR, "Close friends say that Mr. Allen has indicated to them that maybe his brother holds the key to this entire puzzling affair." Nothing was ever printed to explain the insinuation that Floyd—not Claude—had ripped off Target. And yet a mix-up of two African American brothers—one a powerful conservative official who shoplifted, the other a lowly security guard who caught shoplifters—was too haunting to pass over. As was a rumor the *Washington Post* printed that Allen could not afford his legal counsel, intimating that he had shoplifted because he was broke.

But what was striking about Allen was not just these fake explanations, shot through with preconceived ideas about shoplifters. Nor was it that after a brief flirtation with the sort of denial the White House had become notorious for, Allen actually confessed in court and the judge dropped the charge of felony theft scheme to one count of misdemeanor theft. What was striking was the explanation Allen himself eventually used in his testimony at the District of Columbia Court of Appeals Board on Professional Responsibility hearing: shoplifting as exorcism. In effect, Allen was infected with shame. His shameful shoplifting arose out of the greater shame about the administration's inept handling of Hurricane Katrina and George W. Bush's apparent indifference toward the suffering of New Orleanians seen on every TV screen. Allen testified that his shoplifting surfaced because of his inability to do anything about this larger shame. He told the committee that after he visited post-Katrina New Orleans, "I would go to Target just to kind of escape, walk through" to escape his memories of "seeing vividly a gentleman sitting out in front of the Superdome in a chair for days with an [*sic*] sign on him saying, 'I've passed away. Please bury me.' That didn't happen and I felt very much responsible." Allen's psychiatrist, Thomas Goldman, added, in case there was any confusion: "He was outraged that there was so much needing to be done that was not being done that it put a strain . . . on his loyalty."

Four years after Allen was arrested, the discipline board recommended that he be suspended for a year from practicing law in D.C. He had already served ninety-day suspensions in Pennsylvania and Virginia. "We especially are concerned by the repeated and calculated nature of [Allen's] misconduct," the board wrote.

6. | HOT PRODUCTS

Shoplifting, says Ronald V. Clarke, a lanky, matter-of-fact criminologist at Rutgers University, is one of the "most common but least reported and detected crimes" in the world. Clarke is one of the leading experts on the so-called situational approach to crime, which, in the case of shoplifting, focuses on the objects people steal as opposed to who does it or why. In the late 1990s, he invented a catchy phrase to predict what shoplifters would steal: "hot products." He gave the products a catchier acronym: CRAVED, which stands for "concealable, removable, available, valuable, enjoyable, and disposable." He published the particulars in a less catchily titled monograph: *Hot Products: Understanding, Anticipating, and Reducing Demand for Stolen Goods.*

In 2006, in a spare campus conference room at Rutgers's New Brunswick campus, Clarke explained to me that "shoplifting is a neglected area because governments don't want to fund research that benefits private sector, and private sector isn't interested in research." He went on to proclaim his continuing faith in CRAVED and the situational theory as they applied to shoplifting. "The crime is highly concentrated: in certain areas of the city, and of certain goods. In a drugstore, for instance, highly specific goods will be stolen. Many goods will never be. They are too big or bulky or too cheap or difficult to steal."

Clarke added that the levels of shoplifting today "have been created by modern retailing. Historically, you had very few opportunities to shoplift. Because today there are far more stores in relation to people and population and goods are laid out on shelves—you can get them."

In the last ten years, *Hot Products* has inspired retail trade groups to come up with their own "most shoplifted item" lists; these lists look similar year after year. Each one comes with its own biases and limitations; each one's creators claim that gathering information is as difficult as finding black truffles. In America, for the past several years, the most consistent list counted the top fifty items shoplifted in supermarkets, whereas in England, the most publicized one spans all food groups, products, and stores.

To protect stores from competitors, most lists, whose architects keep secret how they determine a product's shopliftability, rarely identify brands. An exception is a newcomer list identifying Jack Daniel's as the most-stolen liquor and Max Factor as the most-stolen mascara in three retailers in the United Kingdom. More common is the 2003 Centre for Retail Research "top ten" list. An annotated version of this list, published in British newspapers, crowned Gillette Mach 3 safety razors and replacement cartridges the most-shoplifted items in the world and tossed the remaining "hot products" into lumpy, unbranded categories:

1. Gillette razors and cartridges
2. toiletries and alcohol
3. clothing
4. lingerie
5. batteries
6. CDs, DVDs
7. vitamins and pregnancy tests
8. luxury toothbrushes
9. instant coffee
10. steak

Much has been written asserting that Gillette Mach 3, the world's most popular brand, is most shoplifted. Criminologists have produced white papers with flowcharts tracking its progress from the Russian mob to your store. But Robin Hoodish theory charged that the Mach 3 is the most shoplifted because it costs a few cents to make and is marked up so steeply. "It *is* difficult to buy Gillette," says Joshua Bamfield, the director of the Centre for Retail Research, launching into a story about grappling with drugstore shelving that sounded more like a trek through the Amazon than a jaunt to the pharmacy.

Though criminologists argue about which brand of razor is the hottest, they agree that the categories of hot products have remained constant in the last decade. The most comprehensive lists today break down hot products by type of store, or "sector." According to the 2009 *Global Retail Theft Barometer*, the most-shoplifted items in the supermarket sector are razor blades and cosmetics, and the most-shoplifted items in the clothing category are "accessories" and "anything branded." The *GRTB* also includes cosmetics, Wii systems, liquor, steak, SatNav systems (including GPS), haute couture, infant formula, and watches. In short, all the products that are sold are shoplifted.

Some older surveys, like the *1999 Retail Theft Trends Report*, elaborated on the preferred times of shoplifting in different sectors. In the auto parts sector, most shoplifting occurs between noon and 3:00 p.m. on Saturdays, whereas in bookstores, it occurs between 3:00 p.m. and 6:00 p.m. on Mondays. Do hubcap thieves shoplift on the Sabbath so they can take a spin on Sunday? Do book thieves steal on Monday afternoons because universities give exams on Tuesdays?

Asked such questions, Bill Greer, until recently the director of communications for the Food Marketing Institute (FMI), which published its last most-shoplifted list for American supermarkets in 2009, said, "We don't drill that deep."

THE SUPERMARKET

Steak first made the top of the FMI's most-shoplifted-items-in-the-supermarket list in 2005. It held the title for four years. To retail security professionals, steak's staying power vindicated their practice of locking up over-the-counter health and beauty products and pharmaceuticals, which had formerly been at the top. Their methods had forced professional shoplifters to switch from Benadryl to beef, they said. To some scholars, carnivorous amateurs were the ones shoplifting steak. "I think it's unlikely that a professional is going to steal something as perishable as steak," said Timothy Jones, a University of Arizona anthropologist, adding that a shoplifted chop would turn into a bloody mess after a few unrefrigerated hours.

Shoplifting meat and fish makes retailers angrier than stealing a loaf of bread: Its causes stem from middle-class feelings of entitlement as opposed to starvation. I first heard this point of view in 2006, when I attended a "Theft Offenders" diversion class sponsored by the Educational Association Service, a not-for-profit company based in New York. In a dour room in a Queens junior high school sat about thirty alleged shoplifters: recent Korean immigrants with their spouses, a trio of college-age men whose parents came from Mumbai, tourists visiting New York for the first time, a professional woman who believed her arrest was part of a conspiracy, and a nurse turned semiprofessional thief. Queens, the nation's most diverse borough, is also home to the nation's most diverse assembly of (alleged) shoplifters.

Group leader James McCall read a word problem from a workbook. An elderly person had shoplifted canned salmon and pork chops. Was the supermarket "mean" to prosecute "to the fullest extent of the law"?

The correct answer was no. McCall argued: If one senior citizen succeeded in her surf and turf heist, she would tell her friends at the assisted-living facility and they would file into A&P "with their walkers." Eventually these oldsters would bankrupt the store. Soon octogenarians all over America would be divesting supermarkets of salmon and pork chops. McCall believed that if senior citizens were shoplifting something they wanted as opposed to something they needed, the store should prosecute. But in our world of a million brands, since the supermarket offers more items "not needed for personal use" than at any other time in human history, it seems cruel to tolerate shoplifting only if the person steals carbohydrates or to observe, as several grocers did, that if shoplifters were hungry they should limit themselves to swiping loaves of bread.

"Where was the beef on the day of August 26, 2009?" a prosecutor joked at the beginning of a jury trial in Orangeburg, South Carolina, over whether Mark Zachary shoplifted an $80 side of steak. Zachary pleaded not guilty. There was no video footage of him shoplifting. There was a hung jury, and the judge had to instruct the jurors to come up with a verdict. Part of the difficulty may have been the severity of the punishment: Under South Carolina law, three shoplifting convictions are punishable by up to ten years in prison. Zachary had nine shoplifting arrests, and once the jury ruled that he was guilty, the judge sentenced him to the maximum amount.

Keith McHenry, the cofounder of the food pantry Food Not Bombs, told me that food shoplifters would otherwise starve. Plenty of people were imprisoned for what he called "lunch related crimes," he said. "I spent time in jail one time where I was caught feeding homeless people with stuff a store threw away and the others had been busted for dining and dashing or shoplifting lunch from groceries."

FROM "ELECTRONIC SHOPLIFTING" TO "BUKOWSKI MAN"

For centuries, shoplifting has meant stealing objects from stores. But if you believe music executives from the end of the last century, we are in the middle of a paradigm shift: Shoplifting may be an endangered species. Like everything else, it has migrated online. In 1999, honest citizens who would never dream of shoplifting a CD were downloading music illegally, which the adversaries of this practice called "electronic shoplifting." Even after peer-to-peer (P2P) file-sharing sites replaced Napster, the phrase stuck. In a 2002 congressional hearing on a bill that advocates hoped would quash these sites, Senator Robert Goodlatte (R-VA) referred to Kazaa "the Home Shoplifting Network." Those who called P2P file sharing shoplifting favored more draconian penalties for the electronic version than had ever been used for the brick-and-mortar one. The fines file sharers (some of whom were college students or housewives) were asked to pay were many times greater than those imposed on shoplifters.

At the same time, just as Abbie Hoffman and the yippies had renamed shoplifting "liberating," Internet gurus, Silicon Valley entrepreneurs, and tech-friendly journalists maintained that P2P file sharing was not shoplifting—it was "trading." File-sharing programs on the Internet, a new frontier, should be exempt from established property laws: The people using such programs, this argument went, would never *shoplift*. They were not criminals. File sharing could not be shoplifting, because music was not a stealable object like a pack of gum. In fact, this argument continued, P2P was saving the music industry by helping to distribute less commercial songs more widely. One Dutch file-sharing company called itself the Honest Thief, dredging up the phrase that nineteenth-century French doctors used for an altogether different purpose. But the most intriguing question about the relationship between electronic shoplifting and CD shoplifting—whether anyone whom the government found guilty of P2P file sharing shoplifted CDs from Tower Records before it went bankrupt—remained unexamined.

The arrival of e-books and magazines inspired a different kind of news story about the Internet promoting electronic shoplifting. Many technology writers have noted how easy it is to download books illegally. Yet the more significant question for stores is whether—as Kindle, e-books, and the iPad replace hardcovers, paperbacks, and print magazines—old-school book shoplifting will disappear or multiply.

Some writers are as vulnerable to the romance of book shoplifting as they are to that of the vanishing independent bookstore. Literary essays keeping count of the most-shoplifted books continue to be published as though they conferred legitimacy—or even creativity—upon the crime. Apparently, to these observers, shoplifting conjures nothing more sinister than a list of readers who have fallen so completely under books' spells that they steal them. The list, after all, includes literary characters, like Augie March. No lowbrow crook, Augie—shoplifter and reader of Plato—when granted a chance to borrow a magisterial work of European history using a library card, observes, "But somehow that wasn't the same." The hero of the late Chilean novelist Roberto Bolaño's *The Savage Detectives* shoplifts poetry and rare books about astronomy.

Many readers and writers make a case for book shoplifting as less reprehensible stealing. "It's not a case of lusting after a particular rare book," Alan Edelstein, a filmmaker, said. "If you love books and you can't keep up with it, it's a little bit different, from, say, shoplifting food. I stole a paperback of William Gaddis's *The Recognitions*, which I haven't read," he added. The writer Luc Sante recalled, about the old Brentano's on Forty-eighth Street in New York, that "it was very easy to shoplift from when I was a teenager." In his salad days, Sante stole *Death of a Salesman* and *Where Do We Go from Here: Chaos or Community?* by Martin Luther King Jr., among other titles. On his first day at Columbia University, browsing at the Papyrus bookstore on 113th Street and Broadway, he tucked a copy of Kafka's *Amerika* into the waistband of his pants. He left the bookstore and crossed Broadway. When he reached the median, he saw that a young man from Papyrus had followed him. The two men stood there, not looking at each other, waiting for the light to change. Then the man turned to Sante and punched him in the stomach, where Kafka was hidden. The light changed and Sante crossed the street. He did not look back.

Thanks to Jean-Paul Sartre, Jean Genet is the most famous writer–book shoplifter in history—the Saint Genet of the famous biography's title. Genet himself describes theft's rush with more depth and humanity than any other writer. "I went to theft as to a liberation, as to the light," is a chapter title in Sartre's opus, a fictionalized account of Genet's love affairs and time in prison. And in *The Thief's Journal*, Genet detailed his pleasure in stealing. "I know the extraordinary calmness one feels at the moment of performing the theft, and the fear that accompanies it." Genet's most memorable phrase about theft categorized it as "a succession of cramped though blazing gestures."

Genet did not start his shoplifting career with books, nor did he limit himself to stealing them. He shoplifted as a child, an adolescent, and an adult. He was arrested for shoplifting a dozen handkerchiefs from the Samaritaine department store in Paris in 1937, at age thirty-six. Genet also stole liquor, bolts of linen, and suits. To accomplish the last, he would enter a tailor's store, try on the suit, and run out the door.

During the German occupation, Genet began shoplifting books from vendors along the Seine. Although he resold them, at a hearing in 1940, he defended shoplifting to the jury as part of his sentimental education: He could list the ten books honored by the Académie Goncourt—"few critics could do as much," he bragged

Book shoplifting is the only type of shoplifting about which entire books have been written, and which even has a book named for it, *Steal This Book*. Book shoplifting is also the only theft to merit its own disease, bibliomania, the disease of wanting to possess books. The literary journalist Nicholas Basbanes, whose six-hundred-plus-page book, *A Gentle Madness*, tells the history of bibliomania, focuses on the theft of rare books—he does not use the word "shoplift"—as the extreme of that disease. Basbanes frames his investigation with the story of Stephen Carrie Blumberg, a rare-book thief who stole 23,000 volumes from archives and libraries across the country, not to sell but to hoard them. Blumberg's defense was the only time that any lawyer used the insanity defense in a theft case, Basbanes said. In 1991, Blumberg was convicted and spent seventy-one months in jail. Basbanes argues that Blumberg's dedication to hoarding Victoriana, though sinister and weird, is more excusable than shoplifting books to resell them. Still, Basbanes wrote: While bibliomania is "the only hobby, so far as I know, that is recognized in the *DSM* of the American Psychiatric Association as a bona fide disease, I don't excuse book theft on the basis of being a disease. Had I been on the Blumberg jury—and I witnessed the entire trial—I would have voted to convict."

I read a passage to Basbanes from the famous 1944 essay *Notes on Bibliokleptomania* by the bibliophile, collector, and classicist (and during

World War II, FBI special agent) Lawrence Sidney Thompson. "The moral questions posed by book theft are considerably more difficult than those involved in deciding the guilt or innocence of a bank robber or a kidnapper." Thompson quotes the collector Gédéon Tallemant des Réaux: "Book theft is not true theft if the books are not resold."

Basbanes responded, "It is true, but I wish it weren't. We don't equate book theft's gravity with other types of crimes. But book theft defaces and destroys books. It's a crime. You're attacking a cultural artifact."

In the age of the memoir, some writers confess to shoplifting to advance themselves, and others profess to be aghast at the crime. Ron Rosenbaum, the author of provocative books on Hitler and Shakespeare, once wrote a column for the *New York Observer* lampooning the white, middle-class shoplifter he labeled "Bukowski Man," whom he described as a "drunk, suburban" poseur "likely to shoplift the Beats, Kerouac's *On the Road*, Ginsberg's *Howl*, Abbie Hoffman's *Steal This Book*, anything by Paul Auster and William S. Burroughs, some French writers, Kafka, Bukowski, and books about sex and marriage." Rosenbaum pointed out that "Bukowski Man" was laboring under the delusion that by stealing he was embracing writers who wallowed in "the lower depths." He said, "Petty and debased ideas of liberation" drive Bukowski Man to shoplift.

Most people who work in bookstores condemn shoplifting as arising from a specious morality and sometimes bad taste. A young salesclerk at Myopic Books, a gloomy used- and rare-book store in Chicago, whispered in my ear that the most-shoplifted book at his store was *Mein Kampf*. Louisa Solano, the former owner of the Grolier Poetry Book Shop—a small, legendary store in Cambridge, Massachusetts—sold it in 2004 in part because of shoplifters. Solano told me that a monk shoplifted from her.

Among editors, a book's shopliftability alternated between a mark of its popularity and proof of a writer's unoriginality. One editor who had worked in academic publishing felt "perverse pride" when one of his books went "behind the counter"—slang for the bookstore putting a title out of shoplifters' reach—but sneered that the majority of such books were written by impenetrable theorists who themselves shoplifted metaphorically anyway. They deserved their fate. Jacques Derrida bragged about graduate students shoplifting the 166-page *Speech and Phenomena: And Other Essays on Husserl's Theory of Signs* more than his lengthier works; another editor confided, adding that "my own conviction is that his entire method and philosophical perspective constitute a form of shoplifting."

"For a time after its release, this book was the most frequently shoplifted book in America," boasted the back jacket copy on Ann Marlowe's *How to Stop Time: Heroin from A to Z*, published in 1999. There's no way of knowing who was shoplifting the book and whether it became notable despite or because of stealability.

A recent surge in stealing rare books inspired the Antiquarian Booksellers' Association of America to protect its members by listing the five types of book thieves in its newsletter: the kleptomaniac,the thief who steals for profit, the thief who steals in anger, the casual thief, and the thief who steals for his own personal use. But many bookstore owners (rare or otherwise) and security professionals reject Bukowski Man, the kleptomaniac, and the rest of them as prime shoplifting suspects: *Professionals*, they insist, are the ones grabbing Harry Potter, art books, sex treatises, computer manuals, anything they can resell. Including the book that commands us not to steal. Which, according to anecdote, is the most frequently shoplifted volume in the Bible Belt.

"It's the best-selling book of all time," explained Melissa Mitchell, in 2006 the director of loss prevention for LifeWay Christian Stores. Mitchell said professionals and amateurs stole Bibles. "As much as we would like to think of it as a spiritual thing, some people think of it as a commodity." She speculated that the amateurs were Christian Yuppies who preferred $40 leather-bound versions with zippers. As to the Yuppies' motives, Mitchell guessed, "It's probably the desire to have nice and pretty worldly things."

The manager of a LifeWay store in Knoxville, Tennessee, who declined to be identified, said, "We have no idea who is stealing Bibles.

We just see the empty boxes, the crumpled plastic wrappers. . . . We live in a fallen world."

LUXURY LIFTING

If book shoplifting is endangered due to the Internet, luxury lifting as an amateur pastime is all but extinct as a result of the new antishoplifting technologies. Women shoplifting lace out of frustrated love, or to get back at their husbands, has fallen from fashion: Madame de Boves is an endangered species. One has to look back to the early 1990s to find essays like Daphne Merkin's "The Shoplifter's High," originally published in *Mirabella* magazine as "Stolen Pleasures." Merkin tells how she and fellow "imbiber[s] of high culture" discussed shoplifting at a high-end boutique as though it were a larcenous version of *Looking for Mr. Goodbar*.

By the time "The Shoplifter's High" appeared in Merkin's essay collection *Dreaming of Hitler* five years later, luxury goods had begun to go mass market. Revered haute couture houses were imploding or being bought by conglomerates. Counterfeit It Bags were flooding Canal Street. Venerated French designers partnered with big-box stores. "The Shoplifter's High" was placed in the section of Merkin's book titled "The Self, New and Improved," which also included accounts of her breast-reduction surgery, tanning, and binge dieting. Shoplifting is a less invasive alternative for aspirational women: If you can't afford liposuction, shoplift a status tchotchke.

Like grocers, luxury retailers connect the professionalizing of shoplifting to their embracing of state-of-the-art surveillance systems: Shoplifting a $6,000 Birkin bag, furs from Bergdorf's, caviar from Petrossian, chocolate from La Maison du Chocolat, $1,700 bras from La Perla, scallops from Citarella, handbags from Prada, or sequined Italian skirts from Barneys is too daunting for amateur thieves. You have to go back to before Merkin's essay—the 1970s—to read a news story about a theft at a luxury jeweler that uses the word "shoplift." Barry Matsuda, the former director of security at Richemont North America, which owns Cartier and a dozen other "mansions," including Chloé and Montblanc, says, "You don't shoplift a $300,000 necklace. You shoplift peanut butter, toilet paper, shirts, skirts."

Matsuda meant that to steal the most valuable jewelry in Cartier required more skill than an amateur shoplifter could muster. In the flagship store on Fifty-third Street and Fifth Avenue, except for a few silk scarves, one or two lonely bottles of perfume, and stationery, there was hardly any merchandise at all outside the glass cases. In the High Jewelry Room, where the most expensive jewelry is displayed, a thick, plaited ruby-and-diamond choker and a platinum ring featuring one emerald as big as a marble were heavily surveilled. (There are ninety-six cameras and eight guards in the Fifty-third Street store.)

Wrapped in a heavy, flat satin ribbon, the catalog—the size of a large, hardcover coffee table book—is sent exclusively to the handful of finicky clients known to spend half a million dollars on a necklace. To even get close enough to such a necklace to steal it, you'd have to be able to impersonate a Greek shipping mogul, a Saudi prince, or a Russian tycoon at close range. You'd have to make small talk about Cannes while you and the sales associate waited for the necklace and sipped glasses of wine or lattes in a small private viewing room—a sort of jewelry confessional. You would have to be a Houdini of jewel theft, volleying banter across the small table, concealing your theft from the camera, slipping the real necklace from the wrap box into your sleeve and replacing it with a paste version in an instant. Not for amateur shoplifters.

In eighteenth-century London, clothing accounted for 27.1 percent of all shoplifted goods. It is impossible to know whether these shoplifters wanted to dress better or resell the clothes for profit or both. But over the centuries, clothing has continued to be a frequently shoplifted item. Defeating clothing shoplifting, the first job the antitheft technology industry took on fifty years ago, is a multibillion-dollar industry today.

Some of the most ingenious clothes shoplifters I heard of were drag queens and transvestites who stole for their pageants—burlesques of Miss America contests and antecedents of reality television competitions. The most "legendary" thefts occurred in the 1980s, when the most important category was "labels," that is, designer labels, Terence Dixon, aka Terrence Legend, a community historian, told me. (Legendary was something all contestants wanted to be.) One time, he said, a group of ball walkers, as contestants were called, lined a Louis Vuitton satchel with tinfoil to make a high-end booster bag and then hit Saks. The contestants were organized into houses, or teams. Tina Montana, a prolific shoplifter, or "crafter," as scam artists are referred to in this community— and one-time head or "mother" of the house of Montana—shoplifted a $25,000 Versace bustier, Dixon told me. A 1997 photo at the Ebony Ball showed her in a full-length Versace gown. Some ball walkers still shoplift haute couture, although many others, Dixon said, have moved on to jeans. Like everything else, the pageants are less formal these days.

First reported in newspapers in the 1880s, filching corsets and women's underwear was for years snickeringly attributed to kleptomaniacs and erotomaniacs. Today, lingerie lifting, though supposedly a for-profit crime, is still treated as a lurid pulp subject with headlines such as "Victoria's Secret Missing Its Panties" or "Undiecover Thief." Although the occasional bold amateur shoplifts from La Perla, and one does read about a panty-swiping cross-dresser or a loving husband stealing a thong for his wife, the most common underwear lifters in the news are boosters rushing into Victoria's Secret with their foil-lined bags, sweeping thousands of dollars' worth of push-up bras and matching low-rise panties from the front table, where they are displayed to lure customers into the store. The boosters abscond with the underwear and then resell them over the Internet, at swap meets, or from warehouses.

The retail industry pays close attention to what professionals shoplift from luxury and big-box stores, but it is less vigilant in tracking what amateurs steal. Some of the items swiped by the latter can never be deemed luxurious—even in our psyches' funhouse interior. The amateur shoplifter takes ill-fitting blouses or high-heeled sandals she doesn't like or other unusable or unsellable items—a piece of gum, a pencil, or a marble. These shoplifted souvenirs languish in the closet or the desk drawer; records of such jejune thefts fade from view or are destroyed.

Perhaps it is to be seen that some amateurs shoplift items that are so big they stretch the definition of the crime. One shoplifter I met dragged rugs out the side exit of a home emporium, another fled carrying a folded-up mattress, and a third pushed small ornamental trees through the garden section at Home Depot into the parking lot. Another person shoplifted kayaks. The scion of a wealthy Detroit family shoplifted so many fishing rods from sporting-goods stores that he needed a tractor trailer to move them. The fishing rod shoplifter countered his outdoorsman pose by shoplifting a $10,000 Montblanc pen and a $32,000 watch.

CONDOM RADICALS

In our anything-goes time, shoplifting forbidden objects is more difficult than you might think. Take cigarettes: A lot of people used to shoplift them, particularly young people. That is no longer possible now that the law mandates that cigarettes be placed behind the cash register. You have to commit an armed robbery to steal smokes. Or take pornographic magazines, once widely stolen. (For the articles.) Today, with Internet porn available at the click of a mouse, why bother shoplifting *Playboy*?

But take condoms. After two decades of selling them on the open shelves, chain pharmacies, citing shoplifting in the 1990s, began locking them up. In the spring of 2006, an article about CVS doing so in its twenty-two D.C. stores appeared in the *Washington Post*. (Walgreens and Duane Reade only lock up Trojan Magnums.)

The article did not just label this obstacle to practicing safe sex as an inconvenience. It condemned it as a public health issue. "Most of the stores that locked up condoms were in poor neighborhoods," the *Post* noted, with populations at risk for AIDS/HIV, adding that these measures tied in with the abstinence-only education movement, which aimed to prevent young people, especially poor young ones, from having sex.

It was this conjecture that inspired graduate students at George Washington University's School of Public Health and Health Services to launch the "Save Lives: Free the Condoms" effort as part of a group class project. After the class ended, four of the students formed a coalition with public health groups, drummed up media attention, and then, store by store, convinced CVS to install "power wings," or "end caps" (stands at the ends of aisles) and "click boxes" (clear plastic dispensers that snap over the shelves), essentially housing the condoms in vending machines. The condoms were more accessible but still unshopliftable.

By the early winter of 2009, the condom radicals had won. Just one of the fifty CVS stores in the District of Columbia still sold only locked condoms—the one at 2646 Naylor Road, Southeast, near Howard University, a low-income, mostly African American neighborhood. But then the Washington-based coalition of labor groups, Change to Win, stepped in. In February, backed by two hundred liberal and community organizations, Change to Win launched the "Cure CVS: Unlock the Condoms Initiative" by sending "Valentines" to CVS's CEO with the message "Have a heart. Unlock the condoms" on them and by staging protests in front of CVS stores. In June, Change to Win released a study claiming that CVS was three times more likely to lock up condoms in poor, minority neighborhoods in cities including New York, Los Angeles, and Chicago. The only places in the country where CVS stores did not lock up condoms, the organization found, were D.C. and Fairfield, Connecticut.

In a prepared statement, CVS responded to Change to Win's accusations by blaming shoplifting. "In stores where condoms have been heavily shoplifted, a selection of condoms may be kept in a locked display to ensure that there is stock available for customers to purchase. This decision is based on the theft experience of the store, not its specific location. In stores that have a locked condom display, we maintain a selection of condoms that are not locked and are available for customers to purchase without asking for assistance from store employees."

When public health leaders, social service advocates, and journalists decried CVS's policy of locking up condoms, they took for granted that condom shoplifting happened because of the shame incurred when young people were forced to push the call button at the pharmacy, ask sales staff to open locked drawers, or wait while an employee requested assistance in the family planning department over the store loudspeaker. By refusing to reveal raw data about shoplifting condoms, CVS has thrust anyone wanting to buy a prophylactic back into the 1950s.

7. BOOSTERS

The flagship mall of the Simon Property Group, Woodbury Common Premium Outlets, is nestled in a valley on Route 32 in the shadow of Averell Harriman's estate, one hour north of New York City. Not that you can see much from the interstate of the 137-acre parcel of land that the former governor of New York and industrialist donated to the town of Woodbury twenty-three years ago. Woodbury Common only bursts into view once you go right onto a long, sloping driveway across from Monroe-Woodbury High School, a good-looking brick building that the Common is partly responsible for. But for years perks like the school barely consoled the locals, who regarded Woodbury Common, the nation's largest luxury discount shopping mall, as a mixed blessing.

When it was built in 1974, Woodbury Common did not look like a mall. Developers had modeled the outdoor emporium after a colonial village with gables peeking from gently sloping slate roofs. All the stores are on the first floor. A steeple rises from a clock tower—if you don't look too closely at the big windows, you might be strolling through eighteenth-century America. The riches of Fendi, Gucci, Versace, Bose, Tory Burch, Tod's, Burberry, Calvin Klein, Jimmy Choo, Kate Spade, Ralph Lauren, Godiva, Frette, Barneys New York, DKNY, and other luxury brands promise silk on every limb, leather on every extremity.

Over the past thirty years, Woodbury has expanded again and again. Today it spans 840,000 square feet and houses 222 stores. Two thousand people work there, or one-fifth of the population of the town. These days, Woodbury draws upward of 10 million people a year, more than Niagara Falls, although still less than Disneyland. Buses slide in six times a day from the Port Authority terminal in New York City.

"It's like an open-air market in the Middle East," said Cliff Weeks, a balding, skinny Central Valley Police Department lieutenant then doing double duty at the mall.

Weeks added: There is a "downside" to the mall's swollen "waistline." Since 9/11, the authorities have declared Woodbury a potential target for terrorists. The FBI and Homeland Security monitor "suspicious" license plates in the parking lot.

But the biggest problem that Woodbury has introduced to the town is a king-size amount of shoplifting. When I asked Michele Rothstein, the senior vice president of marketing for the Chelsea Group, which owns the Simon Property Group, which owns Woodbury Common, about shoplifters there, she said, "A center of that size plopped into the boon-docks. There's going to be a juxtaposition of two worlds."

Robert Kwiatkowski, Weeks's boss, the chief of the Central Valley Police Department, was less blasé: "West, north, east, south, they all come to steal. They're like Fuller Brush salesmen up and down the high-way," he said. In 2005, the "Fuller Brush" shoplifters required Kwiat-kowski to triple the police force from seven to twenty-two men. The thirty-two-year veteran of the force, who grew up in Woodbury and resembles Marlon Brando in his *Godfather* days, cautioned that just as there is no typical Woodbury shopper, there is no typical Woodbury shoplifter: Miscreants range from a member of the Montreal Expos to a pregnant woman who shoplifted $4,000 worth of clothes; from an Asian diplomat's wife to the Newburgh-born pro Willie Mae Adams. Adams was "always a lady," and with twenty-eight aliases, she taught the depart-ment "everything we know about shoplifting," Kwiatkowski added, grin-ning at her memory. "She passed a little while ago."

The chief continued, "There's what we call 'back to school shoplift-ing' in the third week in August." Once, he said with a smile, after a high school senior at Monroe-Woodbury won "best dressed" in her class thanks to her $2,600 collection of pilfered clothes, she was arrested. The town court ruled that she return the clothes along with her ill-gotten title. Fortunately, the yearbook had not yet been published.

In the squad room at the Central Valley police station, Cliff Weeks showed me a folder containing what he described as a shoplifting manual written by boosters or professional shoplifters. "If you are arrested, don't give your name and address," the manual advised. And, "Always carry $500 so that you will be able to make bail."

I asked Weeks how he knew a high schooler who had watched a few hours of *Law & Order* could not come up with the same talking points, which were available for anyone to see on the Internet. He shrugged.

We went down to the basement of the Woodbury PD, and Weeks dragged a couple of the booster bags—also called magic bags or bad bags—from storage to show me. One was from Macy's. It had a false bottom and deep white creases etched into the waxy red paper, and it was lined with tinfoil. A large blue-and-gold-striped wooden box—meant to look like a Christmas package—was suspended inside the bag by a wire attached to the bag handles. At the bottom, a trapdoor swung in and out so that the booster could rest the bag on top of a pile of shirts and suck them inside, where the electronic sensor could not detect them. If she suspected security was watching, she could dump the shirts.

When I cracked that the booster bag had seen better days, Weeks went into the storage room and returned with a booster coat—a long beige wool coat with different-size pockets hand-sewn into the lining—which he hung over the back of the door. It reminded me of what a flasher might wear to a peep show in the old Times Square.

Weeks assured me that the booster bags were effective tools for shop-lifting, as were booster aprons, bras, pants, girdles, harnesses, and bloomers enabling "booster pregnancies" to swell, collapsing nine months into a few minutes as the shoplifter stuffed in hundreds of dollars' worth of garments where the child should be.

Kwiatkowski sat in his fake-wood-paneled office and confided that the shoplifting epidemic at Woodbury had overwhelmed his men: If they're at the mall, they can't be in town. "The Common is a pain in the ass," the chief said in a conspiratorial tone. He pulled from his desk drawer an Excel spreadsheet documenting "calls for service" for the Common.

In 2000, the year before Kwiatkowski became chief and a year after the department opened a satellite office at the Common, the police department made 626 arrests there—about two a day. That's not taking into account the thousands of calls the police answered without arresting anyone. Kwiatkowski was quoted in the local paper, the *Times Herald-Record*, as saying that shoplifting accounted for 70 percent of the town's criminal cases.

Shoplifting had plagued Woodbury well before this most recent spike, townspeople said. The difference was that until the late 1990s, no one cared. According to Sheila Conroy, who sat on the town planning committee in those days, Woodbury's first owner hired janitors to moonlight as security guards, until the town planning committee put the kibosh on that cost-saving measure. Then, for a while, the emergency medical team doubled as shoplifter catchers. "They [the mall leadership] thought all you had to do was change your shirt to be part of security," said Conroy. The Simon Group said that the cleaning crew was only charged with this responsibility for a brief time and only at night.

In 2000, Woodbury created a Business Improvement District (BID) to handle the extra need for policing, to shift the cost of that policing from the taxpayer to the Common, and to siphon more of the Common's taxes to the town. Because of an archaic New York State law, sales tax from the Common goes to Orange County, and Woodburyites thought they were bearing the mall's burden with fewer payoffs than they deserved. After the BID, the mall gave money not just to the police department but also to the schools and the water and sewer systems. Still, the chief complained, it was not enough. When in 2004 the police department exceeded the budget by $30,000 because of overtime and rising benefits and Social Security costs, he assumed that the mall would make up the difference. The mall thought otherwise. "As a major taxpayer, we were entitled to a portion of police and other emergency services," said the Simon Group representative Rothstein. Kwiatkowski took his men off "mall duty" and threatened to keep them out for four months.

Kwiatkowski's lip curled when he talked about this time, because even though Woodbury eventually came through, nothing was ever the same. "I had an understanding. Shame on me. Big business will cut costs whenever they can. Crime goes up when they cut corners. And they're continually cutting corners." He thought for a minute and looked out his tiny window into the parking lot. "What do I think about Woodbury? It's a nice place to shoplift."

THE GOOD BOOSTER

Boosters are shoplifters who resell stolen goods for money. I encountered my first one in a class at Theft Talk, a not-for-profit group based in Portland, Oregon, that teaches thieves not to steal. During the "getting to know you" part of the class, Tamara, a slim, dark-skinned woman, wearing small gold hoop earrings, a jacket with white satin lapels, black jeans, and white Keds, stood out by confessing that she had spent six months in a federal prison.

Tamara had come to the class after "thirty-one years of stealing. I never had this offered in my twenties. So now this is part of the compromise. When I first started, at the age of eighteen, that was fifteen, twenty years ago. I've been running on automatic."

What motivated her to stop shoplifting? "The thought of doing more time." The group leader paused like a teacher who wanted to use someone else's mistake to make a point. "If the only reason you stop shoplifting is a form of punishment, you will steal again," she said.

A few days after the Theft Talk class, I met Tamara at a coffee shop near her apartment. She was fifty-four. She used to be a heroin addict. Since her release from prison, she has worked at a series of jobs at small businesses. "I'm trying to show people you don't need to be a Bible thumper to get clean. I never learned moderation. I can deal with a volcano, but if my shoelace breaks, I can't deal with that. People used to say to me, 'If you put this much energy into something positive, I would back you.'"

When the feds busted Tamara, she had been boosting to support her heroin addiction since the age of eighteen, when she had met her husband, Doug. Tamara grew up on a reservation and spent a lot of time in foster homes.

"My whole perception of life was power and fame." About meeting her much older husband, Doug, she said, laughing, "He had this aura. I was in love." She ran massage parlors and strip clubs with names like Action Unlimited and Playmates' Club, but she switched to boosting because "I got tired of men."

The first thing she and Doug shoplifted was meat, which they called "cattle rustling." She would slip slabs of it into her baby bag and dash out of the store. Many heists ensued. She resold the merchandise to many different clients. "I was doing longshoremen's halls . . . underwear to whatever. Roundup, a weed killer, was in demand in the Midwest. There was this old madam, used to service people in prominent positions. Her son, living in California, used to sell the Indian rugs—we boosted them."

Boosting was easy money: The team could sell bottles of aspirin or Nicoderm patches to a fence for up to 7–10 percent of the market price. On a good day, that meant pulling in between $400 and $600 and the fence would resell the merchandise for 50–60 percent of the price.

Tamara's story was not just about supply and demand: It was an informal history of the eighties' most popular products and also a primer on how boosters blamed stores for making it easy to steal. "When people were stealing those Mach One razor blades, [the stores] would put them right on the floor," she said. "Doesn't make any sense. They were encouraging people to steal them."

Eventually Tamara joined a loose network of boosters selling merchandise to fences and wholesalers. "It was the organized Asian mob," she said. She and Doug worked as a team, driving from store to store, earning enough money to get high. But she soon discovered she also liked boosting. "It was as hard to kick as heroin."

Heroin and boosting helped her escape pain and contributed to her sense of invincibility. Boosting momentarily made Doug feel vital after he got sick from complications stemming from his drug addiction: "He would put his oxygen there and still be there stealing from his [wheel-chair]. It played on people's sympathy. He had a disarming smile. All those things that you need to get someone's guard down."

The best parts were the all-night bull sessions where she and Doug would plan the heist: What if this happens, what if that happens, what if something entirely off-the-wall happens? The product could determine their strategy. Just after Nintendos came out, Doug, Tamara, and Doug's nephew planned a heist at Toys"R"Us. Tamara went to the store and bought a giant plastic wading pool, then carried it aloft into the parking lot, its inside stuffed with Nintendos.

In the bull sessions, ideas flew fast about what items to boost and how to do it. They'd be watching TV and see a commercial about a high-end fishing reel—Abu Garcia. "During fishing season, guys would die for that reel," Tamara said. And they would work up a technique. Doug would slide reels across the counter when the cashier's back was turned. But if the reels were Shimanos, the Japanese high-end brand, after taking them out of the box, Tamara claims, she could fit as many as fifty of them in her purse, evidently a big one. To boost cameras, she would crawl across the floor behind the counter, grab them, and crawl back to the cart. In his younger days, Doug would flirt with the saleswomen to distract them. "He would say, 'Gee, you're pretty. Would you like to go out with me?'"

They usually would.

At 8:00 a.m. one Sunday morning, Tamara and Doug hit a Safeway. In this early-morning scam, Doug would stand in the store and "read" a magazine while directing Tamara as though he were a crossing guard. He would stand next to her holding the magazine or even a piece of poster board so the camera could not "see" her. "Go," he would whisper. "Stop."

But this time, he kept repeating the words, as though he were on continuous loop: "Go stop go stop go stop." Dope sick, Doug threw caution to the wind.

Tamara explained, "A good booster from the time that they go into the store has sixty seconds to assess the situation: Is security there? Is it between shifts? What people are on? Is it a manager that watches people?"

That day, a cashier was looking straight at Tamara during the operation. The Bonnie of boosting violated another of their Ten Commandments: Never stay in a store for more than three minutes. They had been there three hours. Tamara was impatient and she got careless; she "over-rolled" everything she knew because desperation, fear, and anxiety set in. She began to believe she was invincible and adopted a smash-and-grab mentality: She could take anything and no one could catch her. "Not a good thing," she said. "Real tacky. You should have enough finesse to be able to go in again and again and they could say, 'Hello, Mr. Jones.' And you could say, 'How are your grapes?'" In other words, she was blowing her cover.

Instead, Tamara crouched on her knees and loaded up her purse while Doug shouted, "Go—stop." They ran as a saleswoman yelled. They were arrested. "Once you start racking those felonies up," Tamara said, "you bounce in and out of jail."

Shoplifting rehabilitation groups contend that although boosters may be drug addicts, drugs do not make people shoplift. "'She was so drunk and she went to her favorite store and stole her favorite piece of jewelry.' No. They know what they're doing. It's a piece of the puzzle, but not the whole puzzle," explained Lisa Paules, an employee at Theft Talk. She meant that people (drug addicts or not) choose to shoplift. Further, this argument goes, although drug-addicted boosters may steal more in dollars or volume than amateurs, they do not comprise the majority of shoplifters. Only 10 percent of "theft offenders" are drug addicts.

The Oregon Department of Corrections (ODC) does not measure shoplifting (misdemeanors are beneath counting). But after the ODC reported in 2007 that 60 percent of all prison inmates are addicted to drugs, retail industry lobbyists moved to strengthen antitheft laws. Oregon was one of the first states to pass harsher, "enhanced" retail theft laws—putting prescription drugs like pseudoephedrine and ephedrine behind the counter and requiring a state ID to purchase them. (The medicines can be used to make methamphetamines.)

"A 'YOU CAN'T CATCH ME' KINDA THING"

A few days after I met Tamara, I drove to Amity—a town about an hour southwest of Portland, Oregon, in the state's wine country—to meet another Theft Talk alum, John Allen Bradshaw, a recovering methamphetamine addict, ex-booster, and born-again Christian who was also the subject of several local newspaper articles. I found John in the garage where he was working as a welder, blowtorching a hood onto a car. Sparks flew off the torch and around his head. When he turned off the torch and removed his mask, with his round face and spidery mustache, he looked much younger than forty-one.

We went into the office, empty except for a metal desk and two chairs, and sat down. "I'm focused on getting people to love the Lord without throwing the book at them," John began. "But my brother raised me with marijuana and cross-tops and coke," he said, cross-tops referring to a pill form of meth known by its hatching on the top.

After John had been arrested many times, the court gave his wife custody of their three children. In 2004, she lost custody and the state placed them in foster care. John got into meth first, then boosting. To support his habit, he shoplifted electronics from Walmart: "Electronic gadgets, a scanner, two-way radios, digital recording devices, reselling them for methamphetamines." His technique was not polished or thought through. He did not scheme or use props: "Grab things, take them out, out, go in there, go into bathroom, go into stall, take strips off, depackage them. Set off alarm and keep going. Got scared, almost got caught." But like Tamara, John described boosting as an addiction whose power was related to drugs and ultimately bested them. "I started with drugs, but it turned out that taking stuff was more of an adrenaline rush than drugs. The thrill: the adrenaline to see if I could get away with it—knowing the alarms. I'd fill up my backpack with stuff. It's a pretty sick disease. A 'you can't catch me' kinda thing."

For John, shoplifting was also about finding something valuable in dirty, ramshackle houses and anonymous big-box stores. The crime allowed him to be a treasure hunter, a landlocked pirate, to scavenge. After he graduated from shoplifting to burglary, he continued to see himself as a kind of pirate. But when he got caught stealing guns from someone's shed, he didn't feel good about it anymore. As he put it, "The judge gave me such a small sentence, I felt I deserved more. I wanted to be punished more."

John gave up shoplifting. He found solace in a faith-based twelve-step program sponsored by Celebrate Recovery, the national evangelical church, which had opened a branch in nearby McMinnville. It was a drug addiction program, since Celebrate Recovery considered theft a sin. (Now some branches of Celebrate Recovery support so-called theft addiction.)

The next time I saw him, John had progressed to step five, where the addict is supposed to confess. "Made all my amendses [*sic*] since talking to you," he said, happy that he had told everyone he knew about his boosting, sure that confessing would lead to cleansing.

THREE (OR FOUR) STRIKES

In 1929, shoplifting was punishable in New York State by the Baumes Law, a Jazz Age antecedent of our "three strikes" law. First passed three years earlier, the Baumes Law allowed four strikes. Many politicians hoped to use the law to punish *all* shoplifting—not just the felonious version. But a few months after Black Friday, when New York lawmakers utilized the Baumes Law to sentence the first woman to life in prison for shoplifting, it inspired a public outcry. Hundreds of people wrote to Franklin D. Roosevelt, then governor of New York, to protest that the sentence was too much for a shoplifter. Roosevelt overturned it on the grounds that a shoplifter—even a recidivist—did not deserve life.

For the past ten years, the cases of boosters like Tamara and John have convinced many in the retail industry that only a return to a Baumes Law–style punishment will stop the crime. Frank Muscato, the supervisor of Organized Retail Theft Investigation and Prosecution for Walgreens, calls strengthening existing laws "enhancement." Today, if you are arrested for shoplifting a bottle of Sudafed and it is your third offense and you live in a state with an enhanced retail theft statute, you could get ten years for racketeering. In the past decade, eighteen states have passed enhancements, and more are in the works. The enhancements increase sentences for repeat offenders, fences, and shoplifters carrying tools of the trade, such as booster bags and EAS removing tools. Some states now consider shoplifting a felony if the shoplifter leaves through an emergency exit, no matter how much the stolen item is worth. Other states regard it a felony if the shoplifter resells the merchandise to flea market vendors.

Muscato defended the enhancements: "We need specific laws so we can charge cases that way." What would happen to a nice young man who shoplifted Advil for his sick mother? Muscato said, "He is probably going to be charged under the stricter law." In this way, penalties intended to prevent the booster fall on the shoplifter.

Another one of Muscato's causes is lobbying lawmakers to lower the felony level—the dollar amount at which a misdemeanor theft becomes a felony. Since retail trade organizations first began to agitate to enhance these laws in the 1970s, legislators have tightened them in some states and loosened them in others. Now the levels range from zero in Indiana, where shoplifting anything is a felony, to $2,500 in Wisconsin. Some states have built-in exceptions, like California, whose felony level is $400, except for citrus fruits: Shoplifting $100 worth of oranges in the Golden State makes you a felon. In Texas years ago, said Muscato, referring to the obsolete "rustling" statute, shoplifting a can of meat chili could result in jail.

Today judges use felony levels to determine whether shoplifters are professionals or amateurs, boosters or shoplifters, criminal or insane. Retailers complain that raising these levels for inflation, which some Democrats have tried to do in recent years, artificially suppresses the amount of shoplifting being recorded and invites boosters to go on inter-state shoplifting tears.

In the past ten years, seventeen states have raised the felony level for retail theft, but many others have lowered it. In 2001, in the outlet-mall-rich state of Maine, after shoplifting had risen for several years, the Maine Merchants Association got the felony level decreased from $2,000 to $1,000.

In 2009, Senator Arthenia L. Joyner, who represents the Eighteenth District in Tampa, Florida—comprising poor, largely African American areas—sponsored a bill that would raise the felony level from $300 to $600 and place young shoplifters in a diversion program. The felony level had not been raised since 1986, she said at a Criminal and Civil Justice Appropriations Committee hearing, adding that doing so would save money and prison beds.

My main objective was to divert offenders who qualify out of the criminal justice system and into a diversion program. I am concerned that young people are creating barriers to meaning-ful future employment by engaging in what generally constitutes reckless or thoughtless behaviors. The bill was supported by the Public Defender's Association and the State Attorney's Associa-tion. It was a collaborative effort in the end, of all but the retail industry. The bill successfully passed all committees in the Sen-ate and was voted favorably out of the Senate. The bill did not move in the House due partly to the misleading statements made by the retailers that the bill would promote concerted or gang shoplifting.

The Florida Retail Federation's John Rogers said this sort of bill would encourage boosters from areas with lower felony levels to flock to the Sunshine State. Rogers speculated that Joyner supported the bill because she thought the current one unfairly targeted indigent shoplift-ers in her district.

In the past five years, the retail industry has expanded its anti-boosting lobbying campaign to the federal level. In 2006, after several years of attempts, the National Retail Federation pushed Congress to pass a federal bill to fund a Department of Justice Organized Retail Theft (ORT) task force through the House and the Senate. HR 3402 rode through a conservative House and Congress on the coattails of the Violence against Women and Department of Justice Reauthorization Act. Three Republicans sponsored the bill, which would direct $5 million annually for three years to the Department of Justice to fund a database tracking ORT and to train FBI personnel to pursue thieves and their merchandise: James Sensenbrenner, a Republican from Wisconsin; Larry Craig, the then soon-to-be disgraced senator from Idaho; and Robert W. Goodlatte, the libertarian Republican from Virginia who also opposed electronic file sharing. The bill passed; the money was not appropriated, because, according to one source, the FBI already had existing programs to cover organized retail theft. But HR 3402 was only the beginning of the retail industry's crusade against ORT. Four similar bills were proposed in the 111th Congress alone.

ON THE TRAIL OF BOOSTED GOODS

Appearing in the twentieth century's first decade, the word "booster" distinguished those who shoplifted for profit from those who stole because of disease or compulsion. The popular press typed boosters as women, Jews, Gypsies, or Irish Travelers—foreigners or immigrants. But the word also contained a positive meaning. As the *Chicago Tribune* put it in 1911, a booster was "a man or a woman of more than ordinary intelligence." By the Depression, when Americans were obsessed with outlaws, "booster" embraced both skill and deceit. The criminologist Edwin H. Sutherland's 1937 semifictional biography of the professional thief Chic Conwell uses "boost" as a synonym for shoplifting and also defines it as a technique, a sort of "manipulation of suckers by nonviolent methods." At the same time, "booster" was also becoming a synonym for civic pride. Today, however, booster's most powerful meaning as it refers to theft is about what it is not—boosting is not shoplifting. It is bigger and more criminal, and the people who do it are not sick, harmless, or intelligent. Or that is what the retail industry would like you to believe.

Security people sent me photos of recovered boosted merchandise to illustrate the magnitude of the booster epidemic and the necessity to fight it. One photo showed boxes of Monistat, EPT pregnancy tests, Crest Whitestrips, Rogaine, and Oil of Olay cosmetics piled on top of one another. In a second photo, dusty, dented cans of infant formula were jammed in a similar fashion. To those who worked to stop shoplifting, the meaning of this second photo was especially clear: Perishable boosted infant formula was hazardous to the American people's health.

I asked Tamara, the ex-booster, "Who buys boosted Crest Whitestrips and Rogaine?" She said, "Everyone." Doctors, lawyers, she elaborated.

So if boosters are shopping warriors, that makes every person who buys boosted cosmetics and over-the-counter pharmaceuticals accomplices.

Economists disagree about how boosting affects the legitimate economy. One view is that boosting, which feeds the black market, is "constructive," allowing people to buy luxuries that they could not otherwise afford. Another argument is that boosting is linked to terrorism, although there is little hard evidence. A third argument is that the creation of black markets where boosters operate suppresses competition and leads to violence. In this theory, boosting not only drains resources and saps productivity from legitimate stores, it fails to protect buyers from harm or faulty products. To me these theories—especially the second and third— miss the point. The majority of the most-boosted items are cosmetics, not necessities. If the explosion of boosted Crest Whitestrips, Rogaine, razors, and EPT tests furthers the American economy's drift toward that of a third world country, then, though we will have shiny white smiles and full heads of hair and be clean-shaven and know whether we are pregnant, we will also be able to say that we have shoplifted until we dropped.

PART THREE

PATHOLOGY

I suddenly began to realize that everybody in America is a natural born thief.

—Jack Kerouac, *On the Road*

8. | THE THRILL OF THE STEAL

Many shoplifters talk about the crime like a love affair. Here is how they sound: Shoplifting punctures despair, at least temporarily. Shoplifters enjoy stealing. The objects mean something to them, but taking them feels dirty. Shoplifting is a spasm or a seizure. The lesson they learn from the crime—yes, I can!—they might apply to other areas of life. Shoplifting gives them courage to take chances. One shoplifter, who, according to him, over the years stole $25,000 worth of merchandise, wrote:

> It's knowing I'm doing something wrong and the sense of superiority over the store owner or clerk. As I got older and developed more sleight of hand, I had to start stealing more expensive or hard-to-get items . . . to get a bigger rush. There's also this inner fear that a hand is gonna drop on your shoulder as you walk out the door, and when it doesn't, you feel invincible. Making it seem as if I belonged in a place, being so normal that I was overlooked by all. But as I've aged the reverse has happened, in that I've now become the guy nobody notices or pays attention to. Think of the movie [*The Vanishing*]. I identified with the Jeff Bridges character, only my fascination was stealing. . . . Although I've thought I would make a good hit man, if I had been given the opportunity.

For Dahlia, a novelist and former personal assistant who lives in Los Angeles and dabbled in shoplifting for years, the thrill lay in the loot amassed. But for others, the thrill came from proficiency. "You begin to believe that it's a craft and a skill. You get better at it . . . You figure out which store has better security," said Donna, a single mom and ex-journalist who once shoplifted a gym bag on the way home from a court date. "Getting away with it is an adrenaline rush. It evens the score." But, she complained, the rush only lasted for a few minutes. "And you're back to yourself again. In your mind, you think, It was all for a stupid blouse, or stupid soap. For this, I risked everything."

B, an actor who shoplifted with a friend, liked the moment-to-moment unpredictability: "[I shoplifted] every day, like someone with a drug addiction. I could look at G from across the store and that look meant, Go ahead, it's clear. We hadn't planned on taking anything."

Christine, who used to be a flight attendant, found shoplifting apparently unshopliftable items especially thrilling: "Sometimes I'll challenge myself, like one time I took . . . like a door stop, it was a monkey, and it was heavy. It was made out of brass. It was as big as a roll of toilet paper. From a home furnishings store. I put it in my pocket, which is something that I rarely do. It felt great." Adam Stein, an actor and writer who shoplifted for years until he was arrested, said, "I was caught at Barnes & Noble by a floor detective. By that time I had gotten a false bravado . . . I didn't think that anyone would be watching." Sarah, a sixty-one-year-old advertising executive, the daughter of a wealthy judge from a prosperous town, talked of the secret of shoplifting, which "compromised me and made me feel good." Alice, a shoplifting housewife, felt "euphoric and tingly." She said, "I was exhilarated . . . satisfied in a way I had not been for many years." She used to spend hours planning shoplifting. She smuggled cuticle scissors into the store under a big coat, and then she ripped off a plastic wrapper from a DVD, which she would then stuff in her pants while she "made a break" for her car. She shoplifted "at" someone—she didn't know whom. Jennie, another housewife, said, "I had to keep on stealing to keep from remembering all the stealing I had done."

The self-described "elder of filth," John Waters, shoplifted to finance his first films, which were about the crime or used it to advance the plot. Though Waters no longer shoplifts, his obsession with the subject belongs to his brand as much as his caterpillar mustache or designer smoking jackets. In a tongue-in-cheek National Public Radio essay in 2003, Waters joked that he liked Christmas because it was "easier" to shoplift during that holiday, and in an interview for *Filmmaker* magazine the same year, he fondly recalled a shoplifter whose technique involved setting small fires between racks of clothing.

In the spring of 2006, Waters, sixty, a petite, elegant man in a black Isaac Mizrahi jacket with white piping and tuxedo pants, spent a few minutes of an hour-long talk at Columbia College in Chicago lamenting the passing of his salad days of shoplifting. "We were really good at it," Waters said, standing in front of a set consisting of a couple of aluminum trash cans overflowing with garbage. He leaned toward the microphone. "I had a special jacket for stealing LPs," he confessed, adding, "I don't feel bad because today I have to pay $25,000 to use some of these songs in my films, so it's all worked out in the end."

In 1966, around the time Waters made his shopliftungsroman *Roman Candles*, he noticed that Divine (*Pink Flamingos'* obese cross-dressing hero) was talented at the crime. "I saw him walk out of a store once with a chain saw and a TV." Waters minced across the stage mimicking Divine in the scene where, to Frankie Lymon and the Teenagers' doo-wop number "I'm Not a Juvenile Delinquent," he slides a slab of raw meat into his panties and humps it.

Later, I asked Waters why he praised shoplifting in his talks, his movies, and his books. The first thing he said was, "Shoplifting is a cinematic crime." But he was also proud of his own prowess. "I never got caught." He began at age ten, with a 45 of Lawrence Welk's "Tonight You Belong to Me" and continued for reasons whose soundtrack was more Rolling Stones: "It used to be politically correct to shoplift, except from a mom-and-pop store." The thrill egged him on. "You felt a rush of adrenaline when you have that thing under your arm." Besides, he said, shoplifting was as good a standard as any by which to measure friends and foes. "I don't trust anybody who hasn't shoplifted."

Nan, a red-haired, middle-age director and playwright, whispered at a restaurant in Greenwich Village, "If you shoplift once, you forever think of yourself as a thief." The scion of a wealthy suburban family, she (according to her story) shoplifted from the seventh grade until recently, stopping briefly when she became a mom. "During the children's infancy, I had no time to shoplift. . . . I slipped back into my life once they were in school. I went back to that behavior, but never with consistency. I can't risk it." Nan shoplifted solo and in a team, for pleasure and for profit. "I shoplifted a watch that I know I didn't get enough for. It was from a store in the East Seventies, a jewelry boutique. It was $3,500." She stole as foreplay: "This guy who wished he was a girl. I stole with him. I would order him to steal for me and he would and we also stole together." She shoplifted prosaic items and ones that had special meaning to her. She saw herself as a hero in the store, hugging the shoplifted item to her body as she escaped through the aisles. She bragged about it, leaning across the oiled, checkered tablecloth and winking. "I have a close, personal relationship with shoplifting. That sounds glib, but it's true."

Everything was connected to shoplifting, including recycling: "When you get a vintage Balenciaga jacket for six dollars, that's almost shoplifting," she said. One story was more harrowing than the last. When she was twelve, she shoplifted over $500 worth of clothes from a local department store, which was a felony. "It was easier to get sloppy then pre-EAS." What she wanted was a peasant blouse. She put on jeans over the jeans she was wearing. She folded a sundress flat. Her mother bailed her out and treated her to a peach Melba. "Shoplifting was part of a bigger picture, a scary picture in retrospect," she said, alluding to the sex and drugs that lured her. Nan remembered the language of shoplifting as if she had learned it in a school for thieves. "Did you *get* it? If you 'got' it, you'd stolen it."

After she first moved to New York for college in the late 1980s, Nan lived "on the fringe," and not seeing herself as "part of the regular day-to-day world," she went "underground" and shoplifted things she didn't have the money to buy, like spices from a gourmet food store in Greenwich Village. One time a security guard caught her, but instead of reporting her, escorted her back to her apartment. They did not sleep together. Another shoplifting story with an "I escaped in the nick of time" denouement began when Nan and a friend were exiting Bergdorf Goodman with a fur coat, which the friend had slung over her arm. The security guard grabbed the friend but got a handful of fur from the sleeve. The duo pushed through the revolving door and bolted down Fifth Avenue. The guard did not give chase.

Shoplifters like Nan described how they felt while getting ready to shoplift: Their hearts beat quickly; their faces flushed; they knew that shoplifting would release excitement, and they craved that release. Sometimes the excitement began hours before shoplifting and sometimes minutes before they lost the ability to concentrate on anything except going to the store. The thrill of belonging to an exclusive club, and also of being damned to it. The shoplifters were swept up in a dance of pleasure and agony.

Steve, an ex-shoplifter I met in Detroit, leaned toward me and worried that to share his methods was to promote shoplifting, which he was averse to do. But when he spoke of the thrill of it, his face lit up. In Home Depot, "I feel like I know what I'm doing," he said. The crime was his "best friend." Like Nan, he bragged about his technique: "I was the reason why prepaid phone cards had to be activated at the cashier." He shoplifted an X-Acto knife and a price-tag gun so he could shoplift other stuff. "Survival of the fittest," he joked.

In college, Scott Harris shoplifted as others drink Red Bull—for a jolt of adrenaline. His heists included a snowblower and a water ski. "I would get out of class, desire to go down on University Drive or on State Street and hit the stores. It was literally a daily thing. . . . Before long I had over a thousand music CDs, dozens of hats, things that brought no value to my life other than superficial value. Filling voids made me feel better."

"A THRILLING MELODRAMA ABOUT THE SELF"

In his 1988 book *Seductions of Crime: Moral and Sensual Attractions in Doing Evil*, Jack Katz writes about "the neglect of the positive, often wonderful attractions within the lived experience of criminality." Katz, for many years a professor of sociology at UCLA, refers to the French phenomenologist Maurice Merleau-Ponty to tease out shoplifting's affinity with pleasure. He calls shoplifting a "sneaky thrill" and "a thrilling melodrama about the self seen from without and within," and, drawing on the work of anthropologist Claude Lévi-Strauss, compares it to magic. He means that, for transcendence's sake, we create our own sleight of hand when we shoplift. We imagine the borders where objects end and we begin, and we shoplift to shorten the distance. Quoting Merleau-Ponty, Katz muses that we are "seduced and repelled by the world," especially by experiences "present[ing] a thrilling demonstration of personal competence."

After *Seductions of Crime* appeared, a number of novels and memoirs were published in which the heroines shoplifted to demonstrate "personal competence" or to play out a "thrilling melodrama about the self." Ellen Lesser's 1990 short story, "The Shoplifter's Apprentice," describes shoplifting as inspiring "a terrible freedom." The heroine, "as much prey to disproportionate longings as anyone," falls in love with a shoplifting rogue. On shoplifting excursions, she feels "benign even pleasurable panic like she felt at the movies worrying, but knowing deep down that the hero would prevail." After the rogue abandons her, she shoplifts to regain the feeling that "anything could happen now." As a child, Miriam, the heroine of Myla Goldberg's 1999 novel *Bee Season*, shoplifts a pink rubber ball that "tingles against her palm." Years later, shoplifting as an adult, she "luxuriates in the store's atmosphere, lingering over a blue scarf." She is ecstatic when her lover tells her about *tikkun olam*, Judaism's reconstituting of shattered pieces, because it explains her shoplifting.

In Kathryn Harrison's novel *Exposure*, Ann shoplifts at Bergdorf's and Bloomingdale's to block the memory of her father's abuse years earlier and to stop thinking about everything that bothers her. Crystal meth helps, as does Ann's acute impulsiveness. Seconds before she is nabbed, she wonders why she shoplifted. "All she needs in the world is one crummy formal dress so why is there a blue silk jacket, one that she doesn't particularly like, in her camera bag?"

I spent a couple of hours with Harrison one snowy day in the winter of 2006 in her Brooklyn brownstone talking about shoplifting in *Exposure* and in her life. Reclining on a velvet chaise longue in her living room, the novelist said, "Dumbo has his feather and we have our stolen objects, which are more powerful for having been acquired illicitly." Harrison launched into a story about her own shoplifting as part of a girl duo in California, complete with monikers—hers was Edwina—and wigs. "I had this friend Nicole—she and I were quite opposite physical types in every way. She was sort of this very dark creature. Daydreamy. We were good girls, late bloomers. This was when we were twelve, thirteen."

After a while a guy named Jeff joined them. Harrison resented Jeff. He changed the character of their crime. But she nonetheless deconstructed shoplifting as a girlhood rite of passage and as a force that focused her chaotic spirit. She kept shoplifting until she was sixteen or seventeen, when a supermarket detective at Ralphs in Sherman Oaks ended her career. "They called my grandfather, who was apoplectic. . . . My grandmother . . . believed the worst of me. It was Tampax—all the checkers were guys. I didn't want to pay for it."

But, Harrison mused, shoplifting was also a game grown-up women played, like flirting or courtship. There is a secret language that shoplifters speak, she said. "Intuitively, I know which women among my friends steal," she added, repeating that shoplifting amplified the value of any object because of the trouble one took to acquire it. "When you steal, there is a frisson of being connected. If I said, 'Can you give this to me?' that would be less powerful. Stealing can make you feel *more* than you are, arriving at yourself in some way. The act in and of itself is a fetish. Objects then lose their value and you have to do it again."

9. | THE RISE AND FALL OF
THE SHOPLIFTING CELEBRITY

"My little shoplifter," Gaston coos to Lily in *Trouble in Paradise*, Ernst Lubitsch's movie about two thieves disguised as wealthy Europeans. For the bounders in evening wear sharing dinner in their hotel room, stealing is an aphrodisiac. By the time Gaston utters his endearment, gazing into Lily's eyes, they are already entwined on the couch. In the next frame, a Do Not Disturb sign hangs on their hotel room door. The movie ends happily as the thieves escape in a taxi. For these sexual shenanigans and for its celebration of lawbreaking, *Trouble in Paradise* was censored by the Hays Code in 1932.

After that, the movies depicted lady shoplifters as femmes fatales who feel toward objects the way they are supposed to feel toward men. We learn so much from watching the movies—everything from kissing to smoking—so it's not surprising that Hollywood's definition of shoplifting sticks in our minds. Or that we're still saddened to learn that the reality of movie stars shoplifting is grimmer than that of the lovestruck kleptos that you see on the screen. In the golden age of film noir, at the dawn of postwar American consumerism, some of the era's most ambitious directors saw the kleptomaniac as a woman driven by the contradictions and ambiguities of the genre to shoplift clothes. Preston Sturges's *Remember the Night* (1940), a romantic comedy with noir accents starring Barbara

Stanwyck; Otto Preminger's *Whirlpool* (1949), starring Gene Tierney; William Wyler's *Detective Story* (1951), starring Lee Grant; and later, Alfred Hitchcock's *Marnie* (1964), starring Tippi Hedren, begin with a mysterious woman shoplifting (or having stolen). This woman lacks a history, perhaps an identity. She doesn't know why she steals. A wry, troubled man—sometimes a detective—investigates her. He is trying to solve a crime, but also to find out who killed her capacity to love. Mostly, that villain is the woman's father. As in most noir, even when the hero saves the girl, the story does not necessarily end with a wedding.

Remember the Night opens in Meyers jewelry store in Manhattan at Christmastime with a close-up of Stanwyck's arm in an opera-length velvet glove; a bald salesman is fastening a diamond bracelet watch around her wrist. While he dives into the cabinet to look for a different bracelet, Stanwyck escapes. Briskly walking down Fifth Avenue in her muff, matching fur jacket, and diamonds, she blends into the crowd. Her pawnbroker turns her in. Fred MacMurray, the prosecutor with the heart of gold, is reluctant to send Stanwyck to jail over Christmas. He finagles her bond. They go out for a bite to eat at a supper club. As a torch singer croons, Sturges sets the stage for their romance by making MacMurray hope that Stanwyck is a kleptomaniac.

"How long have you been swiping things?"

"Always."

"Did you take beautiful things you didn't need?"

As a flirtation, she explains that she is just a common thief. "Oh no . . . you see, to be a kleptomaniac, you can't resell any of the stuff afterwards or you lose your amateur standing."

Stanwyck goes on to say that her mind works "differently" and that MacMurray will never understand her. En route to the MacMurray homestead in Indiana, after a local judge arrests the pair, using her "different mind," Stanwyck sets fire to a garbage can. The couple escapes. A glimpse of Stanwyck's unhappy family is enough to make MacMurray fall in love. At the end of the movie, he proposes to Stanwyck after she pleads guilty to shoplifting. But she demurs: If he feels the same way when she gets out of prison, she'll marry him. Sturges could not end a film in which a district attorney falls in love with a shoplifter any other way. He was no Billy Wilder.

Written by Ben Hecht, *Whirlpool*, which Otto Preminger directed a few years after his hit film *Laura*, takes place in traditional noir territory: Los Angeles. The film suggests that shoplifting—kleptomania, really—is a symbol for being a woman. In its first seconds, a shadow falls across the interior of the Wilshire Shops in Beverly Hills. Don't worry. It's just a crisp piece of paper that a hatbox is going to be wrapped in. The camera cuts to Ann Sutton (Gene Tierney), a beautiful, icy kleptomaniac leaving the store. She asks the valet for her convertible. But in the next moment, a detective confronts her and demands that she empty her purse. A shoplifted brooch falls out. Tierney feigns shock. On the way back to the holding room, passing David Korvo (José Ferrer), an oily hypnotist, she faints and when she comes to, surrounded by security guards, he vouches for her.

Apparently, Tierney, the wife of a distinguished psychoanalyst who ignores her despite her many décolletage-revealing gowns, shoplifts to get his attention. Korvo at first seems interested in curing the lonely woman, then in having an affair with her. But finally, he frames her for murder. Because she is a kleptomaniac, she is vulnerable to charlatanry. A crook who forgets that she has stolen is capable of worse crimes. "I'm a bad girl! I'm a thief!" she cries, ashamed. Preminger ultimately resolves the Oedipal roots of her problem—her tightwad father—by restoring her husband's love to her.

A recurrent theme in the era's movies is the lonely female shoplifter stealing luxury items. "I didn't need it. I didn't even like it," Lee Grant whines about the purse she lifted in the hard-boiled film *Detective Story*, as though stealing were part of the feminine mystique. *I Was a Shoplifter* (1950), a cold war noir film preaching against kleptomania's dangers, is also a love story. Tony Curtis and Andrea King are the heads of a gang of professional shoplifters. After Mona Freeman, a socialite librarian, and kleptomaniac, is caught shoplifting in a department store,

King blackmails her into joining them. A love triangle among Scott Brady (an undercover agent on the gang's trail), Freeman, and Curtis—Pepe, a small-time hood—underscores how shoplifting can lead to that "dark and lonely place" where so many kleptomaniac heroines wind up if they don't meet Mr. Right. Hitchcock's *Marnie* follows a similar arc, tracing Marnie's kleptomania back to her childhood, when she witnessed her mother killing a man, and forward to marital happiness.

By the early sixties, the crime became less dangerous, a pretty party girl's lark. It is little more than a ruse to steal a kiss in the movie of *Breakfast at Tiffany's*. In Truman Capote's 1958 novella, Holly Golightly says to the "Capote" character, "Let's steal something," and the duo lift two masks from Woolworth's. As he puts it, "Successful theft exhilarates." In the novella, Holly is a prostitute who swears like a sailor. But in the 1961 movie, as played by Audrey Hepburn, she is an insouciant charmer, a wayward feminist. Thanks to Hollywood's prudishness, the Capote character morphs into Holly's beau, Paul (George Peppard), a self-described "bookish type." Shoplifting becomes a zany lovers' adventure.

"Ever steal anything?" Holly asks Paul. Wearing a tangerine-colored day coat, she ambles through the aisles of Carter's five-and-ten until, eyeing two detectives, she picks up a frilly lampshade and sets it on her head. She covers a fishbowl with her mink hat and moves it from one shelf to another. Paul watches. After trying on a Huckleberry Hound mask, Holly slides a kitty-cat one over her face, Paul seizes a doggy one, and the two miscreants flee down the street. They run right into a policeman. "I can't see," Holly yells. At the apartment, exhilarated, they rip off the masks, look into each other's eyes, and fall into each other's arms. Shoplifting was never more romantic.

SHOPLIFTING CONFIDENTIAL

A biopic about a Hollywood star shoplifting would be terminally depressing. But the real stories about stars and shoplifting rivet us to the crime. The same year that *Breakfast at Tiffany's* was released, the *Saturday*

Evening Post quoted Dean Martin confessing to shoplifting from haberdasheries. "Even today . . . I steal a necktie or a pair of gloves or a pair of socks. I'm sure that the owners know it, but I'm such a good customer they don't really care. Everyone has a little larceny in him," Martin told the magazine, whose editor worried about the interview: "We better send it to the lawyer. Maybe this guy is libeling himself."

Stores stopped tolerating celebrity shoplifting a few years later. In 1966, former glamour queen Hedy Lamarr was arrested for stealing a $40 knit suit, $1 worth of greeting cards, a $10 pair of bikini underwear, and an eye makeup brush at May's department store on Wilshire Boulevard. The luscious creature whose near-naked body and smoldering sexuality had lit up the screen in the German film *Ecstasy* in 1932 (it was released in 1940 to scandal in the States, where Lamarr was under contract to MGM) was the first shoplifting celebrity to stand trial. For several days, she commanded front-page headlines reminding readers of how far she had fallen: "Ex-Star Seized as Shoplifter Booked," read one.

On the night of January 28, after shopping in May's with her business manager, Lamarr left the store. A guard chased her into the parking lot, shook Lamarr from behind, and said, "You're under arrest." Later, Lamarr would say that she had protested, "Don't hold my arm so tight. I just had a shot"—a vitamin shot, she clarified. The guard testified that she had witnessed Lamarr shoplift before but had never made an arrest until now. She was processed as Hedy Boies (her last husband was Lewis Boies).

Fifty-one, cast in her first film in twelve years, a small role in a Paramount thriller, *Picture Mommy Dead*, Lamarr flung out defenses like an ingénue auditioning for a part. First, she explained, she had attempted to pay for the items by waving $14,000 in checks she was carrying in her purse. Later, at a press conference at a Beverly Hills restaurant, she was "mystified" as to how she could have shoplifted. In February, she collapsed under stress, and Paramount replaced her with Zsa Zsa Gabor.

Both of Lamarr's children protested that their mother had contributed too much as a patriot to be accused of shoplifting. "For the past thirty years my mother has been doing a good deal for the people of this country . . . and in return she has received a slap in the face, for nothing," her teenage son said. (Lamarr had collaborated with the composer George Antheil in the invention of an antijamming device for radio-controlled torpedoes, which would later be used in pagers, cordless phones, cell phones, and the Internet, but she never earned a penny from it.)

May's pressed charges, unheard-of at the time. Lamarr insisted on a jury trial to clear her name. When the trial began in April, the *Los Angeles Times* covered it in obsessive detail. Hundreds of Angelenos stood outside the courthouse every day to gape at the beautiful star who had raised wartime morale with her pinup photos and lent her brain to the war effort.

During the trial, prosecutor Ira K. Reiner, future district attorney of Los Angeles County, then just out of law school, contended that Lamarr stole "systematically and methodically." The police report seemed to support his argument. A security guard who said that she had seen Lamarr shoplifting sweaters earlier in the year testified that she saw her slipping a suit and blue slippers into her handbag. A salesclerk swore that she spotted Lamarr slipping on a headband underneath her scarf. When the guard stopped the star in May's, she protested that the same thing had happened at I. Magnin and Neiman Marcus before and they had let her pay.

More reasons why Lamarr might have shoplifted emerged. Her psychiatrist testified that his client might be confused, but she was no kleptomaniac. Lamarr's son ventured that his mother was upset about her fading beauty. When Lamarr took the stand wearing a "dark, one-piece Italian knit suit and high heels," she played the amateur psychologist, throwing out still more possibilities about her motives: She had neglected to pay because she was upset about the failure of her sixth marriage. She described herself as forgetful, and she pleaded poverty. She was broke. She was about to be evicted from her Coldwater Canyon home; she had an infected tooth. Having just seen the 1964 movie *The Pawnbroker*, starring Rod Steiger as a Jewish man living in the Bronx who suffers from flashbacks about Nazi Germany, she was plunged into memories of her traumatic escape from that country in 1939. "Our president was killed. I knew him very well," she said on the stand, referring to the assassination of the German chancellor Engelbert Dollfuss.

In his closing argument, Lamarr's attorney, Jordan M. Wank, said that the star fell victim to the security guards and their "Gestapo tactics." When the jury acquitted Lamarr, applause erupted in the courtroom. Reflecting on the trial years later, Reiner said, "It was my first celebrity trial and I was too soft on her. Afterward, three or four members of the jury came up to me and said, 'We all agreed she did it but it was clear you didn't want her to be convicted.'"

The publicity brought Lamarr offers of work as well as attention. Commenting on the case, the Supreme Court justice Earl Warren said, "When poor people are afflicted with the disease they are jailed. When rich ones are, they are given a chance to return the property."

In 1991, Lamarr moved to a modest condominium in Altamonte Springs, Florida, where she covered the walls with Hollywood memorabilia, including pictures of her and Clark Gable. She wore big picture hats and dramatic scarves to run errands around town. One day that summer, in an Eckerd drugstore in nearby Casselberry, Lamarr, accompanied by her assistant, was arrested for allegedly shoplifting a magazine, laxatives, and contact solution. As years earlier, she denied it, claiming that while the assistant paid, she had absentmindedly walked out holding the items. Eckerd wanted to prosecute, her lawyer, who was chosen because he "spoke German," said, whereas the police wanted to dismiss the charge. Although Lamarr's daughter insisted she was not financially insolvent, the seventy-six-year-old actress received money from fans. The daughter protested, "My mother used to go to Nieman [*sic*] Marcus and Saks, and they used to say, 'Miss Lamarr, take anything you want.'" At the arraignment, the assistant state attorney agreed to drop the charges if Lamarr refrained from shoplifting and shopped with her companion for a year. "Lamarr Gets Off Easy," one headline read.

"THE BESS MESS"

If Lamarr was the quintessential Hollywood shoplifter, the archetypal New Yorker with sticky fingers was Bess Myerson, who shared beauty with the movie star, as well as a drive to escape her circumstances and transform herself. If Lamarr represented the unattainable studio sexpot, Myerson stood for the troubling possibilities of conspicuous consumption for everywoman. In the 1960s and 1970s, she wrote columns and articles about spending money and her struggles with her weight. What was different from Lamarr was the public reaction to Myerson's crime, the degree to which and means by which she was punished.

Myerson grew up poor in the Sholem Aleichem Cooperative Houses, a housing project in the Bronx. She was the daughter of a housepainter and a stay-at-home mom, Russian immigrants determined to give their children all the benefits of the New World. Born with a beautiful speaking voice, Myerson became the first Jewish Miss America in 1945, refusing advice to change her name to the less ethnic-sounding Bess Meredith or Betty Merrick. But her principles hurt her. In the aftermath of World War II, before the full extent of the Holocaust had been revealed, many Americans blamed Jews for having lost their sons. "Because of the Jews, we got into this war," the mother of a wounded soldier screamed at her. Several sponsors declined to support Myerson (she suspected anti-Semitism). She ended her tenure as Miss America before the year was over. Instead, she toured the country, campaigning against discrimination and racism for the Anti-Defamation League.

Myerson married. After her daughter was born, as a spokesperson for *What's My Line*, *I've Got a Secret*, and other game shows of the 1950s and 1960s, she proved that she was more than just a pretty face. In 1966, she became the first commissioner of Consumer Affairs for John Lindsay, then mayor of New York. She set about exposing dishonest merchants, from those who sold "shamburgers"—hamburgers made from mystery meat—to those who stuffed shrapnel inside baby rattles. "Bess Myerson on the Prowl for Stores That Cheat Us" was a *Life* cover story headline. She was enormously popular. Nelson Rockefeller conducted a poll that found her to have a 90 percent approval rating. After backing out of a run for the U.S. Senate in 1974, in part because of ovarian cancer, she worked in private industry. She tried another bid for the Senate, but lost in the primary. After helping Ed Koch win as mayor in 1982, she became the New York City Cultural Affairs commissioner.

Five years later, Myerson had to resign due to accusations of bribery and conspiracy. She had allegedly tried to lower the alimony payments of Carl Capasso, a wealthy, hunky, formerly married contractor who had been her lover for six years. Capasso himself was under investigation for tax evasion—charges that were eventually dismissed. In the spring of 1988, Myerson was already occupied with publicity from the pretrial investigation (the trial would be prosecuted by the up-and-coming district attorney Rudolph Giuliani) and had taken the Fifth Amendment in front of a grand jury. Capasso was in prison.

On Sunday, May 8, 1988, the *New York Daily News* reported that while vacationing in London eighteen years earlier, the then Consumer Affairs commissioner had shoplifted from Harrods. When the Metropolitan Police chased Myerson, she ran. In 1987, she paid a $100 fine. But neglecting to mention the theft when filling out paperwork for a stint as Cultural Affairs commissioner was a felony, the prosecution pointed out.

Nineteen days after the *Daily News* story, the police arrested Myerson for shoplifting at a Hill's department store near Allenwood prison in South Williamsport, Pennsylvania, where she was visiting Capasso. Myerson had entered the store carrying a Hill's bag. She walked out with a pair of white espadrille flats, a pack of AA batteries, several pairs of plastic earrings, and four bottles of nail polish. She left through the side entrance. When caught, she was carrying $160 in her pocket. She supposedly asked the store detective who caught her, "Can't I just pay for the stuff?" as she signed the store's confession. After being told at her arraignment that the court had to report the incident, she turned philosophical. "So be it," she said. Publicly, she denied the charges. "I was leaving the store to go to my car to come back and pay for the merchandise," she told reporters. With the help of a local lawyer, she made sure that the shoplifting charge could not be raised at the New York trial.

The photo of Myerson taken at the crime scene in the Susquehanna River town that spring bears no resemblance to the elegant sophisticate once beloved in New York. She looks nothing like the vibrant young woman who won the Miss America pageant, the habitué of swank nightclubs and power restaurants, and friend of the glitterati. Her hair is flattened back across her head, her face wan. In July, after failing to delay her hearing until after her New York trial, she pleaded guilty.

Twenty years after Abbie Hoffman and "Lizzie Liftwell" advised Americans to shoplift as a revolutionary tactic, the shoplifting of the ex–beauty queen with the sparkling smile inspired the first trend story blaming the women's movement for the crime. Whereas in the 1960s and 1970s shoplifting was understood to be part of the youth protest, now journalists were pinning it on women's lib. Newsmagazines attacked Myerson as a menopausal shrew who, thanks to feminism, had missed out on stay-at-home wives' happiness and stole as compensation. They borrowed clichés from nineteenth-century kleptomania to evoke women rushing stores to satisfy their desires. "Why Do Aging Women Steal?" "Midlife Shoplifters Often Feel Robbed of Love."

Writing about Myerson in *Ms.*, Shana Alexander intoned, "As for the women's movement, I often think we may have opened Pandora's Box." In the group biography of four women involved in "The Bess Mess" that grew out of this article, Alexander painted Myerson as Venus, the goddess of love. She attributed Myerson's problems to excessive self-sacrifice and to men and to what New York women "would and would not do for love." Other unsympathetic articles about Myerson's shoplifting that year expressed contempt for a celebrity who was stupid enough to make up stories about why she committed the crime. *Life* published a color photo spread of the shoplifted objects and depicted Myerson as representative of the shoplifting crisis trickling down to all Americans.

"It could be you," *Life* cautioned in an article highlighting the social problem.

Initially, Myerson was concerned that the shoplifting, along with her other erratic behavior, would cause the jury to find her guilty. In the fall, when the trial started, the defense was leery of calling character witnesses whom the prosecution might ask about the crime. But in the end, "the Queen of the Jews," as she had often referred to herself half-mockingly in more prosperous years, was acquitted of the charges levied against her. She disappeared from the public eye.

The most far-reaching consequence was that after "The Bess Mess," the media outed more celebrity shoplifters than they had in all the previous decades in the twentieth century. Some of these were celebrities' children, but a surprising number were adults. An incomplete list includes pool shark Minnesota Fats, a Miss Minnesota, gymnast Olga Korbut, tennis player Jennifer Capriati, ex-spy Felix Bloch, ex-secretary of the army John Shannon, Felicidad Noriega, Noelle Bush, and Al Goldstein. Since 2002, the Internet aggregator Notable Names Database (NNDB) has included shoplifting as a celebrity category—a criminal best-dressed list. NNDB lists which celebrities have allegedly shoplifted, when, where, and whether they pleaded guilty. What's next, a Hollywood map of which boutiques shoplifting stars have hit and a reality TV show about the crime?

WINONA RYDER—CARRYING "THE SCARLET LETTER S FOR SHOPLIFTER WHEREVER SHE GOES"—AND INJUSTICE

From the Gilded Age, when Emma Goldman and Mark Twain ridiculed the light punishment for kleptomaniacs in comparison with the severe penalties for starving single mothers, there has been in America the idea that treating rich shoplifters as sick, not criminal, reveals an ugly class bias. But in the 2000s, the contrast between how rich and poor shoplifters were sentenced was amplified: Now rich shoplifters became fashion icons, and poor ones were given life sentences. At Christmastime of 2001, the case of Winona Ryder, or SA044291, as it was later known in the Los Angeles Superior Court, redefined celebrity shoplifting. This trial, examining the relationship between fame and shoplifting, trivialized the crime. Another case—a Supreme Court case involving shoplifters serving life sentences under California's three-strikes law—magnified the sense of a double standard.

"Anywhere else, this petty crime by a first-time offender would have quickly ended with a plea bargain," a *New York Times* editorial concluded during Ryder's trial, deploring the municipal resources squandered on it, which by some accounts added up to hundreds of times the amount typically spent on a shoplifting offense. The Ryder trial also provided a poignant contrast between decades of glamorizing shoplifting on the screen and the real-life tawdry crime.

On December 12, 2001, when the Beverly Hills police arrested Ryder for allegedly shoplifting just under $6,000 worth of designer clothing from Saks Fifth Avenue on Wilshire Boulevard near Rodeo Drive, she was a thirty-year-old icon. Like many earlier celebrity shoplifters, Ryder had transcended her beginnings. She started out as Winona Laura Horowitz from Minnesota and later Northern California, daughter of the rare-book dealer Michael Horowitz and goddaughter of Timothy Leary. She began acting at age twelve. In the 1980s, she became one of the young actors known as the Brat Pack, starring in *Beetlejuice*, *Heathers*, *Edward Scissorhands*, *Little Women*, and *The Age of Innocence*. At twenty, the actress lauded for her portrayal of characters on the edge and for her brown eyes was briefly hospitalized for depression. In 1999, she played Susanna, a mentally ill young woman in the movie adaptation of Susanna Kaysen's memoir, *Girl, Interrupted*. In one scene, Valerie (Whoopi Goldberg) tells the Ryder character, "You are a lazy, self-indulgent little girl who is driving herself crazy." That description hung over the proceedings.

Right away, Ryder's case raised questions. It is company policy for

Saks to call the police in instances of felony shoplifting. But it was not long before the district attorney's office began to pursue the case with more prosecutorial zeal than some observers thought it merited. "Money Talks, Celebrities Walk" was the campaign slogan that got Steve Cooley elected, referring to the previous administration's lax handling of the O. J. Simpson case. But in the Ryder case, a blooper made Cooley's ferocity look vindictive or worse. The day after Ryder was arrested, Lieutenant Gary Gilmond, the spokesperson for the Beverly Hills Police Department, read a statement at a press conference: "The security officers observed both visually and by video Ms. Ryder to remove Sensormatic tags . . . and place the items in a bag that she had, and then she was observed to leave the store without paying for the items." Based on Gilmond's statement, Sandi Gibbons, the media relations person for the district attorney's office, wrote a press release asserting that "the actress was seen on the store security camera using a pair of scissors to cut security tags off the merchandise."

On March 12, 2002, still eight months before the trial, a *Los Angeles Times* reporter viewed the video and discovered that Ryder was not seen anywhere cutting off tags. In May, the star used it all performing the monologue on *Saturday Night Live* with Tracy Morgan, producer Lorne Michaels, and the rest of the cast.

Ryder: "They set up security cameras because of me?"

Morgan: "No! No! No! No!"

After the two stars scrutinize the cast in their dressing rooms with the security cameras, Morgan says: "See? They watch everybody. Nobody thinks you're gonna take anything." A video of Ryder thanking Lorne Michaels for inviting her on the show the previous day extends the joke. After Ryder exits, the camera catches Michaels checking to see if he still has his wallet. In a later skit, "Winona Loves Mango," Ryder, Chris Kattan, and Moby go shopping at Barneys. After all of them confess to having left their wallets at home, the two men stare meaningfully at Ryder. Kattan, who is struggling to hold the heaps of clothing he supposedly intends to purchase, recommends that they shoplift, and Ryder announces, "Stealing is wrong," twisting her face into a wry grin. A security guard swoops in to detain Mango (Kattan), who goes to jail. But not before he vogues for his mug shots in the stolen merch, including a Marabou bed jacket. He even blows kisses at the camera. Later Ryder visits him in jail.

The jokes at the expense of the district attorney—at anyone who dared accuse Ryder of shoplifting—continued. Over the summer, Y-Que, a T-shirt company whose name in Spanish means "So what?" printed "Free Winona" T-shirts, which quickly became hipster best sellers. In June, Ryder vamped on *W* magazine's cover in one of the shirts, which, as Y-Que's founder Billy Wyatt pointed out, "hit a Warhol level of parody."

In September, after negotiations over Ryder's plea halted, *National Review* columnist Joel Mowbray defended her as a victim of big government run amok: "According to an NBC News study of L.A. County records, none of the other 5,000 people prosecuted for shoplifting in the last two years has been hit with such harsh charges—and in two specific cases in Beverly Hills where the alleged amount stolen exceeded that in Ryder's case, both defendants pleaded out with misdemeanors—something that prosecutors have adamantly refused to do for the movie star."

Asked about Mowbray's allegation, Sandi Gibbons wrote in an e-mail:

Ms. Ryder was not prosecuted for shoplifting, which is a misdemeanor charge. She was prosecuted on felony charges of grand theft and vandalism. A Superior Court jury in Beverly Hills heard all the evidence at trial and convicted her of the charged felony crimes—grand theft and vandalism. Those charges were reduced to misdemeanors after she successfully completed her probationary sentence.

Gibbons said that *Ryder* declined the attempts of the district attorney's office to strike a plea bargain. It was speculated at the time that one reason Saks pursued the case so assiduously was that the star was unwilling to plead guilty even to a misdemeanor.

The trial was not televised. The 1,019-page transcript begins on October 24, with a hearing. Before the attorneys presented their motions, Ryder asked, "Your Honor, may I approach the bench?"

The court: "Not at this point."

The defendant: "Do you have a gavel? I've never seen a gavel."

The court: "No gavels."

The defendant: "A real one. Really?"

The court: "Judges don't use gavels—honest . . ."

The defendant: "It's only on TV?"

The court: "The only gavel I have is a crystal gavel, and that was a gift. I'd never bang that."

A few pages later, Deputy District Attorney Ann Rundle raised the question of Ryder's two prior alleged acts of shoplifting, which she characterized as a "scheme"—a series of linked crimes. According to police records, Ryder shoplifted three times in 2000 and 2001—twice at Barneys New York in Beverly Hills—and a third time at nearby Neiman Marcus. Arguing that these alleged thefts should be inadmissible, Ryder's lawyer, Mark Geragos, contended that the security guards' search of Ryder's purse for the scissors she supposedly used to snip the tags from the clothing was illegal, since only police officers could legally conduct searches. After listening to Rundle read from the transcript in which one of the security guards asked Ryder to hand over the scissors (she supposedly said, "I need those scissors," and Ryder allegedly reached into her pocket and took them out), Judge Elden Fox ruled the scissors in.

Geragos's final attempt at suppression involved one of Ryder's alleged explanations for her shoplifting. At the hearing, Ann Rundle, riffling through the pages of her transcript, summarized them:

At one point she indicates that she was doing research for a role as a kleptomaniac. At one point she indicates that her director had told her to do this, that she was very sorry, that she wasn't very good at it. One point she claims to have been doing research for a part in a movie called *White Jazz* and that at another point she indicates that she is researching a role in a movie, I believe, called *Shop Girl*, written by Steve Martin.

Rundle argued that Ryder volunteered her confession, including the bits about the movie, and therefore did not need to be Mirandized. She further noted that Ryder had signed a civil demand confession, which begins with the phrase "I, Winona Ryder, agree that I have stolen . . ." But, Geragos countered, although his client may or may not have confessed, in the holding room, the male security guards asked her to "lift up" her shirt, he said. "And my skirt," Ryder added helpfully from her seat.

Judge Fox ruled that Ryder's alleged lines about doing research for a role could stay but suppressed the confession.

Besides Peter Guber, a movie executive whose studio had produced several of Ryder's films, the jury included a legal secretary who worked at Sony and a program developer for television. A representative of the Radio and Television News Association of Southern California filed a motion to unseal the records the judge had sealed, which inspired Mark Geragos to say, "My client's right to have a fair trial on the evidence that is admissible in court greatly overwhelms the *L.A. Times* . . . desire to report on this shoplifting trial as opposed to the war in Iraq."

Ann Rundle presented Ryder's case as one of "a simple theft," and Geragos claimed that Saks had fabricated evidence. Ryder never testified. She wore one designer outfit after another, representing "the woman wronged," as Geragos would later call her.

Of the six witnesses Ann Rundle called, five were Saks security guards. The first, Ken Evans, introduced the jury to the "researching a role" story. Evans spent two days delivering a rambling narrative about Ryder's hour and a half in the store, beginning with an account of every item she shoplifted. He tracked her on several of Saks's sixty cameras. He began early on, when she was still on the first floor in the accessories area, he said, displaying an impressive command of haute couture.

In his cross-examination, Geragos's characterization of Evans's overzealousness could neither erase the "researching a role" story nor the damning testimony of other Saks employees. Shirley Warren, a "Donna Karan specialist," saw Ryder's finger bleeding and got her a Band-Aid. "She just appeared to be a little nervous." A salesperson from the third floor testified that she saw Ryder holding the very garments that the prosecution now presented as evidence, except that now they had holes in them, ostensibly from where the movie star cut out the security tags.

It was Colleen Rainey who first saw with her own eyes a shoplifter cutting the tags off a Natori handbag and a Dolce & Gabbana handbag and failing to cut tags off several other handbags. And it was Rainey who first realized that the shoplifter was Winona Ryder. This epiphany occurred when Rainey stood outside the fitting room. Peering through the slats, she watched Ryder kneeling on the floor and stuffing hats, socks, and hair bands into one of her bags. Rainey could detect the star reflected in the mirror on the wall opposite the door. She whispered to the saleswoman that it was Ryder and returned to her post.

Throughout the trial, Geragos tried to spin his client's silence to his advantage by asking witnesses whether anyone had touched her, thrown anything at her, called her names, asked her for movie premiere tickets or phone numbers, and otherwise making it look as though she was a victim. But in the end, the prosecutor won points with her no-nonsense approach. Trying to get Ryder's signed confession admitted into evidence, Rundle responded tartly to the defense attorney's assertions that store employees had invented it—made up, indeed, every single thing that happened in the holding room that pointed to her guilt. "Why would they need to go back and change their story to make up evidence against the defendant to prove that she did it when in fact, from the very day on December 12, 2001, they had her signed statement?"

Saks had bullied his client into signing, the defense attorney replied. And there was another thing that made Saks seem like a bully: Although she allegedly shoplifted $5,500 worth of clothing, Ryder, Geragos claimed, gave Saks an imprint of her credit card when she bought a pair of shoes that day. Saks acknowledged that Ryder did pay for the shoes, a leather bomber jacket, and two shirts—worth around $3,000—but denied that any tab was started or that there was any arrangement between the star and the store.

So Geragos lost points here just as he did in another key battle. In early October, a few weeks before the trial began, he gave the prosecutor a sworn statement signed by one Dr. Jules Lusman, asserting that the doctor had provided Ryder (under the name Emily Thompson) with Oxycodone. The intention of this was to defuse one of the counts against Ryder—felony drug possession—because she had been carrying Oxycodone the day she shoplifted. The judge agreed.

It was not until sentencing that a report of the other drugs Ryder was carrying (liquid Demerol, liquid diazepam, Vicoprofen, Vicodin, Percodan, Valium, morphine sulfate, and Endocet) became part of the public record. A Medical Board of California report posted on the Smoking Gun website described Ryder as visiting Lusman a week before the alleged shoplifting. In November, Rundle petitioned Judge Fox to suppress Lusman's statement, likely because if the jury knew that Ryder was in pain, or addicted to drugs, it might sway them to acquit. If there was even one person on the jury who had taken a painkiller, the result might be a hung jury or worse.

SA044291 was ultimately a trial about a celebrity shoplifting designer clothing, and journalists shifted from analyzing the witnesses' testimony to deconstructing Ryder's sartorial taste and demeanor in the courtroom. "This is not a film performance that is going to garner Winona Ryder any Oscar nominations," one article began. *Slate*'s Dahlia Lithwick called Ryder "Felony Barbie." According to some fashion writers, Ryder looked "splendid" in the courtroom, but because she chose to wear Marc Jacobs in court—Jacobs, among the designers whose clothing she had allegedly shoplifted—others thought that she was sneering at the proceedings. They also criticized her "demure" attire, including one dress with a faux collar and matching black Mary Jane shoes, a ladylike yellow dress, a black cardigan, a preppy hair band. She was trying too hard to play an innocent person, the logic went.

Geragos used Ryder's style to argue that someone who dressed so well in court—who was herself wealthy—wouldn't shoplift. He held up an Yves Saint Laurent blouse with holes in it from where the security tags had been ripped out to argue that his client could not possibly wear damaged merchandise. But the repetition of the most expensive items on Ryder's designer shoplifting list—including a Marc Jacobs cream-colored thermal top ($760), a Natori handbag ($540), an Eric Javits hat ($220), the white, sleeveless Yves Saint Laurent blouse ($750), and a pair of Donna Karan tan cashmere socks ($80)—inflamed public opinion against Ryder. The full list of the items in the exhibits submitted by the prosecution, which included a turquoise bag, a beret, a Calvin Klein purse, a black beaded purse, a purse with flowers, a headband, a pony-tail holder, a hair clip, a rhinestone hair bow, two pairs of gray Calvin Klein socks and one pair of purple Calvin Klein socks, one pair of brown DKNY socks, "handled" scissors, and sensor tags "with fabric attached," was exhaustive in its evocation of waste and luxury.

In her closing argument, Rundle turned her adversary's contentions about Hollywood on their head. "We've presented the truth; they've presented a story that could only be written in Hollywood." She listed her "top ten of what the law does not say" about shoplifting, including "only poor people steal." She alluded to a scene in *Girl, Interrupted* in which Ryder's character, crouched in a dingy basement, whimpers, "Have you ever stolen something when you had the cash to pay for it?" as if life imitated art. "She came, she stole, she left."

On November 7, 2002, after a day and a half of consideration, the jury declared Ryder guilty of grand theft and vandalism. In California, grand theft is shoplifting whose dollar value is more than $400. Vandalism and trespassing are lesser charges aimed to prevent shoplifters from returning to the stores they've stolen from. But the jury ruled Ryder not guilty on the most serious charge, second-degree commercial burglary, in which a person enters a store with the intent to steal.

A month later, at sentencing, Judge Fox gave Ryder 480 hours of community service, five years' probation, and drug counseling—more or less standard for first-time shoplifting offenders. Once Ryder completed that sentence, he would reduce her charge to a misdemeanor.

In the fashion world, the crime raised Ryder's status. Marc Jacobs hired her to represent his spring collection. The hyperreal images from German photographer Juergen Teller's ad campaign are all staged in a brightly lit hotel room. In one, Ryder, grimacing, perches on an armchair, wearing a white terry-cloth robe and light-colored pumps. A Jacobs handbag rests at her feet. In another photo, a pair of scissors is placed on a nightstand. Ryder models a sweater next to a large bag full of clothing. Marc Jacobs president Robert Duffy told a London newspaper that the campaign would be "controversial but not in a negative way." (A few years later, the Festival Market Mall in Pompano Beach, Florida, used the final minutes of the Saks surveillance video, when Ryder exits the store, along with the song "The Best Things in Life Are Free" in its ad. "Winona Knows. Why Pay Retail?" the caption reads.)

Not everyone found Ryder's shoplifting amusing. In 2003, Woody Allen cast someone else in *Melinda and Melinda* after he failed to get insurance for Ryder. Five years later, after a series of lackluster roles, Ryder told *Vogue* that she had shoplifted because she was addicted to prescription drugs and because, being famous, she was allowed to take things out of stores without paying for them. She added that since she was iconic, she provided a distraction from 9/11. The following year, she divulged to British *Elle* that her family had shopped at the Salvation Army. New rumors about recent heists and new motives emerge every time she stars in a film.

Haute couture continues to use shoplifting as a sales tool. At Christmas of 2009, Karl Lagerfeld's short video *Vol de Jour* appeared on Chanel News, an online magazine advertising the spring/summer 2010 collection. Dutch supermodel Lara Stone and French boy muse Baptiste Giabiconi zoom over cobblestoned Paris streets on a motorbike. The carefree beautiful people alight at several Chanel boutiques to shoplift. Accompanied by a spy movie soundtrack, they run through a dark hall, carrying the stolen clothes in a big white Chanel shopping bag. The leggy blonde's stilettos clatter on the marble floor. At a second boutique, Stone grabs dresses and suits from the wall and drops them unceremoniously into the Chanel bag. The duo lopes by a salesclerk, stuffs the stolen goods in a car, and hops on their bike. In a final sequence, Stone tries on one slinky dress after another, tossing them to Giabiconi, who lets them fall into a bag. Again, the dresses wind up in the getaway car and the supermodels on their bike, leaving the non-fashionista viewer puzzled. In a world where haute couture is endangered, Lagerfeld treats supermodel shoplifting as an eccentricity, a taste to be indulged and a billboard for his own reinvention of the brand. Ordinary mortals need not apply.

At Ryder's sentencing in 2003, the prosecution and the defense bickered over whether to burn or auction the allegedly shoplifted designer clothes. Geragos pointed out that they might fetch a good price on eBay and the profits could go to charity. A representative from Saks said, "Shoplifting is a serious crime" and told Judge Fox that the company lost $7 million the previous year because of shoplifting. "I certainly don't want my children to think it's not against the law to shoplift from Saks."

Geragos decried Saks's use of a "victim impact statement"—a tool that the state of California had designed for families of victims of violent crime—to bemoan the store's woes. Profits were up, so for Saks to cast itself as victim was to make a mockery of real victims, he said, adding that Ryder had already been punished. "She will carry the scarlet letter S for shoplifter wherever she goes."

In his sentencing statement Judge Fox asked the question judges have asked of wealthy shoplifters since the nineteenth century: "Why would Winona Ryder steal . . . when she has enough money to buy?"

But Ann Rundle complained that the presence of a real victim in the courtroom—Marc Klaas, the father of Polly Klaas, who had been murdered by a drifter in 1992—distracted the jury from the defendant's alleged shoplifting. "What's offensive to me is to trot out the body of a dead child," she said.

Under the three-strikes laws the California legislature passed after the murder of Polly Klaas, shoplifters could be sentenced to life imprisonment. In 2002, there were about four thousand "three strikers" in prison in California for nonviolent offenses: Of these, 368 involved shoplifting. Although many states had passed three-strikes laws in the 1990s, California is the only one where the offender's third strike can be a "wobbler"—a misdemeanor that can turn into a felony if the first two strikes are violent crimes, including robbery or burglary.

Two of these cases had just reached the Supreme Court. Leandro Andrade, a nine-year army veteran, father of three, and heroin addict, had been arrested in 1995 for shoplifting five children's videotapes including *Batman Forever* and *Snow White*, worth a total of $84.70, from a Kmart in Ontario, California. He was arrested a second time for shoplifting four tapes worth $68.84 from a different Kmart, in Montclair, California. He had been arrested for burglaries in 1983. He either planned to give the videos to his nieces or resell them to buy drugs, depending on whom you believe. But none of his thefts added up to more than $150, and none of them were violent. The other defendant, Gary Ewing, a drug addict, shoplifted three golf clubs, a total of $1,200. He had many prior theft convictions, including one for robbery with a knife.

In his oral argument for Andrade, Erwin Chemerinsky, the esteemed First Amendment lawyer, contended that giving his client two twenty-five-year sentences was not just "cruel and unusual," it was "cruel and unique." No attorney general had ever tried to put a shoplifter in jail for life. Chemerinsky continued, "The State can't point to even one other person in this history of the United States who has received a sentence of 50 years to life for shoplifting a small amount of merchandise. Even in California this sentence would be regarded as quite—much larger than, say, second-degree murder, manslaughter, rape, which shows that it is a grossly disproportionate punishment." Ewing's lawyer also used the word "shoplifting" to contend that his client's crime did not deserve three strikes. "This still remains shoplifting three golf clubs."

Some justices did not buy it. "You say the principal focus has to be on the three golf clubs, like we're some judges out of Victor Hugo or something. . . . But . . . there's a long recidivism component here, and that's the whole purpose of the California law that you're asking us to ignore, it seems to me," Justice Anthony Kennedy said, referring to Hugo's 1862 novel *Les Misérables*, in which Jean Valjean is sentenced to nineteen years in prison after he steals a loaf of bread.

In two 5–4 rulings, the Supreme Court ruled against Andrade and Ewing. In the majority opinion, Justice Sandra Day O'Connor wrote that the three strikers' sentence was proportionate for both men even though Andrade, then thirty-seven, would not be eligible for parole for fifty years. So whereas in Beverly Hills, a jury found a movie star shoplifter guilty of grand larceny and gave her community service, in Washington, the conservative Supreme Court found that two poor shoplifters deserved the twenty-five-to-life sentence they had received in California.

Marc Klaas was in the courtroom at the Ryder trial to show his support for the star who years earlier had donated $200,000 to help him find his daughter. "She may be a double felon, but she has a big heart," he wrote in a letter to the judge.

10. | THE SHOPLIFTING ADDICT

"Do you think that we're damaged people?" Alice, a raven-haired, rail-thin thirtysomething housewife shoplifter with a Bettie Page haircut whispered at dusk one summer day in 2006. Her husband was an attorney. We were sitting on a slate patio outside a mall at the merger of two interstates, a pretty, semirural area of wooded, rolling hills and white-shingled houses. Alice wore cutoff jean shorts, a tank top, and white Keds. Her nickname was tattooed on her biceps. "We would not want to hurt a particular person," she said, striking a familiar note about shoplifting as a victimless crime. She guiltily confessed to "shop hopping"—an act verging on shoplifting—with her kids. She roamed from PetSmart to the ASPCA, pretending to be in the market for a kitty when all she was doing was encouraging her children to get over their fear of animals. She called shop hopping "the gray area." Buying a hardcover from Barnes & Noble, reading it, and returning it the next day was equally shameful. Coveting is a prelude to shoplifting, she said. She once opened a hundred boxes of cereal to find a toy for her young son, which she then stole.

Alice led me into the mall, through a door, and up some stairs to a corridor on the second floor. A sign announced that Shoplifters Anonymous was meeting in room 6. Weight Watchers was next door at 9:00 p.m.

Alice closed the door. Inside the small, windowless room, seven women of varying ages, classes, ethnicities, and marital statuses began chanting the Serenity Prayer: a coed in her twenties with long blond hair, a tight sleeveless top, and jeans; an agitated Realtor in her fifties; a Chinese woman with red lacquered nails and a black lacy long-sleeved T-shirt. A woman who had lost a child.

The objects shoplifted included a can of turtle soup, a bottle of cough syrup, a bag of *herbes de Provence*, and a small bottle of black truffle oil. The women admitted temptations unsuccumbed to, such as yearning to "shop and dash" while waiting in an interminable line at Walgreens. Alice vowed to live a shoplifting-free life.

Wasn't it hard to meet at the mall, I asked?

"I just drive around and around until I find a space right near the room where we are meeting so I won't be tempted to steal," said Sandy, who wore a huge diamond ring and came from a family of shoplifters.

What was the difference between shoplifting and other addictions?

"Shoplifting does not let you forget," said Melinda, a middle-aged woman with Turner syndrome, a chromosomal abnormality that can result in shortness as well as cognitive defects. Melinda had served three months in jail after shoplifting while on probation. Keeping her out of jail was one reason Alice started the group. When the women went around the circle talking about their crimes, Melinda complained that it was hard to find a job once her criminal history had been revealed. She added that shoplifting felt distinct from the emotion alcohol or heroin addicts feel, because it dragged her back to the moment of the arrest. "Memory is a luxury that only those who are straight can afford," she said.

"I want to feel guilt or shame," Alice protested.

SHOPLIFTERS ANONYMOUS

Shoplifting came late to the self-help movement. One pioneer, Lawrence A. Conner Jr., the postmaster of Glen Mills, Pennsylvania, a small town outside Philadelphia, according to an apocryphal story, started Shoplifters

Anonymous in 1977 after a friend could not stop shoplifting. In the golden age of self-help, Conner was the first reformer to connect the uptick in shoplifting with the introduction of self-service in stores, the first to use the phrase "theft addict," and the first to believe that shoplifters could be rehabilitated. Like drug addicts or alcoholics.

Conner's 1980 book, *The Shoplifters Are Coming: Don't Steal This Book*, furthered his aims. Yet at times, his views seem at odds: Conner wanted to draw a sharp line between shoplifters and honest customers and to establish that "shoplifters R us." He traced the roots of "me generation" shoplifters to the advent of the self-service emporium. He contrasted the tiny corner store, where the grocer handed items from behind the counter to the customer, to the hurly-burly of supermarkets of the 1930s. After World War II, he argued, the vast number of products flooding stores enticed Americans to shoplift. But the former postmaster's most significant contribution to our conversation is his taxonomy. He divides shoplifters into four categories, the first three of which were already in existence: professionals, kleptomaniacs, and amateurs. The fourth, the shoplifting addict, a phrase of Conner's invention, refers to Americans who shoplift regularly but do not resell the merchandise. But they are not kleptomaniacs either. Conner rejected the nineteenth-century disease and replaced it with the more palatable—at least in the 1980s—addiction. He predicted that shoplifting addicts would crimp retail industry profits for decades.

In 1988, two years after Conner died, Peter Berlin, a cherubic-looking former Bonwit Teller security executive, bought parts of Shoplifters Anonymous from Conner's son. Berlin was unable to get a judge to agree to turn Conner's ideas into a for-profit company that, as the company's website now puts it, would "create public awareness regarding the root causes of shoplifting." He had already been obsessed by this goal for a decade, since one person after another he stopped at Bonwit's "did not know" why they had shoplifted but told heartbreaking stories about their lives.

The following year, Berlin incorporated Shoplifters Anonymous as a not-for-profit company. Three years later, he added an educational arm,

Shoplifter's Alternative, and started a for-fee newsletter, *The Peter Berlin Report on Shrinkage Control.* Today the newsletter, which surveyed antitheft technology as well as all types of retail theft, reported from conferences, and published studies on ethics and employee behavior, no longer exists. But the National Association for Shoplifting Prevention (NASP), evolving out of Berlin's dream, has become, according to its promotional materials, "the biggest and most reputable organization committed to raising awareness about the hazards of shoplifting." It serves five hundred communities across the country.

By the time Berlin's rival, Terrence Shulman, founded Cleptomaniacs and Shoplifters Anonymous (CASA) in 1992 in Detroit, he had shoplifted many times. (He uses the "C" in "cleptomania" because *casa* is the Spanish word for "home.") Shulman endured his parents' divorce at age ten. His father was an alcoholic, his mother was a teacher turned long-suffering housewife, and he began stealing at around age eleven. His was first arrested for shoplifting in 1986, when he was twenty-one. He shoplifted chronically throughout law school, stopping when he was twenty-five. Cycling through financial deprivation and heartache, through psychiatrists, medication, and jail, through clinging to sanity and arriving at recovery, Shulman credits many people with helping him recognize his shoplifting addiction. But ultimately, neither a psychiatrist nor a pill was enough to overcome it. That credit goes to the Forum, the motivational organization.

As part of CASA, the self-described "expert" on shoplifting recovery launched a self-help group modeled on the twelve-step program. In 2003, Shulman self-published a book, *Something for Nothing: Shoplifting Addiction and Recovery,* in which he elaborated on the popular understanding of shoplifting, expanding on some academic researchers' arguments that there are many more kleptomaniacs than we think. Shulman's contribution was to assert that according to his research, there are many more *shoplifting addicts* than we think.

The following year, Shulman went on *Oprah.* The September 21, 2004, episode, "Living a Secret Life," presented former governor of New Jersey Jim McGreevey's confession that, while married, he had been having an affair with a gay male employee. A chronic gambler came on. But shoplifting addiction, which *O* magazine had run a story on in the September issue, was a fresh addition to the show. The shoplifting addicts were Alice, the stay-at-home mom and attorney's wife, and Shulman.

When Oprah asked him, "Are we calling it a disease?" Shulman, slouching on the butterscotch leather conversation couch, and clasping his hands around his knees, replied, "I'm calling it a disease." Shulman told Oprah the story of how he first realized that he was sick. Then he confessed that he had recently shoplifted "a piece" of a lamp, although he did not specify whether it was the shade or the stand. Only when his wife chastised him at home did he realize he had "slipped." Stealing from Oprah's playbook, he said, "It is the secrets that make us sick."

After the commercial break, Oprah asked Shulman whether he had returned the "piece" of the lamp.

"I finally took it back this week," Shulman replied. "I knew I was coming on the show and I wanted good karma." Oprah's last words on the show that day, as usual, advocated telling everyone "who you were" even if you had done something bad: "Outing yourself . . . the people who love you will still love you."

In between Shulman and Oprah sat Alice, wearing a long wig and thick black-rimmed glasses. She confessed that two months earlier, she had been arrested for shoplifting "blue cheese dressing, a small plastic bottle of play bubbles, red wine vinegar, three DVDs, and one VHS tape." But Alice later complained to me that among those who knew she shoplifted, not all of them had—as the guru from Chicago had promised—loved her. Some of her friends no longer spoke to her.

In November 2005, Shulman hosted the first International Conference on Theft Addictions and Disorders at the Courtyard Marriott River-view Hotel and Spa in Detroit. Wednesday night, before the conference began, Shulman invited me to his weekly Theft Addicts group, which that evening met in a nondescript room at Clean House Holistic Treatment Center in Southfield, Michigan, just outside Detroit city limits. Before anyone arrived, Shulman shared his disappointment about the conference. Although he had promoted it, no one from any judicial branch had registered. Nor had anyone from the National Association for Shoplifting Prevention or any security people. He said, "I put out the olive branch. Loss prevention does not like me because I try to play both sides of the issue."

Shulman meant that while he conceded that shoplifting was a crime, he understood better than most people that it was a pathology too. Shoplifters needed to be punished, but they also needed to be treated. But although Shulman compares CASA's mission to that of Alcoholics Anonymous, which in the 1970s convinced the public and medical authorities that alcoholism was an illness, whether theft addiction will reach the same acceptance is open to doubt. Neither the Division on Addictions, a center affiliated with Harvard Medical School, nor the National Institute of Mental Health employs a specialist in shoplifting addiction. Christine Reilly, who was until 2009 executive director at the now defunct Institute for Research on Pathological Gambling and Related Disorders, housed at the Division on Addictions, said, "We don't do theft . . . we deal with substance abuse. But theft is not a substance. You need to call someone who deals with criminals."

Still, Shulman achieved some success. In the last five years, Shoplifters Anonymous franchises have popped up all over the United States and in Mexico. In 2004, he created the not-for-profit Shulman Center for Compulsive Theft and Spending, and he is now developing a trademarked treatment process, the Shulman Method. Shulman's book and his website, filled with stories of despair and recovery, stand as testimony to these methods. By subsuming his life into his work, he has parlayed his authentic wound into a self-help typhoon. On *Oprah*, *48 Hours*, *Fox Files*, *Inside Edition*, *Extra!*, the *Today* show, *The Early Show*, *Ricki Lake*, *Queen Latifah*, the Discovery Channel, at conferences on addiction, he sells inspirational talks. He consults, and writes books on employee theft and related topics, such as compulsive shopping.

In November 2008, NASP filed a lawsuit against Shulman over his use of "Shoplifters Anonymous," the phrase Peter Berlin had trademarked twenty years earlier. According to the lawsuit brief, Shulman, "an admitted recovering shoplifter himself," had been drawing on NASP's materials without crediting the organization. NASP was suing Shulman for false advertising and trademark infringement.

Initially, Shulman tried to fight, writing in his newsletter, "I am increasingly aware of the opportunities this 'inconvenient event' may be offering me, not the least of which is to stand up for myself as well as to ask for 'divine guidance and support.'" And, "while I'm certain the organization suing me feels equally righteous in their position that I am, in essence, 'stealing' from them, I continue to choose to see the world as a big place where there is enough room for many different voices and contributors. Nobody has a monopoly on the term 'shoplifters anonymous,' or, at least in my mind, nobody should." Soon after his lawyer advised him to "limit discussion" of the matter, he was still convinced that he was going to win. In the fall, he remained optimistic. "Likely, we will be filing and arguing our Motion for Summary Judgment to have this case dismissed so that anonymous self-help groups for those interested in recovery from shoplifting/theft behavior might continue to exist and expand without fear of being sued." Later in the year, Shulman signed over the rights to the domain ShopliftersAnonymous .com to NASP.

"YOU CHOOSE A TARGET AND RUN"

No matter how preposterous it sounds, shoplifters do lose consciousness while stealing, said Dr. Eda Gorbis, the director of the Westwood Institute for Anxiety Disorders, Inc., in Beverly Hills and a faculty member at the UCLA School of Medicine. Gorbis specializes in treating illnesses whose sufferers go into trances for relief—eating disorders, body dysmorphia, and kleptomania. She and the handful of other research scientists who study the emotions of kleptomaniacs believe that, as with other risky activities, a dopamine and/or serotonin disorder is indicated. When the kleptomaniac shoplifts, dopamine focuses her brain's attention on a particular object, like a scarf or a saltshaker. If her dopamine system works, she can resist the urge to shoplift. If not, in order to flood the brain with good feelings, she will want to grab something. Gorbis talked about the grabby moment in mythical terms, comparing it with the one when Diana, the goddess of the hunt, out for a moonlit chase, sees the stag. "You choose a target and run," she said, drawing back one arm as though she were about to shoot an arrow from a bow.

Gorbis described two categories of kleptomaniacs—those who shoplift because of impulse control disorder and those driven by obsessive-compulsive disorder. Obsessive-compulsive disorder starts with anxiety, which shoplifting can assuage, whereas impulse control disorder cannot be assuaged. But kleptomaniacs shoplifting out of either kind of disorder are suffering, she said. They are not merely criminals.

The University of Minnesota's Jon Grant, a prolific scientist studying impulse control disorders, has made it one of his life's projects (gambling addiction is another) to convince others that shoplifting is a pathology. In 2001, after he used neuroimagery to compare kleptomaniacs' brain waves with those of cocaine addicts, he found that the addicts' brain activity more resembled each other than that of nonaddicts: "Consistent with the hypo-frontality of addictions, cocaine dependent subjects have demonstrated compromised white matter microstructure in inferior frontal regions. Similar white matter microstructural findings have been demonstrated in individuals with kleptomania," he wrote. But the point of the study was not just to demonstrate that shoplifting resembles substance addictions; it was, Grant said, to prove "there's actually a pathophysiology as to why some people can't control [shoplifting]."

Grant is as fascinated by the trances kleptomaniacs endure as he is in their brain matter. In 2004, he studied chronic shoplifters displaying trancelike symptoms and "altered state[s] of consciousness" in the store. Shoplifters scored "slightly higher than . . . groups of patients with social phobia, alcohol use disorders, or anxiety disorders." But some of the recent conclusions seem as much advocacy as science: A 2005 study found that kleptomaniacs "would report poor quality of life," as if Grant felt it necessary to prove that his subjects suffered.

One reason Grant and other researchers belabor this point may be the *DSM*—the *Diagnostic and Statistical Manual of Mental Disorders*. Published in 1968, the second edition excluded kleptomania. Twelve years later, the *DSM III* grouped the disease under the category of "Impulse Control Disorder not elsewhere classified," but defined kleptomania narrowly, cautioning that if the patient shoplifted for personal use or out of anger, she was probably a common thief. Ditto if she planned to shoplift. Resurrecting the nineteenth-century anxiety about confusing shoplifting the crime with shoplifting the disease, the *DSM III* warned physicians to be careful of impostors. When the *DSM III-R*, a revision, was published in 1987, it delivered the first estimate of the number of kleptomaniacs at "less than 5 percent of arrested shoplifters." Yet the revision also widened the definition to include the shoplifter who planned her crime and the shoplifter who worked with others.

Striving to make sense of the *DSM* definitions, some researchers protested. "Stealing is an almost universal developmental behavior," wrote Marcus Goldman, a psychiatrist who once specialized in kleptomania and thought that the disease was underrepresented. Others argued that because modern people could buy products that nineteenth-century people lacked access to or could not conceive of, a new way of thinking about kleptomania was necessary.

Today, if you call shoplifting "kleptomania," no health care plan in America will reimburse you for treating it. If you use the word to defend your client in court, no jury will declare her innocent. A psychoanalyst I spoke to speculated that the psychiatrists on the relevant *DSM III* committee may have defined kleptomania as an impulse control disorder because they realized that that is how they could most easily get insurance companies to cover it. Doctors who treat kleptomania (whatever they call it) with means besides pharmaceuticals tend to use cognitive behavioral therapy, which, with lists and exercises, concentrates on the moment as opposed to what happened during the first years of your life. It is easier to hope that a neurochemical zap or a list will stop shoplifting than to talk about the Oedipal lack. "Psychopharmacology is big now and everyone wants to get into it," says Eric Hollander, a psychiatrist and professor of psychiatry at the Mount Sinai School of Medicine.

Hollander studies how kleptomania fits into the larger category of compulsive behavior. Freudian ideas are less relevant than the possibility that shoplifting may be one symptom of a compulsive disorder. He has identified a link between impulse control disorders and obsessive-compulsive disorders. On a 2005 broadcast of the science program *The Infinite Mind*, devoted to shoplifting, he explained:

> We believe that there is this very important connection between the frontal regions, which are involved in putting the brakes on impulse, and the limbic regions that really are associated with the drive to obtain sex or procreate or aggression. Individuals with impulsive behavior really fail to be able to utilize their frontal lobes efficiently to put the brakes on limbic impulse. And this results in two problems. One is a difficulty in delaying or inhibiting, acting on impulse. And another is a fundamental decision-making difficulty, where people choose behaviors that are associated with a small amount of reinforcement despite long-term negative consequences.

Charlene Alderfer, a family therapist based in New Jersey, said, "From my experience, a secret [such as shoplifting] can keep a family in balance. It's positive for the family system, but negative for morality. My theory is that people who feel excluded in one way or another are the most likely to steal. From a family systems perspective, I don't think it's useful to talk about stealing in ways that pathologize it. I would not prescribe drugs, except in some instances where people are severely depressed. I'm not knocking a biomedical approach but to treat it as part of OCD is ridiculous."

Asked whether shoplifting is an addiction, Dr. Steven Grant, a member of the Clinical Neuroscience Branch, Division of Clinical Neuroscience and Behavioral Research, at the National Institute on Drug Abuse, said, "We can learn a lot by looking at the ways addictions are similar to behaviors and we can learn a lot by looking at the ways they are different. But we don't know if any of these things happening in the brain are causes of addiction, consequences of addiction, or predisposing factors for addiction. We are on a shifting terrain."

"SHOPPING IS LEGITIMATED STEALING"

I wanted to find someone who could anchor shoplifting in the modern world without reducing it to an addiction or measuring it biochemically. That is why I finally visited Adam Phillips in London. Phillips is a psychoanalyst and author of many brilliant aphoristic books on topics like flirting, kissing, tickling, boredom, Houdini, sanity, and monogamy. He sees the bad characters in literature as more interesting than the good ones. He regards psychoanalysis as "a set of stories about how we can nourish ourselves to keep faith with our belief in nourishment, our desire for desire." He evokes rather than cures. "Psychoanalysis, of course, does not reveal what people are really like, because we are not really like anything; psychoanalytic treatment is productive of selves, not simply disclosing selves that have been there all the time waiting to be discovered, like Troy or Atlantis," he observes in his book on Houdini.

Phillips is also heir to a group of British psychoanalysts who are part of the object-relations school, and whose most illustrious member, child psychiatrist D. W. Winnicott, is known for his interest in how infants, having been failed by their parents (the "objects"), retreat into a world of fantasy.

When I knocked on the door of Phillips's office, an apartment on the third floor of a walk-up in the chic London neighborhood of Notting Hill, in 2006, the analyst, who has been said to resemble Bob Dylan, ushered me down a hallway to a bright and sunny front room filled with books, paintings, and photographs. A legal pad with some notes in ink lay on the floor next to the bookshelf nearest me. Phillips retreated to a yellow armchair by the window at the front of the room.

I asked Phillips whether he thought the word "kleptomania" was outdated. He said:

> Patients would use it. I have a different working model that doesn't fit with that word. I sort of favor, broadly favor Winnicottian picture theory. The way I would think about these things is as an individual story, about some state of mind that is unbearable, but the person doesn't think "I'm in unbearable state." They have a prior state of entitlement. . . . They're stealing something that belongs to them. Originally belonged to them. With socialization it becomes, from the outside, stealing. But symbolically [stealing] is a restorative story. There's a prior state of entitlement in anybody who steals. And I assume that impulses become compulsive. If there's trauma.

Phillips named three works he thought I should read: one by Melanie Klein, the radical Freudian psychoanalyst, about "children wanting to steal unborn babies"; one of Anna Freud's most famous essays, the 1953 "About Losing and Being Lost"; and Christopher Bollas's book *The Shadow of the Object*. Freud first explained losing, Phillips said, as a desire to tame an infantile intention into a rational act. When we lose a beloved item, it is not because our attention wavers, but because the unconscious mind overpowers the conscious one. Stealing might arise out of similar crossed circuits, Phillips said, warming to his subject.

Anna Freud's "About Losing and Being Lost" explains that kleptomania might begin when the child, trying to retrieve the mother's love, steals the first object from her purse. Since stealing objects, like any other concrete means of protest, cannot compensate for bad mothering, the crime blossoms. Believing that the Oedipal complex starts as early as the womb, Melanie Klein connected infantile loss and stealing by describing how children wanted to tear their siblings from their parents' wombs to metaphorically destroy the parents. As for Bollas, he wrote, "A man who burgles may be violating a home to steal the internal objects of a family, and in that moment his act may mirror his own experiences as a child, compulsively reversing his life pattern through violent redress."

The second-generation Freudians described an unpleasant psychic landscape emerging in one's infancy, continuing with the dour circumstances of one's childhood, and resulting in sometimes criminal acts—such as shoplifting—because one failed to bond with a mother.

But there is also a cultural dimension. Phillips shifted in his chair and slyly inverted ideas about shopping and shoplifting. "Shopping is legitimated stealing," he quipped, dismissing the phrase "theft addiction" as "a violent narrowing of behavior."

I mentioned a shoplifter who stole only LEGOs. What might that mean? Did his mother forbid him from playing with the toy as a child, so in some neo-Dickensian scenario, he was now avenging himself?

Phillips cautioned, "When the object stolen makes perfect sense, you have to wonder if the story is too seamless. It is not just about shoplifting socks because you were forced to go shoeless as a child."

I went downstairs. I walked through Notting Hill, first passing high hedges and tiny boutiques crammed inside Victorian houses. And then I found myself on Portobello Road. Stalls shaded by turquoise awnings sold new white linen shirts and silky skirts, necklaces embossed with greenish Roman coins, linoleum blocks of antique wallpaper patterns. Hot cross buns, fruits, vegetables. Antique furniture, flowery scarves, smoky sunglasses, Murano glass perfume bottles, eighteenth-century fountain pens, canes, and Victorian silverware. One shop was devoted entirely to mechanical corkscrews. It was a kleptomaniac's paradise. Imagine the stories the things could tell.

PART FOUR

REMEDIES

The not paying for things is intoxicating. The American appetite for ownership is dazzling to behold. This is shoplifting. Everything free that everyone craves, a wanton free-for-all free of charge, everyone uncontrollable with thinking, Here it is! Let it come!

—Philip Roth, *American Pastoral*

11. | TO CATCH A THIEF

"God is a loss prevention agent," I was told in 2005, the year I began attending the National Retail Federation Loss Prevention Conference and Exhibition, according to its website "the industry's leading" annual conference for the men and women who used to be known as store detectives or floorwalkers. Held in June either in San Diego or Minneapolis, the conference hosts almost three thousand people.

The new job titles coined a few decades ago—loss prevention agent or associate, or assets protection agent—represent a schism in the profession. If the word used is "agent," it is likely that the person talking is old school, invested in connecting LP to private security forces from earlier times. If "associate," then the person is probably younger and wants to be thought of as a white-collar worker. Confusing matters further, since 9/11, some industry consultants, giving the job a paramilitary twist, call loss prevention staff "shoplifting operatives." Assets protection suggests that the most important thing about the job is guarding products, while loss prevention implies that you might have to put your hands on an actual shoplifter. But whatever you call these men—the profession is mostly male—the most important thing about their duties is cutting shrink, "solving shrink," or even "shrinking shrink."

Thus, although he is responsible for handling all sorts of security and fraud issues, the LP agent is only interested in the Winona-style klepto-maniac as the icing. The cake is the boosters. LP sells the booster story in trade magazines such as *Loss Prevention, Stores, Chain Store Age,* and *Drug Store News,* and on LPInformation.com and Private Officer News Network. The two major retail lobbying organizations in Washington have staffed loss prevention divisions to advocate for boosters' promi-nence to anyone who will listen.

To those in the field, shoplifting is a battleground, LP is a spy versus spy world, and LP agents are soldiers who, though winning the battle, lose the war. Each new piece of antishoplifting technology promises to vanquish the shoplifter, and yet none ever achieves that goal.

Most of all, the new job title signaled a change in who was guarding the store. Store detectives had drawn their ranks primarily from for-mer or off-duty cops and ex-military personnel. Their methods came from their experience in those professions and until the 1990s can be described in five words, "Hook 'em and book 'em."

But although LP would like to leave violence behind, it follows the profession into the twenty-first century. Between 1995 and 2005, many people detained for shoplifting began to sue stores for coercing confes-sions and for engaging in racial profiling. As the retail industry became more cutthroat, stores increased pressure on LP departments to justify their financial existence. The industry was asked to become both kinder and gentler *and* more technologically sophisticated—to catch shoplift-ers, some of whom are armed and high.

These days, stores defend LP's occasionally rough practices by say-ing that shoplifters often carry weapons and wound or kill people and their staff needs to protect themselves. A much-discussed incident was a teenager's shooting of a store detective at a Shoe Carnival in Tennessee.

Not all LP agents enjoy catching shoplifters. One wrote, "My first time I caught someone . . . I saw him put a couple of record albums under his T-shirt and head for the exit. I stopped him in the vestibule and asked him to step back into the store. He stood motionless and nodded his head that he could not. When I asked again, I followed his eyes to the floor and saw that the poor chap was so scared he had urinated."

"In reality, your life is not worth a pair of pants or a steak," Gregor Housdon, an LP agent, told me at a Mexican restaurant near the Walmart where he worked in Baldwin Park, a suburb southwest of Los Angeles. Housdon, one of the few agents who allowed his real name to be used, no longer chases shoplifters into the parking lot, because "too many bad things happened out there." Also, it's not worth it to detain people who shoplift little things. "This one guy stole five packs of beef jerky and I said, 'Look, man, I just want to get my beef jerky back. We're not going to have a knockdown over the jerky.' This judge stole batteries for his pager. 'I didn't feel like paying for it,' he said. . . . I let him go. They take underwear, stupid stuff."

Housdon, who described himself as a "shoplifter catcher who got five to eight a day" has since worked at several Walmarts across the country. He said, "I always say 'thank you' to my shoplifters. I say, 'I just want to say thank you. The reason I have a job is because of you.'"

The renaming of LP is not the only change in the industry. Marketing guru Paco Underhill points out that whereas nineteenth-century department stores were designed to entice the customer, big-box stores make it easy to catch shoplifters. They are square, like the boxes they are named for. The "cash wrap," as the check-out counter is called, is generally five steps from the door; cameras hang above most aisles, although according to Underhill, it doesn't matter whether these are real or shells, since their mere presence dissuades some shoplifters. Other antishoplifting decorating techniques include placing desirable items on low shelves, staggering aisles, or setting them far apart so that salespeople standing at one end can see shoplifters at the other. Some cash register lanes resemble the TSA.

When the flagship Gimbels store opened in New York in 1910, it attracted consumers with rows of doors opening directly onto the Herald Square subway station, the better to race from straphanging to shopping;

by the time the store closed in 1986, the ease of exiting Gimbels had helped give it one of the highest shoplifting rates in the country. It would be unthinkable to construct stores this way. No retail chain could be further from Gimbels than Neiman Marcus, but its design tells much about where we are. The four-story store in Chicago, built in 1982 to resemble, as architect Adrian Smith put it, "a postmodern stage set," offers but two exits. Inside there are no clocks on the wall, nothing to mark time spent shopping or to indicate that you are being watched.

At any of the discount retailers, an earpiece-wearing guard stands by the only exit checking bags, in case the pedestals made out of white plastic are not up to the job. From time to time the alarm on the pedestals bleeps, but you rarely see the guard give chase. Midrange department stores acknowledge that some people shoplift, but the crime must be kept secret, like an adulterous affair. At Bloomingdale's, the pedestals at the exits are hooded with fake wood paneling or Plexiglas, as if giving antishoplifting technology prettier "skins," as the covers are called, makes shoppers forget their purpose.

But the most dangerous element of store surveillance may be the guards. In many states, they are exempt from laws binding the police and protecting individual rights and due process. In general, no authority requires store security to Mirandize detained alleged shoplifters. Some receive training to use handcuffs; others do not. Some stores require all shoplifters to be handcuffed, while others forbid staff from touching them at all. No store condones guns, but I read of some security people carrying them in stores in bad neighborhoods or in states with "open carry" gun laws. Screening for a security position, though stricter than it used to be, is still lax in many states. In a throwback to the seventeenth century, before the appearance of the modern police force, some stores use mystery or secret shoppers—spies who pose as real shoppers to catch shoplifters in the act, to do what loss prevention cannot. Many stores set shoplifting-arrest quotas.

Scott Barefoot, director of security at Richemont, which owns Cartier and many other luxury goods companies, said that Richemont does not use quotas but that "one retailer two blocks south of here had an unwritten quota system." Barefoot meant Saks Fifth Avenue, where he used to work. The Saks LP staff posted the quotas on a whiteboard, he said. "Your pay was based on apprehension. No one received direct financial compensation for it, but as you were reviewed, your status would come into play in terms of how much money you made."

I wondered whether these quotas had anything to do with Winona Ryder's detainment.

SWB

African American shoplifters have been more harshly punished than white ones ever since colonial times. But according to reporting in the *Houston Chronicle* and other newspapers and court documents, since 1994, six alleged shoplifters, all but one African American, have died in confrontations with LP agents at Dillard's. Headquartered in Little Rock, Arkansas, the family-owned store seems even more secretive than others about how it handles shoplifting. Four of the deaths were in Texas. In the most publicized incident, LP agents hog-tied an alleged shoplifter, whom Dillard's later described in depositions as "psychotic," to a table. He died. A jury voted to give his family $800,000, plus interest.

Security experts attribute the deaths at Dillard's primarily to the fact that the store is the only one in the country that still hires off-duty police officers. "Cops moonlighting as LP agents treat shoplifters like criminals," one told me, explaining that off-duty police officers tend to use handcuffs and guns more freely than those who have been trained as LP agents. The practice benefits the store: If an off-duty police officer shoots a shoplifter in a store (or in the parking lot), he can say he was acting in his capacity as a peace officer, and in some cases, the store has not been considered liable for the shoplifter's death or vulnerable to personal lawsuits brought by the families.

Dillard's has said that it hires off-duty police officers to protect customers from armed robberies and that it does not do background checks or (until recently) provide training because those provided by law enforcement agencies where the police officers work are superior to anything the store could offer. But according to a 2004 investigative article in the *Houston Press*, Dillard's stifled negative publicity about these issues by canceling—or threatening to cancel—advertising from newspapers and television stations reporting on the deaths.

Jerome Williams, a professor of business at Rutgers University, who studies racial profiling in stores, also known as shopping while black (SWB), said that since about 1990, more than one hundred alleged shoplifters have sued Dillard's for this offense. "There is a persistent misperception that minorities account for most of the shoplifting. . . . The reality is that nonminority shoppers account for most of the criminal activity," he said, adding that SWB may have risen in the past twenty years.

Rewarding quotas may lead to SWB. In a deposition from a 1997 hearing in Kansas, Byron Pierce, a police officer and former LP agent at Dillard's, testified about the rewards stores give to those who make large numbers of shoplifting arrests. "Officers get more hours based on the arrests that they make. . . . If you arrest X amount of violators, you kind of move up the list from No. 1 to, say, No. 25 if that's how many officers are there. If you don't arrest that many violators, you kind of get bumped down to the bottom of the list."

Dillard's is hardly the only offender. In 2003, after the New York State attorney general's office found Macy's LP agents guilty of SWB, the company allowed a *New York Times* reporter an unusually frank look at what is, according to Robert McCrie—a professor of criminology at John Jay College of Criminal Justice—the "most extensive" LP agent training program in the country. The Macy's coverage in the *Times* contained three revelations. First: If you are caught shoplifting, your civil rights as they are understood by public law enforcement are irrelevant. Some Macy's stores allowed LP agents to handcuff any shoplifters it considers dangerous, "not simply ones who showed violence," said Brian Kreiswirth, the assistant attorney general handling the case.

Second: Macy's is flooded with shoplifters. Macy's LP detained more than twelve thousand people for shoplifting nationally in 2002, and while only 56 percent of the detained were ultimately arrested, over 95 percent of them confessed. The relatively small percentage of arrests is due to a combination of factors: Many shoplifters pay a fine before leaving; the police are often too busy to deal with them. Of the detained shoplifters, a tiny fraction comprises what the industry calls "nonproductive stops"— stops that fail to find shoplifted merchandise. These are litigable and can be fireable.

Third: Shoplifters cost Macy's a lot of money. In 2002, nationwide, the chain spent over $20 million on security. But $15 million was stolen from the Manhattan flagship store at Herald Square.

Kreiswirth said that Macy's was "remarkably" cooperative with the investigation. One of the attorney general's sanctions was that Macy's had to report any instance of security surveilling, for longer than five minutes, of African Americans not "exhibiting suspicious behavior." Among Kreiswirth's jobs was to monitor the store, and although from January 1 to June 30, 2005, only one such incident occurred, in-store apprehensions of African Americans remained slightly higher than those of white people, at around 10 percent. Kreiswirth added, "You shouldn't be prosecuting black people more than white people. That makes it as though black people are stealing more."

To critics of LP, lack of training leads to the most lethal tragedies. After three African American shoplifters were killed in Detroit in 2000 and 2001, it emerged that Michigan was among the thirty-two states that then did not require unarmed contract security guards to undergo any state training at all. The first death took place at Lord & Taylor at the Fairlane Town Center, a mall in Dearborn, Michigan, where half of the customers are African American, but only .04 percent of the population is. Five security guards—some in plainclothes—followed

Frederick Finley into the parking lot after his eleven-year-old daughter had allegedly shoplifted a $4 bracelet. Several of them confronted him, he punched them, they ganged up on him, and one of the guards, a firefighter moonlighting at Lord & Taylor, held him in a headlock until he lost consciousness. He yelled, "Get off me," before passing out.

Media reports initially alleged that Lord & Taylor security might possess a video showing Finley and his family removing the electronic tags from the bracelet. The insinuation that Finley was a booster proved wrong. On July 5, between five thousand and ten thousand people— including Martin Luther King III, Al Sharpton, and Dick Gregory— gathered in front of Lord & Taylor, demanding a public apology. Sharpton said, "This is part of the racial profiling that goes on across the country." Local activists demanded that Lord & Taylor provide them with copies of training manuals that they believed would prove the department store engaged in racial profiling. Democratic representative John Conyers Jr., then the ranking member of the House Judiciary Committee, asked Janet Reno, then the attorney general of the United States, to investigate. But apparently, shoplifting, even when someone died, did not merit federal intervention. The family sued for $600 million, but after a judge threw the manslaughter case against the security guard out of court, Lord & Taylor paid them $6 million, according to news sources at the time.

Six months later, at a Kroger store in Royal Oak Township, another suburb outside of Detroit, a shoplifter died in a similar fashion. After attempting to steal meat, he fell and hit his head, and a guard sat on him until he stopped moving. Some of the witnesses said that the guard, who weighed over three hundred pounds, sat on the shoplifter's thighs. But one witness provided a different picture: the guard had sat on the man's back. Paramedics tried to revive the shoplifter in the ambulance, but he died at the hospital, where diabetes and traces of crack cocaine were found in his blood. In this case, the family asked for $750 million and settled for an undisclosed amount.

A few months after that, a security guard at a Rite Aid on the city's

East Side sat on a shoplifter who stole cigars and a hair dryer. She had diabetes. Knee surgery had made it difficult for her to walk. A toxicology report showed several painkillers and opiates in her system. Her husband said they had no money problems. The family filed a billion-dollar lawsuit and also settled.

Security specialists aver that the deaths in most of these cases are due to positional asphyxiation, a medical condition in which the victim's windpipe shuts. "This can happen when someone is on top of a suspect who's facedown with hands handcuffed behind their back," one expert told the *Houston Chronicle*. The obese, those with heart conditions, and drug users are particularly vulnerable to positional asphyxiation. Murder charges against guards tend to be dismissed in court because of the shoplifters' preexisting health conditions or drug use or, as in the Rite Aid case, because they fought back.

In Michigan, with the help of some security professionals and Philip Hoffman, then a state senator, Senator Hansen Clarke proposed legislation requiring increased training standards, bigger badges on uniforms, increased fees for permits, federal criminal background checks (as opposed to state ones), and a concealed weapons permit for store security to carry firearms. The statute on file, they complained, had not been amended since 1968; security guards, for example, were only required to hold an eighth-grade diploma. (The amendments advised a GED.)

Although not all of the original legislation passed, according to Clarke, the amendment did raise the standard of training. He pointed to the Michigan Contract Security Association's founding that year and to more stringent background checks for guards as proof of progress. Today, in Michigan, you can no longer be a convicted felon and work as a security guard. But a related problem, Clarke acknowledged, is competition in the private security industry. "Today, many of the legitimate companies are being underbid by companies that provide neither training nor standards."

Another problem is that 60 percent of all security guards are proprietary—in other words they work directly for stores—and are therefore not required to follow the laws. That was the case in two out of three of the Detroit deaths. But whoever the guards are working for, since 2001, at least thirty shoplifters have died in the parking lots of Walmarts and in the alleys behind CVSes, in the aisles of Kmarts and in Price Chopper and Family Dollar stores.

"NECESSARY FORCE"

Joseph LaRocca, the former vice president of loss prevention at the National Retail Federation (NRF), assured me that racial profiling, tackling shoplifters, putting them in choke holds, and sitting on them in the parking lot was not industry "best practice." "Cowboys" were ancient history, and anyone who profiled was a "bad apple." Most states require certification and background checks for LP agents and some of these checks are extensive. But ten states—including Alabama, Alaska, Colorado, Idaho, Mississippi, South Dakota, and Wyoming—currently have no licensing requirements for LP agents. In some states, like California, a convicted felon can technically become an LP agent. And although many stores have implemented policies forbidding the most aggressive practices, *LPInformation Convention Daily* lamented that "there will always be individuals who go beyond the training format, policies and procedures set by their company."

On LPinformation.com, several LP agents posted about the death of a shoplifter by a guard's choke hold at a Houston Walmart, worrying that the company would sustain damages from a wrongful death lawsuit. LP agents described sneaking up on a shoplifter from behind or tackling her in the parking lot or running after a getaway car with a bravado and a rage that matched the one shoplifters used to describe their crime. Some voices cautioned against store policies prohibiting them from tackling shoplifters, and others argued that without training to understand what constituted reasonable force, shoplifting would skyrocket.

A forum titled "Shopping While Black" offered a similar range of posts. Some voices deplored racial profiling.

I see what the agents see on cameras and follow certain customers. And it seems its always the same race most of the time and of course which bugs me also is the young customers that come in with hats backwards, pants and shorts half way down. . . . And I catch myself doing that every now and then. And have to say, HEY!!! The ones that are nicely dressed and dont even look like they would shoplift do shoplift.

But another poster wrote, "What is wrong with demographic profiling?" "There's good profiling and bad profiling," someone said to me.

Thus the LP agent remains troubling. Although a director of LP can make $100,000 or more, a starting salary for an LP agent can be $24,000 a year or between $8 and $12 an hour. Despite the new name, the position of "floor detective" has changed little since the nineteenth century. Some entry-level positions still do not require a high school diploma, although you need one to move up the ranks, and a BS in criminology helps. There is one university program for retail loss prevention and some specialized advanced certification programs teaching would-be store detectives about how to do certain parts of the job, such as detecting fraud. The best in-house programs that include training future LP agents how to deal with shoplifters last forty days. Some programs advertised on television or the Internet last forty hours.

Even more troubling, a language for catching shoplifters exists, but not an agreed method of identifying them. Many assets protection agents talk about the difference between shopper behavior and shoplifter behavior as though it revealed elemental psychological truths. "Picking up a piece of Baccarat crystal and holding it next to a coat is not behavior typical of people shopping for this type of merchandise. Yet picking up merchandise, holding it next to a coat and inspecting it inside and out is normal shopping behavior in the handbag department," an ex-vice president of LP at Bloomingdale's told *Stores* magazine.

In a white paper of which he declined to share more than a few paragraphs (he charges retailers thousands of dollars for a peek at it), security consultant Read Hayes—who looks young for someone who, by his own account, has been in the business for thirty years—listed what is known in his industry as "shoplifting behaviors," now thought to be the best predictors of the crime: "Signaling to others, hands-down, concealing items, removing or switching tickers, or attacking tag systems, flushed face, continuous 'scoping' or searching for people, moving closely to fixtures, repeated stops in a particular area and inordinate nervousness (stretching, yawning, pacing, etc.) are probably better indicators of possible theft activity than physical cues such as race."

But Shaun Gabbidon, a professor of criminal justice in the School of Public Affairs at Penn State Harrisburg, said that loss prevention agents may ultimately pay less attention to these tics than they do to your shoes. "If you walk into Neiman Marcus wearing scruffy shoes, you will be watched more closely."

HOW TO MAKE A THIEF CONFESS

Along with nineteen male and eight female loss prevention agents, I attended a two-day workshop to learn this skill, sponsored by Wicklander-Zulawski (W-Z), a national firm with offices in a western suburb of Chicago. Before joining W-Z, the instructor, Thomas Masano, was a special agent in the air force, where he conducted felony investigations. With the help of a young woman assistant—the Vanna White of shoplifting prevention—Masano began by describing the challenges retailers face to get shoplifters and other thieves to confess. "This isn't Guantánamo. You cannot hold a shoplifting suspect in a room for five hours; you have to let them go to the bathroom. If they have heart pains, don't keep them in there. Lights on table, battery, we don't want to do that."

But there are some things LP agents can do: Unplug the phone while interviewing, but hide the handcuffs. The holding room should be neutral. It should not contain any personal artifacts, since a person looking at family photos and thinking about what they're going to lose will not confess.

Don't let the suspect have a clicking pen. It will relieve stress and we don't want that. A drink can be a weapon—a hot cup of coffee. A paper clip can be a weapon. The worst type of chair is one with wheels, which allow the person to swivel. Arms also allow you to relieve stress. You sit in a higher chair and you have authority. Room temperature will change behavior. Don't give the suspect a drink of water, because that relieves tension. Don't give them a tissue if they haven't confessed. Let them wipe their eyes on their sleeve.

Masano asked the LP agents where they conducted interviews: the boiler room, the stock room, the back of the store by the Dumpsters, the ladies' room, which Masano called the "female bathroom." He continued, "Depending on the store policy, if you are interviewing a suspected thief, you generally have a forty-five- or fifty-minute time frame to get the person to confess. So you basically have fifteen to twenty minutes to get the confession. How many people have interviewed an innocent person?"

A lot of people raised their hands.

Masano quoted Groucho Marx: "There's only one way to find out if a man's honest: Ask him." But then he elaborated on the W-Z method's doctrine of body language: 55–65 percent of behavior is nonverbal; 30–40 percent is tone; less than 10 percent are the actual words. Masano said that telling a thief that he is a bad person will not produce a confession. "People want acceptable reasons for doing what they did. So you have to break them down. Everyone is programmed to deny, and 90–95 percent of the time it happens. One of the key elements of getting a confession is to crush the thief's hope. So, for example, you don't want to shake their hand."

Masano shook his pretty assistant's hand firmly. A damp hand is a sign of guilt. He continued his lecture. "Establish a behavioral norm. This is what you do in the first few minutes of the interview, so that you can tell henceforth when the person is lying. You try to build a rapport." He paused. "Who's made people cry?"

Half of the hands in the room went up. "I like that," Masano joked. But then he got serious. "The idea is to get them in submissive posture." He slumped over to demonstrate. To do that, a three- to four-foot distance is the best, chest to chest.

Masano next played a video of a suspected thief about to take a polygraph.

One way to tell if alleged thieves are lying is how they breathe.

On an instructional video, Brett, a six-foot-five W-Z staffer, oozed sincerity. Hunched over, he was speaking softly to console a woman who had stolen from her company. He crooned about protecting the assets of the company. He said the word "dollars," and her hands jumped. He said, "People make mistakes."

Masano paused the tape to deliver some editorial commentary: "She doesn't go into full submission . . . she never tells you why. That's the most important thing. People are impulsive."

Brett said to the suspect, "People play blackjack at Tunica." He told her a story about a good person who just wanted to take her kids to a good Thanksgiving dinner. "We are all good, hardworking people. We like to help people get out of these situations. We would like to talk to the good people," he said. Masano delivered commentary: "She nods, yes, she sees herself as a good person." The suspect began to tell some of her sad story, but Brett cut her off. "Time is running short. We need to get this resolved." He recommended the hard sell. "We're past the facts. We need to find out why. Drugs are different than putting food on the table, and I can understand putting food on the table. I don't care if you're honest."

Finally Brett shattered the suspect into confessing. "Good, I'm glad," he purred. "The important thing is the company wants to know if it would ever happen again."

"No, sir," she whined. And then the reasons why she stole the money: "I used it to pay bills. My car got repossessed."

One of the LP agents in the room interrupted. He had busted the same woman at Walmart. The class laughed. Masano said, "She didn't learn her lesson."

12. | THE FUTURE OF LP

Video surveillance cameras have curbed shoplifting less than the retail industry hoped. London is the city with the most cameras in the world—by some counts 1 million. England, as a whole, is said to have 4 million cameras. Yet last year shoplifting rose 34 percent in the United Kingdom. The 2008 *Global Retail Theft Barometer* found that the United Kingdom's shrink rate was 5.4 percent—higher than that of many other European countries. In America, the Winona Ryder trial proved that even sixty cameras monitoring an alleged shoplifter in the store does not necessarily result in a commercial burglary conviction. Some studies suggest that the cameras are only as good as the people watching them, many of whom get tired after ten minutes. One paper, "To CCTV or Not to CCTV," found that cameras are more effective at stopping theft in parking garages than in stores. More optimistic (from the store's point of view) results concede that closed-circuit television may "displace" shoplifting—if a shoplifter sees a camera in Bergdorf's, she will run across the street to Bonwit Teller. The most positive finding (again, according to the store) is that CCTV gives LP staff the courage to confront a possibly dangerous shoplifter.

But stores keep installing more and more powerful cameras. Remote feeds connected to camera networks allow security cells, sometimes located hundreds of miles away from the stores, to monitor what is going on, and if appropriate, to initiate action. I visited a busy one in west Des Moines that resembled Batman's cave, complete with a metal roll-down screen installed in the event of a terrorist attack.

Jay Stanley, the director of the Technology and Liberty Program at the American Civil Liberties Union, predicted that as stores train more and more cameras on shoppers and shoplifters, the result will "lead to a Wild West environment legal system."

Cameras initially became necessary because in 1982, Earlest J. Carter, a mostly self-taught engineer from Chicago, figured out a way to beat electronic article surveillance. Carter designed a booster bag—a shopping bag lined with material to resist radio waves and foil sensor tags. Carter lined his bag with tritium, a mildly active isotope used in nuclear fuels and illuminated watch faces, and advertised it in a local alternative weekly for $110. The ad caught the attention of the police. The alternative weekly declined to run a second ad; the retail industry defamed Carter, and the national media cast him as a criminal. According to Carter, the FBI and the Department of Energy investigated him. Tritium is a controlled substance.

After that retail stores diversified their antishoplifting strategies. "Benefit denial devices" "demotivated" shoplifters before they stole as opposed to catching them afterward and gave stores legal relief from false-arrest lawsuits after multitudes of people were caught with EAS. The most successful of these, the ink tag, threatened to spurt ink all over shoplifters if removed. Department stores across the country piped in sentences like "I am honest. I will not steal. If I do steal I will be caught and sent to jail" through teenybopper lyrics and Muzak. An academic named David Riccio tried to sell his version of a subliminal antishoplifting tool based on sounds. "Which is more impactful—the words 'a baby is crying' or a baby crying?" he asked, adding, à la *The Manchurian Candidate*, that he aimed to turn a store into "an environment that people are apt to not have an immoral thought in," by interpolating church bell chimes and choirs.

Civil restitution, whereby shoplifters paid stores in lieu of being prosecuted, caught on. As did closed-circuit television (CCTV), which would shortly upgrade from analog cameras to digital ones, allowing loss prevention agents to sweep a wider footage. In some stores, so-called mystery, honesty, or secret shoppers pretended to browse while waiting to catch thieves, whereas in others uniformed—and sometimes armed— store detectives stood by. Nearly every retail company switched from the onerous (and often unsuccessful) process of training salespeople to attach antitheft tags in the store to "source tagging"—attaching the tags to products at factories in Asia and Mexico where they were manufactured.

"Aggressive hospitality," a phrase used to describe sales associates chirping "hello," supposedly thwarts shoplifters' attempts to steal. "If you see a young lady in Department 46 stealing or trying to steal some lip gloss, use 'aggressive hospitality' to help drive her someplace else," said J. P. Suarez, the former director of Assets Protection at Walmart, on a 2006 staff training video. But as Gregor Housdon, the Walmart LP agent, noted, aggressive hospitality isn't appropriate for all employees. "Senior citizens, they don't get paid for hassling with the dude," he said, referring to his company's practice of relying on septuagenarian cashiers to double as loss prevention agents.

The retail industry justified these enhanced measures by saying that legally, it is harder to prove shoplifting than other types of theft: The burglar never has the right to be in anyone's home but her own, the bank robber should never be in the bank, but the shoplifter strolls through the store, a private building, passing as a customer. Yet like capital punishment, transportation, psychoanalysis, shame, civil restitution, the ink tag, subliminal messaging, and CCTV, aggressive hospitality has failed to stop shoplifting.

Since the advent of the Internet, it is easier for ordinary people to see how much shoplifting is going on. When I plugged the word "shoplifting" and the time frame "one week, 1988" into the LexisNexis newspaper database, two or three hundred newspaper stories came up—from a policeman shoplifting nutrition bars in a New Jersey convenience store to a kleptomaniac shoplifting designer purses from a luxury mall in

Singapore. But the tsunami of shoplifters was not just a mirage created by technology. According to the Department of Commerce, between 1980 and 1994, an era of unprecedented financial growth (the go-go years), shoplifting offenses swelled 50 percent.

I spent many hours in online news archives reading about shoplifting in the 1980s and 1990s. Shoplifters who got a lot of attention in this era captured the tension between the personal drama they relived while stealing and their larger-than-life criminal exploits. Since then, as the economy has foundered, and as Americans scramble to get into the middle class, some shoplifters resell enormous quantities of LEGOs or *Star Wars* paraphernalia. Others shoplift and hoard tiny, unusable items. The financial boat that lifted many Americans left a lot of people behind, stealing.

Pressed for the secrets of distinguishing between shoppers and shoplifters, LP agents retreated to fatalism. Some cited the "80-10-10 rule": 10 percent of the people will never steal from you, 10 percent always will, and 80 percent will if given the chance. Or they slid into banalities: Shoplifters carried shopping bags from other stores, wore sunglasses, hats, or dirty shoes. "You can tell they're about to steal if they have shifty eyes," one LP agent said. Or, as it is known in the lexicon, "thrown eyes."

Mismatching of knockoffs and luxury clothing might also be a warning sign for shoplifting, LP agents told me: bad shoes and a blue pinstripe suit; a Chanel-swathed woman in costume jewelry. And then there is the sixth sense. "A lotta academic stuff doesn't prepare you for that," said an LP agent who sneered at a college education as a prerequisite for the job. "Sometimes people who are too good in school are not good defenders of evil," he said, recalling one colleague who "was working part time and he aspired to be a police officer and he only bagged two shoplifters a month, whereas the rest of us were in the double digits." He said of another colleague, "If you gave her an SAT, she'd flunk, but she had this radar."

The closest thing LP agents have to a method is the "six-step rule," first popularized in 1992. Here are the six "tells" an LP agent should witness before detaining a shoplifter.

1. You must see the suspect approach the merchandise.
2. You must see the suspect take possession of the merchandise.
3. You must see where the suspect conceals it.
4. You must maintain an uninterrupted surveillance to ensure that the suspect doesn't dispose of the merchandise.
5. You must see the suspect fail to pay for the merchandise.
6. You should approach the suspect outside.

The six steps exceed what retail statutes require in most states for a shoplifter to be detained. In Virginia, all you have to do is observe someone concealing something and you can stop her. Retail stores apply the steps unevenly. Sears and Macy's use five steps. Walmart uses four steps, which may be why there are so many shoplifting stops there.

THE EXHIBIT HALL

The NRF conference's most popular sessions focused on boosters, which generated a new openness and aggression in an industry traditionally loath to talk openly about shoplifting. The Gap could announce it had recovered $830 million in shoplifted goods and arrested "101 habitual offenders" the previous year without offending its middle-class customer base. Gap managers rarely detained shoplifters and stores did not have dedicated LP staff: Boosters changed that.

But the real action was in the exhibit hall. Each year I attended the conference, I saw creepier antishoplifting devices there. The Smoke-Cloak, when attached to a security system, can fill a room with dense smoke in seconds. The brochure promises a "remarkable, unforgettable experience," although I wondered who was going to be doing the unforgetting. Other vendors sold all shapes and sizes of fish-eye mirrors—convex mirrors and smoky orbs for the ceiling or the wall—just the thing to turn the store into a surveillance funhouse. There was a "roundtangular" one for those hard-to-surveil spaces, and shiny oculi hanging everywhere.

Thick and thin metal alarm cables of varying lengths can be snaked up the sleeves of minks or inside It Bags and iPods, locking them to metal racks, or "fixtures," as they are known in the trade. I recalled seeing these at Best Buy, where it was impossible to examine the cell phones because, as in a slapstick comedy, when you pulled them to your ear, the cables snapped back into the fixtures. For those with Superman fantasies, infrared thermal cameras measure heat in dimly lit areas. "Intelligent" shopping carts' wheels lock when shoplifters push them out of the parking lot. A metal detector supposedly stops those dressed in booster clothing, or "steal wear," from exiting the store with boosted property. "The secure store," a model store outfitted with the latest in antishoplifting technology, featured floor mats implanted with sensors to detect booster bags and mirrors that can "understand" the clothes the shopper brings into the dressing room, as well as those the shoplifter is stealing.

The most charming antishoplifting device I saw—though maybe not the most effective—was in a high-end consignment store in Chicago. The store sold pre-worn Diane von Furstenberg wrap dresses from the 1970s and pre-worn Jil Sander sheaths from the 1980s. On the wall of the dressing room, someone had hung a typed poem in a small silver frame:

DEBS IN JAIL
It's not a pretty story, to say the least
Bread and water, group showers
And worst of all no designer clothes
If you're tempted to grab our items all we can say is
Think twice
It's no more Mr. Nice Guy when
Our security commandos catch you
We do the whole bit

No offense but we've got to warn you by law
We don't play cute.

Less literarily inclined merchants inked more direct messages on their front doors. "We have surveillance cameras and prosecute shoplifting and vandalism" read gold cursive lettering on the front door of a lingerie store that would soon go out of business.

But the future of loss prevention lies in high-tech electronic surveillance tools, some of which use the Internet. Others—like radio frequency identification (RFID) smart chips, or "spy chips," rely on radio waves to track products from the factory to the consumer—are still little used because of privacy concerns. In 2003, after a media maelstrom, Gillette, the maker of the Mach 3 razor, had to abort an RFID trial in England in which merely picking up the razor from the shelf triggered a CCTV camera. But in 2010, Walmart launched RFID on clothing.

One of the most successful devices to hit the market in the last few years is made by IntelliVid, a high-tech retail security and marketing start-up that was purchased by the multinational security corporation Tyco/ADT in 2008. I met IntelliVid's founder and then CEO, Patrick Sobalvarro, in San Diego. His premiere product, Video Investigator (VI), was the first device to solve LP's problem of how to track shoplifters without violence. Sobalvarro grew up in Puerto Rico, where he read encyclopedias and "everything I could get my hands on in English." In the early 1980s, he attended MIT for engineering, but dropped out to join the research staff at the robotics group at the MIT Artificial Intelligence Laboratory, then run by Rodney Brooks, the inventor of iRobot, the robot vacuum cleaner. Brooks would star in the 1997 Errol Morris documentary, *Fast, Cheap and Out of Control*. Sobalvarro later returned to MIT to get his BS, his MS, and his PhD.

Sobalvarro's and Brooks's careers have intersected many times since then. But it was in the 1990s that Brooks hooked up Sobalvarro with Flagship Ventures, a venture capital firm and start-up incubator.

Sobalvarro was researching vision tracking technology, the science of making robots see. He'd reengineered the two tools he wanted—intelligent video analysis and video article surveillance—to stop shoplifters.

VI would turn store detectives into "knowledge workers," Sobalvarro said, using the phrase Peter Drucker introduced in 1959. VI promised to shift the paradigm and to propel LP from its "Wild West" origins into lean, clean cyberspace. VI software would sense the frequently shoplifted items (through a series of algorithms). Then an LP person could highlight such an item by dragging a cursor across it. The next time someone tried to steal the item, an alarm would go off. The system is supposedly alert to techniques such as fast sweeping—shoplifters ransacking shelves in minutes. Another algorithm alerts the LP person when people linger around a security gate. The software can also watch the video in every camera and determines which of the hours of footage contain theft.

VI works "like a velociraptor," said Brooks, referring to the dinosaur made famous by *Jurassic Park* for sensing its dinner scurrying around in the brush. "It gets intrigued by motion." When a shoplifter snatches items off the shelf, an alarm in VI's "brain" goes off. The technology then focuses motion detectors on that area, alerting the store detective. VI can also supposedly tell the difference between a shoplifter and a consumer by sensing *how* he grabbed the item from the shelf. And whereas a CCTV camera can only follow one person at a time, VI can follow many people all over the store. In early trials IntelliVid installed beta versions in Macy's, Bloomingdale's, and CVS, which, unlike the first two retailers, uses sales associates to apprehend shoplifters. In initial store reports, according to IntelliVid, VI drove shoplifting down 40 percent.

A group of IntelliVid staffers and I drove to a CVS in Somerville, Massachusetts, where we all pressed into a tiny office with a bird's-eye view of the store. On his VI handheld device's video screen, a recently hired sales associate demonstrated "painting" areas where he thought items were being shoplifted. If BIC razors were vanishing, he could "paint" the shelves where they were stocked. Then, if someone shoplifted one, an alarm went off on his handheld device. After that, he could scroll through video footage in real time and see the razor snatcher or he could actually head over to the shelf in question until he came upon the shoplifter in the middle of stealing. At that point, he would say, "Can I help you?" to scare him away. We stood around for a while waiting for a shoplifter to steal razor blades, but no one obliged that morning.

Over lunch in a hamburger joint near IntelliVid's Cambridge office, I asked Sobalvarro why he thought stores did not want to talk about shoplifting, and he said, "shame." LP people are ashamed of shoplifting, he continued, because they recognize that their initial response—outrage— is too ferocious an emotion to feel for the loss of an object. "Shoplifting is a hush-hush issue because it is a violation, an evidence of something out of control, a weakness."

"CAN'T STOP WATCHING"

Though I tried many times, the closest I came to seeing LP staff catch a shoplifter was in Gaithersburg, Maryland, when a young agent agreed to bring me "backstage" at the local Target one afternoon as long as I did not use his name. From the parking lot, the store looked like a giant mausoleum. Although it was not peak shopping time, Target was packed. Shoppers clustered near the front door, studying the bargains in that week's circular like touts studying racing forms at the track. It was right after Christmas, and sales were in progress.

My host escorted me around the store and showed me how he walked around to see if anything was being shoplifted. Sometimes he checked inventory as many as three times on his shift.

We went into his office. It was gray: walls, carpeting, metal desk, computer. Along one wall ran the kind of metal bar that you find in handicapped bathrooms. LP agents handcuff shoplifters if they cause trouble, he explained. A doorway led to the command center, a tiny windowless room, about 10 x 10, with rows of monitors bolted into three walls. Target uses a medium-old system with cameras that came out about seven to eight years ago.

The two LP agents had piled surveillance videotapes high on every available surface. One LP agent, Don, an African American man in his twenties, wore elegant braids; Joseph was a pimply white youth in his late teens. Without shifting his gaze from the monitors, Don joked that the tapes of shoplifters were better than anything on *America's Funniest Home Videos*.

Swirling around the room was the masculine feeling one notices when one has the misfortune to be in the same room with men watching a sporting event. Someone muttered, "I'm gonna get them." Someone else grunted and cried, "Aw," as if a favorite player had fumbled a ball. The LP guys expressed opinions about stops and compared rules in various states. "What do you think about surveillance in dressing rooms?" Don asked me. I said I expected privacy, and he rolled his eyes.

The LP agents kept up a hopeful, sly patter, both connected to what was going on in the store and floating above it. "Look at the bag. We need a camera down that aisle," Don, the more experienced one, said. He shifted to camera 4, where a man he thought he had seen shoplifting in the past was—we hoped—about to do it again. When he zoomed in, though, we were disappointed. "It's not him. We know him," he said, grabbing the joystick as though he were playing a video game and switching to another screen, where a young black girl was examining a curling iron.

The girl turned over the box and read the information on the back. Finally, she put it in her cart and wheeled into another lane, out of the camera's reach. "Stop being so indecisive," Don said, cajoling and reprimanding her. Joseph shook his head. "She's in a bad spot."

But Don replied, with disappointment in his voice, "I think she's going to be a law-abiding citizen." He began to chant, "Stop watching. Can't stop watching." On another monitor, a guy in a blue hat riding the up escalator seemed familiar to the LP guys. But Curling Iron Girl had made it to the cashier, and we had to pursue her if we wanted to stop her. Don zoomed in on her credit card, printed out its info, and compared it to a list of fraudulent credit cards. It passed. Hours had gone by. All I had to show for it was a cramp in my leg.

When I stumbled from backstage into the store, it was bright, like a power plant on the highway at night. The sun shone like a metal disc, and the gray sky pressed down on piles of slushy, dirty snow pushed to the parking lot's edges. I have yet to see anyone catch a shoplifter.

13. | THE DISEASE IS INCURABLE

As loss prevention efforts, though providing a diversity of methods, cannot erase the crime, so approaches in the self-help industry hold a false nostrum for curing the disease. The handful of not-for-profit groups across the country aiming to help shoplifters stop differ a good deal in their approach and success rates, such as they are revealed. Some imitate twelve-step programs, and others juggle behavioral approaches with varying doses of compassion. I met no one who forbade shoplifters from stealing. "This is not a morality play," the head of one antitheft group based in Denver explained to me.

A group claiming a method specifically designed to stop shoplifting is Portland's Theft Talk. Shoplifters come to Theft Talk in three ways: Before sentencing, after sentencing, or of their own volition. The first two options are part of the alternative sentencing movement that began in the late 1960s to keep petty offenders and the mentally ill out of jail. The third reflects the self-help approach.

By "going at it from the viewpoint of the thief," as Lisa Paules, the daughter of the organization's founder and director Steve Houseworth, puts it, Theft Talk is unique. Whereas other programs specializing in treating thieves weed out recidivists, Theft Talk allows all shoplifters, including boosters and "theft addicts," to attend meetings.

Theft Talk began in 1983, when Steve Houseworth and Patrick Murphy were trying to forge an alternative to the existing social service organizations' smorgasbord approach to addressing theft. Houseworth had graduated from Portland State University with a BA in psychology, and Lewis & Clark College with an MA in counseling. He and Murphy, juvenile probation officers just outside Portland, borrowed lingo ("cops and robbers thinking," "licensing," "mental rehearsing") from psychiatrists Aaron T. Beck and Lawrence Kohlberg, and from psychologist Stanton Samenow. Stereotyped as either a "dewy-eyed liberal" or "a hard-line reactionary," Samenow, in his 1984 book *Inside the Criminal Mind*, challenged theories blaming society, one's parents, and mental illness for criminals' actions. Echoing other anti-Freudians of his era, Samenow believes that "a person may steal so often that others become convinced that he is compulsive and a 'kleptomaniac' [his quotes] but a thorough examination would show that he is simply a habitual thief."

Murphy left Theft Talk after the first or second year to become a schoolteacher. But Houseworth remained. A few years ago, he created a research arm for the organization, the National Center for the Study of Theft Behaviors, to sift through the piles of data he had accumulated over the past twenty-five years. "I am actively working on a database of 35,000 clients to be completed by the end of the year," he wrote in a catch-up letter in 2008. Like Samenow, Houseworth dismisses kleptomania. "If you have kleptomania, why are you taking jewelry? . . . Why didn't you steal kitty litter and garbage bags?"

Houseworth concluded that the criminal justice system has failed to stop "theft offenders"—the penal system's term for thieves—from stealing. "People are taught to be obedient—'don't steal.' Or they are given family counseling, which also doesn't work. They are told, 'You better not be stealing or you will go to jail.' Criminals don't like to follow rules, so here instead of making them follow rules we like to understand—let's talk about why."

Houseworth uses cognitive behavioral theory to sidestep the question of what to call shoplifting. "Let's not deal with whether you are an addict or not or a kleptomaniac or not. Let's just deal with the fact that you are regularly attracted to stealing." But Theft Talk can also sound a little like Nancy Reagan in her "Just Say No" phase. The organization explained thieves' motives on its website:

> Don't make it complex. They steal out of SELFish greed, to get what they want. They fail to develop a sense of an OTHERSness. Isn't it to get attention? NO. Absolutely not! If they wanted attention, why did they hide the item and try NOT to get caught? If they wanted attention why didn't they waive [*sic*] the item over their head and yell as they were leaving the store, "I'm stealing this." Isn't it a poor SELF image that makes people steal? NO. Absolutely not! Do you realize what a positive self image a person must have in order to steal? The person who steals is thinking "I'm smarter, I'm better, I can do it. They're so stupid, I can beat the system, etc., etc." To the contrary, the theft offender has enough of a SELF image, they are lacking in an OTHERS image.

Theft Talk seminars last four hours. " 'You must have eighteen months to restructure behavior'—that is not our approach," Houseworth says, adding that most courts in Oregon believe that half a workday is the amount of time it should take to teach someone that shoplifting is wrong.

The monthly shoplifting session conducted by the National Association for Shoplifting Prevention or NASP (founded by Peter Berlin) at its office in Jericho, Long Island—about an hour west of Manhattan—could not be more different. NASP takes the stand that people shouldn't shoplift—it is after all, a crime. The organization, which says that it has been "nationally recognized for encouraging the lowest recidivism rates among shoplifters," compares on its website a rate of between "1.5 percent and 3.0 percent for the more comprehensive programs" and "up to 25 percent in communities without effective programs."

NASP argues that stores would be closer to ending shoplifting if they acknowledged that the biggest problem is that ordinary Americans—not boosters—commit the crime. The organization draws shoplifters from all five boroughs of New York City, as well as Westchester County and other parts of New York State. At one fall session a few years ago, six regulars—one man and five women—sat around the conference table. Caroline Kochman, Peter Berlin's daughter, attended, as did Gina Hoelderlin, who ran the sessions until 2008. Hoelderlin placed a large stack of dog-eared folders in front of her. A plate of store-bought cookies rested in the center of the table.

Peter Berlin, who is now retired, made a special appearance to introduce the shoplifters. "We have a teacher, a doctor, a homemaker," he began. He said a few words on shoplifting and shame. "Shoplifting is shameful because there is the feeling that something is wrong with you for a nonacceptable reason. This is different than drinking or taking drugs. Those things are understandable. You can see the effects. But not if you're a shoplifter."

Candace was silent. She had sworn off stores. She didn't even put gas in the car for fear that she would become too confident and shoplift. She sent her daughter. Jane, a shoplifting grandmother, regularly left the grocery store carrying a stolen object under her arm, such as a plastic container of cut-up fruit. "Supermarkets are hard for me," she said. Sometimes at night she would spill milk on the counter so she would have an excuse to return to the store, where she could shoplift. Arrested three times, she swore off her habit and slipped back in an endgame of anguish and celebration. "My stealing inspires disgrace and disgust. I am like a yo-yo," she said, arguing that she deserved whatever punishment she got. She did not want her children to know that she was "a bad person." Her husband, whom she described as "an honest man," prayed for her.

Peter Berlin suggested that Jane forswear shoplifting on Mondays and Thursdays, but she worried about bingeing the rest of the week. Jane lamented being so brazen and wondered if she was crazy. Then she grinned. "Tomorrow will be a week since I've stolen anything."

Gina Hoelderlin recalled the time Jane quit for a couple of years. "It gave me chills," she said. But Jane only remembered her agony and her pitiable life. "How will I satisfy myself? Cooking for him?" Jane asked. "My accomplishment is to shoplift." She slumped into silence.

Darren, an older man with white hair, glasses, a round face, and a big belly, shoplifted from the supermarket and switched price tags on meat. He had whittled down his habit to two or three times a week—much less than in the old days. He preferred coming to the group to seeing a doctor, who "treated him with kid gloves." Darren saw shoplifting like baseball. He had to "get to bat, get to the plate." He declared himself a bad person too.

"It's morally wrong," Alana told Peter Berlin. Although she had first started coming to NASP in 1992, Alana had been stealing since childhood. According to her story, rummaging through her mother's pocketbook, she found something her mother had shoplifted. After that discovery, she stole a potato or a loaf of bread now and again. As an adult, she was unable to separate the addiction to shoplifting from a plain old desire to have things. But she felt it. "I must say that during those initial years, the habit was strong."

After a few arrests, the judge put Alana on probation. She didn't stop, and the judge sent her to jail for three weeks. Now every time she and her husband drive by the jail, they nod at each other. (She hid her habit from him for twenty years.) Shortly after her release, Alana shoplifted again. That time, the judge mandated an ankle bracelet. Alana begged to be punished and then complained of the "pressure of being good for too long."

From month to month the population of the group changed. There were regulars and newbies. Generally meetings were peaceful, but arguments did break out.

"My mother taught me how to steal. Put that in your book," Erica, an ex-gambler, shouted across the table one Tuesday night. She and a more timid shoplifter had just finished arguing over whether stealing was an illness or a crime. Coming from the world of twelve-step programs, Erica preferred the "I am sick" explanation.

"I'm still a bad person," the other woman insisted.

"I don't look at myself as a bad person. I look at myself as a sick person," Erica countered. Her sidekick, a well-dressed newbie in her thirties, asked the group, "Am I a klepto?"

The newbie had shoplifted $50,000 worth of clothing with a partner over three years. Now, about to go to her hearing, she was upset. "I can't figure me out," she said, pulling a pair of needle-nose pliers and a pair of scissors out of a brown LeSportsac change purse and throwing them onto the middle of the table. She carried the tools of her trade and a pillowcase whenever she went out to shoplift. If the store detective stopped her, she said she was trying to match the pillowcase to whatever she was fingering. Later, she expressed contempt for another attendee who shoplifted from the clearance table. "If I'm gonna steal shit, it should be big," she said.

"YOU ALTER YOUR STATE OF MIND"

Just as there is no agreement about whether these groups help, there is none about how to treat kleptomania. While selective serotonin reuptake inhibitors (SSRIs)—the drug category that includes Prozac—work for depressed people, there has only been one SSRI study on kleptomania, at Stanford, in 2002. But the prognosis the team published in 2007 in the *Journal of Clinical Psychiatry* was dim. They observed: "Kleptomania has no definitive treatment" and "kleptomania . . . may respond to various medications." Over the past fifteen years, fluoxetine, topiramate, naltrexone, fluvoxamine, valproic acid, lithium, tricyclic antidepressants, trazodone, and buspirone have sometimes performed well and sometimes less well in studies on kleptomaniacs. These tiny studies—some used as few as three people—can hardly be called conclusive.

The paucity of research boils down to dollars and to the stigma surrounding shoplifting. Drug companies are not going to make money by curing kleptomania. Yet shoplifting crops up as a symptom of many types of mental illnesses—bipolar disorders and anxiety disorders as well as substance abuse, eating disorders, and depression. Eric Hollander, one of the research scientists most influential in promoting brain chemistry (as opposed to society or personality) as kleptomania's cause, is the lead author of many articles about impulsivity, which he describes as "a core behavioral symptom domain that cuts across a vast range of psychiatric disorders and contributes to various public health problems."

When the *DSM V* is published in 2013, it may group kleptomania with other behavioral and substance addictions. Hollander favors adding diagnoses to the encyclopedia, explaining, "There was a decision to recommend grouping the behavioral and substance addictions together into one unified category." But in a letter titled "Warning on the Road to the *DSM V*," Dr. Allen Frances, formerly the head of the *DSM IV* task force, argued against creating new categories of disease out of these old vices: "None of these suggestions is remotely ready for prime time as officially recognized mental disorders."

Whereas there is a good deal of empirical research on alternative remedies for depression, no one has spoken of using these remedies for shoplifting. Biofeedback, which measures brain waves, has never been mentioned as a treatment for shoplifters. Nor have I ever heard about Saint-John's-wort or acupuncture being applied to stop shoplifting as they are applied to people suffering from depression. I found only one shoplifter who hypnotized himself. Imaginal desensitization, which has been found to cure gamblers, was studied on shoplifters in the 1970s and 1980s. Two small peer-reviewed studies suggested that the technique, which forces shoplifters to envision the negative consequences of the crime, might help people stop.

But asked the secrets of conquering their illness, ex-shoplifters give mundane answers: yoga, diet, exercise. Many grab on to New Age cults or adopt self-esteem dogma. Now in her midforties, married for decades with three children, Susie, a stay-at-home mom who lives with her husband in a prosperous suburb of a large midwestern city, described stopping shoplifting as "a journey." She traced her crime to her mother's rages, her father's coldness, and her childhood isolation. Like many adults who began shoplifting as children, she returned to it when things went bad. In the 1990s, she lost some money in investment. "It was my inheritance. I was mad. And I went right back into [shoplifting] like I had never stopped. I got to the point where it was every day. I wanted to quit but I didn't know how." And then she got caught. "I was out of my mind. I said to my husband, 'You have to do the shopping. I can't do this.' I had to pay a $250 fine."

In 2002, while working out at her gym, Susie met a woman who belonged to a self-help group and who encouraged her to sign up for seminars in which members discussed their "innermost secrets." Susie told me: "I said, 'I can't tell you my innermost secret—I'll tell you my second secret.' But they were on me, they made me say it even though I said, 'I can't talk about it—it's really painful.'" Next, Susie discovered Terry Shulman, who advised her to give her shoplifted stuff to charity, but not to take a tax deduction for it. "It makes you feel like Robin Hood," she said.

When she "outgrew" Terry, as she put it—by which she meant she grew impatient with his methods—she read a book online: *Why Honest People Shoplift or Commit Other Acts of Theft*, by Canadian forensic psychologist Will Cupchik. She flew her family to Toronto, where Cupchik performed what Susie now understands to be Gestalt therapy: He made her itemize everything she had ever shoplifted; he asked her to analyze the photos in her family album; he instructed her to go on a spending spree, the first step of which was, in a surprisingly Abbie Hoffmanish gesture, to rip up a $5 bill, except Cupchik told Susie that henceforth she would buy everything at full price. After she looked at photos and discovered that she liked the one in which she wore a longer hairstyle, he advised her to grow out her locks to boost her self-confidence. Susie described Cupchik, who charges roughly $1,000 a day, as "expensive but worth it."

Perhaps the most controversial therapy used to deter shoplifting is exposure and response prevention (ERP). Historically applied to drug addiction and alcoholism patients, ERP recalls the Ludovico technique in *A Clockwork Orange*, which dissuaded Alex from violence by feeding him nausea-inducing drugs and making him watch acts that earlier gave him pleasure. ERP has been tested on behavioral addictions, with widely varying results. Advocates say it works "like a recipe." A counselor at an in-patient facility using the therapy described it. A shoplifter is brought into a small, darkened room with a couch and a coffee table. There she is sat down and asked a series of questions—a "cognitive script"—to impel her to think about how stealing will affect her family and friends. The darkness lulls the shoplifter into a trancelike state; her pulse is taken. Next, the counselor escorts her on an imaginary shopping trip, describing objects that she is drawn to. Sometimes he spreads them out on the table in front of her.

In the case of a hardware shoplifter, the counselor recalled, it was, "wrenches, hammers, shovels, even though she had plenty of money." This process goes on—sometimes for weeks—until the shoplifter is deemed ready to go on a real shopping trip. By then, she might be desensitized to the hand tools that once overmastered her.

But can any of these methods, even one that sounds like a séance or a movie, dissuade shoplifters from a crime that feels good? A shimmering passage in Dostoevsky's novella *The Gambler* in which young Alexei Ivanovich loses his fortune at the roulette table for the first time lays out how the attraction of such risks could overpower every rational "cure."

> I confess my heart was beating and I was not cool. I knew for certain and had made up my mind long before, that I should not leave Roulettenburg unchanged, that some radical and fundamental change would take in my destiny; so it must be and so it would be. Ridiculous as it may be that I should expect so much for myself from roulette, yet I consider even more ridiculous the conventional opinion accepted by all that it is stupid and absurd to expect anything from gambling. And why should gambling be worse than any other means of making money—for instance commerce? It is true that only one out of a hundred wins, but what is that to me?

Shoplifters expect more from their crime than it can ever give, just as Alexei expected more from the dice than even snake eyes could provide.

In the store lies the stuff of dreams, which might disappoint if you did anything as pedestrian as buying. But shoplifting differs from gambling. In these dire times more than one political hopeful has proposed black-jack riverboats to close budget deficits or add to Social Security's diminishing pot, but it would be absurd to think that any elected official would suggest enticing shoplifting games to do the same.

Then, too, Americans have stretched rehabilitation's possibilities to sex offenders, prostitutes, gamblers, shy people, people with restless legs syndrome. But the idea of rehabilitating shoplifters, though it leans heavily on American faith in the march of progress and in second chances, may never gain the acceptance that other types of addictions have earned. There is too much resistance to seeing stealing as just another appetite. Besides, not every shoplifter can be rehabilitated.

INCURABLE

SLS Residential is a private clinic in Brewster, New York, which no sign identifies. The main building resembles the other Victorian homes lining the leafy road in this depressed town off Route 84 just over the Connecticut border, not far from the Danbury Mall. Only a low picket fence separates the facility from its neighbors.

Elizabeth, whom I met at SLS shortly after I began work on this book, is one of the apparently unstoppable shoplifters. Four years ago, the then thirty-five-year-old daughter of well-to-do parents received a Solomonic choice from a judge in the state where she had most recently shoplifted: She could either spend another three months in a drug program in the county jail, where she had already spent fifty-six days (she was also at the time a drug addict) or she could spend one year in a treatment facility of her choice. If she opted for the latter, she would be on probation for ten years.

Elizabeth chose the path all but the most sainted would take: She elected to go to a treatment facility. Her parents helped her find SLS, which is not for those who depend on Blue Cross Blue Shield. The average cost is $400 a day, but it varies depending on how intensive the "residency," how long, and what kind of care the "resident" subscribes to. Although most leave after two to three months, Elizabeth stayed for over two years, until, according to her, her parents suggested she try a less expensive cure. She checked out of SLS and got a job in a nearby town.

Elizabeth and I spent several afternoons in the SLS building called the Carriage House talking about her story. Fluent in psychology, she attributes her shoplifting in part to childhood rootlessness. "Back and forth, back and forth," is how she described the many moves from East Coast to West Coast and back. She had a round, friendly face, brown eyes, and brown hair swept into a scrunchy. Though she complained she was gaining weight from the SLS food, she looked as though she might break in two. A hearing aid was wedged in one ear, and an iPod dangled around her neck. She wore long sleeves and pants to hide her many tattoos, orange Keds, and a green David Yurman ring, a garnet ring and bracelet, and a heart and diamond necklace. Her ears were pierced multiple times, and in one hole was a silver earring flipping the bird.

Elizabeth had shoplifted every piece of jewelry she was wearing except for that silver earring. "They got some of my stuff, and I get to keep some of their stuff," she said, adding that while she was in jail, someone threw away all her earthly possessions and "liberated" her cat. For a minute, she looked like she was going to cry. "If you boil off the sauce, you get a reduction. That's what I'm left with."

Some of Elizabeth's earliest memories involve stealing. At age four, she stole the family babysitter's toothpaste, which she felt entitled to, since the babysitter lived in her house. Next she stole a Snoopy Band-Aid from a Hallmark store, but she got caught and returned it. Her dad was at soccer practice with her brother; although her mother says she has forgotten the theft, Elizabeth remembers conspiring with her to keep it secret. During her early adolescence, Elizabeth shoplifted on and off. Stores caught her a few times, but hardly anything compared with the "380,000 other times I got away with it."

Elizabeth explained her technique. "You watch the salespeople. You

pretend. You manipulate. You act like ritzy clients. You dress appropri-
ately. You have self-confidence like 'I own the place.'"

Elizabeth shoplifted books, art supplies, and food. "I hated wasting
money on food," she said. "I would binge and purge. I would switch
prices. Shoplifting was my comfort food," she said. After graduating
from college with a 3.0 grade point average in her major, social psychology, she moved back home and enrolled as an MA candidate in
a program in exercise physiology. Two years later, she checked into a
private clinic for an eating disorder and for burning herself. She began
to recover memories of her father abusing her. A few weeks before the
shoplifting spree that landed her in jail in 2005, Elizabeth checked into
a motel. In the back of her mind, she was planning to go to the mall to
shoplift. Her parents were only paying her rent but not expenses, and so,
Elizabeth told herself, they drove her to steal. By the time her mother
visited after Thanksgiving, she had unraveled further. Although she was
going to therapy once a week, she had cycled through five hostess jobs in
four weeks. At the same time, she dreamed that she could change her life.
She planned to enroll in a graphic design program in January.

One explanation Elizabeth gave for shoplifting was that it reminded
her of the childhood years she spent shopping with her mother. "It was a
fun-loving activity: creative, comforting, fulfilling, theatrical," she said,
adding that when her mother came to visit and they went to the mall,
if her mother didn't buy her anything, she wondered, as she often did,
whether it was because she was too fat. Elizabeth, who weighed ninety-
five pounds, knew she should be grateful for her mother's company. But
the "old" feeling of "you must show me love through objects" haunted
her, even though rationally she knew that it was silly.

Elizabeth's mother returned home. A few days later, Elizabeth found
herself in a Saks Fifth Avenue in a mall. She looked around and thought,
"I want it all. The Chanel and different little boutiques like on the first
floor, purses and shoes and accessories, and I want one of each. I want
to be Paris Hilton and walk in and money is no object." She warmed up
by shoplifting from a few other stores and then returned to Saks, where

she took thirteen Burberry scarves in different shades of plaid, a bottle of Dior Addict perfume, and a Dior eye shadow and then, "exhilarated," she tried to leave the store. The moment she stepped outside, security grabbed her. She did not cry, but she felt ashamed and disappointed, although mostly she was mad at herself for being sloppy. In the security office, she signed a waiver saying that she would return the merchandise. She spent a couple of days in jail. Her parents paid the bond.

Elizabeth rode one city bus after another through the winter rain, first back to jail to get her Klonopin prescription, then to a pharmacy to refill the prescription, then to pick up her property at City Hall. The property department was closed. While riding the bus to get bonded out, she began to plan a shoplifting trip to a second mall, more suburban— "but still affluent." She craved a black coat from White House/Black Market, but she also wanted to do a return at Nordstrom—a store whose commitment to service means that it gives customers cash for returns.

By the time she arrived, Elizabeth was mad that she got caught the first time—mad at herself and mad that Saks reclaimed the merchandise. She was mad that she had to use public transportation. She shoplifted a couple of sweaters and shirts from one store and a key chain and a pair of sunglasses from another. She shoplifted from a third and bought a gift card and exchanged it for boots. A pair of Seven jeans on the second floor of Nordstrom's beckoned. By this time Elizabeth was anxious, and she could only extinguish the anxiety by shoplifting more. She started stuffing items into her shopping bags and raced to the third floor. She began to shuffle toward the exit, but two security guards stopped her. She started crying.

Two years later, Elizabeth was arrested for shoplifting $2,500 worth of Ed Hardy shirts at another mall. She was sent to a minimum-security prison. She spent over twelve months there, and since she had also violated her probation, she faced a possible ten-year sentence. The first letters she sent me edged between hope and fear. "It's then that I need to become a poster child for compulsive shoplifting. . . . If Clinton can be excused from the whole Monica L. episode because he had sex addiction,

I need to be able to voice how strong of a hold this compulsion has over me, how frightening, how powerful, how life destroying, how crippling, how uncontrollable I feel it is."

"It breaks your heart," her mother said over the phone. "She's a regular girl. But if they let her out, she'll shoplift again."

14. SHAME

Bank robberies and jewel heists command daring, skill, and technical know-how. But shoplifting is a more exhibitionist and mediagenic theft. The crime is committed during store hours, in broad daylight, in well-lit stores armed with surveillance cameras, mirrors, and shiny, reflective surfaces. Shoplifters use the body—since Genesis the site of shame—to hide shoplifted objects. I read about a shoplifter who, caught with seventy-five eight-ounce glass bottles of hand lotion stuffed in his pant legs, could not be wedged into the squad car. He was arrested as he waddled away from the police. I heard a story about a pack of shoplifters who returned to their host's apartment after a stealing expedition and started pulling one item of clothing after another from beneath their clothes, like circus clowns piling out of a VW. There is a catch-me-if-you-can quality to shoplifting.

If loss prevention can't stop it, if the law can't deter it, if drugs can't cure it, can remoralization, a society-wide strengthening of the inner check, curb the epidemic? Where fear has failed, can shame succeed?

Shame is ubiquitous, or nearly so. Among primitive peoples, the anthropologist Bronislaw Malinowski tells us, shame governs conduct. The late Japanese studies scholar Ivan Morris has written about how, from the fifth century, samurai committed hara-kiri rather than let the enemy capture them: "A warrior's self-destruction was accepted as a release from shame." Some psychologists have compared public officials' committing misdemeanors like shoplifting to those public suicides. Indeed, some shoplifters kill themselves rather than endure shame. As recently as 1982, Lady Isobel Barnett, a British surgeon and former talk-show host, committed suicide after being tried for shoplifting a can of tuna.

To the liberal believer in individual dignity, making a shoplifter parade up and down wearing a sandwich board with the logo "I Am a Thief," or posting her mug shot (on a wall, on the Internet) sounds barbaric, something a sheriff in the Deep South might do before the civil rights era. Today the South is at the front lines of so-called shame punishment—or, as some advocates often call it, "public punishment." Yet although this punishment is scorned—by legal scholars who find no evidence that it works—and questioned by psychiatrists, it is even on the rise in shameless New York and Los Angeles, where its methods include public tip lines, Facebook, MySpace, and reality TV shows.

Judge James McKenzie, one of shame's most vocal promoters, believes that it can make a difference. McKenzie lives in Dayton, Tennessee (population 6,180), in the eastern half of the state. One hour north of Chattanooga, Dayton was the site of the 1925 Scopes Monkey Trial, where a landmark battle was fought over the teaching of evolution in Tennessee schools.

In 2005, McKenzie started using shame to discipline young shoplifters. He believes that it is an attractive alternative to sending them to overcrowded prisons. "I hate liars and thieves," he said as we walked from the Rhea County Courthouse, where the Scopes trial was held, and toward Dayton Coffee Shop, a country diner wedged on Second Avenue, which slopes away from the courthouse square.

Over a lunch of grits and catfish, McKenzie explained that shame was necessary to punish shoplifters because it used to work: "When I was growin' up and I took something and I didn't pay for it my father took me back to the store and I had to be shamed. It was enough for me.

[Today] if they're first offenders, I give them an option—ten days in jail or four days walking in front of the store they stole from wearing a sign. They don't like the ten days in jail. The sign says 'I stole from Walmart. I am wearing this sign by order of Judge McKenzie.' People take pictures of it. It's a tourist attraction. And it's cut down shoplifting quite a bit."

McKenzie attributed shame's success to Dayton's size. "We're not a metro area. It's easy for people doing it to be known."

Two hundred miles west of Dayton, in Memphis, a poor black city with a tourist strip, a ring of white suburbs and malls, and a legacy of racial tragedy, the police and the retail industry used TV to shame shoplifters. In the summer of 2008, I went there to meet Andy Wise, the executive producer and host of the show, who got the idea for it when, between 2001 and 2005, the theft rate in Memphis jumped 30 percent. The year before Wise began his crusade, the *Commercial Appeal* published an article comparing FBI shoplifting statistics in different cities: Memphis's per capita rate of shoplifting was higher than that of Detroit and Los Angeles.

From January 2008 to May 2009, Wise hosted the first TV show in America dedicated to catching thieves. *Stop Thief!* ran at 10:15 p.m. every Friday night on WMCTV Channel 5, the NBC affiliate. "We had fifteen captures in thirteen months," Wise said. "It made a difference."

Just in the few days I was in Memphis, *Stop Thief!* helped the sheriff's office catch three thieves. The show begins with a talking head (Wise) telling the story of a recent shoplifting incident. One was about a TV. The "NBC scam cam" panned to the man running through the store carrying it aloft.

The voice-over shouted, "Theft like his means YOU'RE STUCK paying an extra $3.30 on every TV sold at discount merchandise stores to cover the loss."

Back to the footage of the shoplifter rushing across the screen.

More voice-over: "Think you know who he is? Where he is?"

I asked Wise whether an extra $3.30 really motivated people to call in to bust the shoplifter. It wasn't the amount of money, it was "the principle of the thing," said Wise, who attributed the high shoplifting rate in Memphis to its having "a violent inner city, liberal politics, and suburbs surrounding the city where people can go to steal." Although he said that shoplifters "cross genders and races," he conceded that there were fewer white ones. One was "a Caucasian perp," a gang member. There were three white boosters. A prolific shoplifter specialized in digital readers. The NBC legal department saw no problem with legal challenges to outing shoplifters because tips are anonymous. But television has its own rules about what makes a good shoplifting story. Whereas one segment omitted the particulars about a man who played in a local church band and shoplifted a Yamaha keyboard, another aired about the manager of a fast-food joint who shoplifted a $100 bottle of whiskey. The whiskey thief made an easier target for TV-style shame.

Stop Thief! ended, according to Wise, in part because several local stores declined to share thief-catching techniques. They thought shame worked best behind closed doors.

Using shame punishment to police shoplifting seems archaic, yet shame is the secret terror of shoplifters. Publicity is their death penalty. Although in the post–Winona Ryder, post–Terry Shulman era, some writers sign magazine pieces admitting to shoplifting, few chronic (nonwriter) shoplifters would let me use their names or incorporate significant clues to their identity. Typical was a sixty-three-year-old retired shoplifter who, when I called her back to check her story's particulars, wailed, "If you put those details in, people will know who I am!" Also typical was the self-disgust voiced by Laura MacKenzie, an eighteen-year-old who'd stolen almost $1,000 worth of merchandize from a Filene's in Manchester, New Hampshire. "For me just the word 'shoplifting' makes me cringe and feel dirty, like I need to take a shower and get it off me," she wrote me. "I cannot express how quickly I want November to come, so I can go to court, as much as I dread it, to get the whole thing over and done with." In the event, dread of exposure overcame the desire to be cleansed of her crime: On the day of her hearing she disappeared and was located five months later by the police in Florida.

Merely being connected to shoplifting by rumor evokes shame. In 2004, Janis Karpinski, the highest-ranking officer in Abu Ghraib, was accused of the crime just after she had revealed in public that she was not the only one who knew about the torture of prisoners. The army, Karpinski said, charged her with shoplifting because "they had nothing about Abu Ghraib to use against me. So they pull this flakey allegation out and use it to demote me." The army has redacted Karpinski's file so heavily that it is impossible to determine whether she shoplifted or whether the army was indeed trying to shame her to cover up a greater shame.

"Shame is the universal emotion," the psychologist Jonathan Haidt told me. "We are one of the societies that have tried to do without it."

Yet for the most part, shoplifting still falls outside the culture of confession, suggesting that in an era when speaking or writing openly about previously taboo subjects is an entrepreneurial frontier, stealing household trinkets from stores remains too shameful for words. Shoplifting may be the last species of creepy conduct of which that is true. The silent epidemic grows in a medium of silence.

CONCLUSION

According to the 2009 *Global Retail Theft Barometer*, the only worldwide survey of the crime, the percentage of losses from retail theft, including shoplifting, rose 8.8 percent in the United States during the first year of the Great Recession. It also rose in many other countries. Although this book has focused on shoplifting in the United States, where the crime has reached epidemic levels, it is currently flourishing all over the world, and will only become more prevalent as globalism intensifies. "The main crime problem that retailers faced is shoplifting," the 2010 survey proclaimed.

Shoplifting manifests itself differently in different regions, but one global trend is high-tech antishoplifting vigilantism accompanied by renewed efforts to make a case for the crime as a symbol of enduring social inequality. In 2010, a British company called Internet Eyes launched a CCTV "online instant event notification system." After paying a modest subscription fee, couch potatoes anywhere in the European Union can earn up to £1,000 a month by catching British shoplifters they see on live CCTV feeds streamed in from stores to their televisions. The company plans a worldwide launch in 2011.

In the city of York, about a year earlier, an Anglican vicar made international headlines by counseling starving congregants to shoplift. Father Tim Jones advised, "I would ask that they do not steal from small, family businesses, but from national businesses."

The British Retail Trade Consortium, the Yorkshire police, the arch-deacon of York, and Lord Carey, a former archbishop of Canterbury, condemned the vicar's advice. A representative from the British super-market chain ASDA, which is owned by Walmart, said that shoplift-ing did not steal from the rich, but from its hardworking staff. Another quipped that Jones was "one psalm short of a sermon."

Jones replied, "Walmart is a trade union recognition short of an ethical employment policy." He reached back into church history to defend himself: "What I said is nothing more than St. Ambrose, St. John Chrysostom and St. Thomas Aquinas said. What is more, everything I said . . . is backed up by all the relevant papal encyclicals of the 20th century."

Writing in the *Times Online*, Julian Baggini, author of several books on ethics, disagreed. If people shoplift when they cannot afford food, "it just mimics the theft at the top," and ultimately creates a vicious cycle, he wrote. If we all act desperately in desperate times, society will crumble.

Over the past few years in Japan, as social structures protecting fami-lies fell apart, senior citizens began to commit the biggest proportion of shoplifting; jails added low-sodium diets to their meal plans and safety bars to their cells. In Russia, where only after the fall of communism did enough products appear on store shelves for people to shoplift, one entrepreneur offers a shoplifting game: Businessmen pay a fee to run through supermarkets for a half hour, vying to steal the most expensive item without getting caught. Of course, not every incidence of shop-lifting ends with the loser taking the winner out to a lavish dinner; the crime more often results in tragedy. In 2009, on the sidewalk outside a Walmart supercenter in the city of Jingdezhen, China, five employees beat a woman to death after she allegedly shoplifted.

The opening of supermarkets, hypermarkets, and luxury shopping malls and districts worldwide has made shoplifting more visible and forced modern psychological, legal, and retail remedies to collide with corporeal solutions from ancient cultures. In Singapore, where the crime can result in a seven-year prison sentence, some shoplifters still seek spirit doctors to exorcize the stealing demon. In Dubai and Abu Dhabi, where, according to common wisdom, shoplifting has historically been low, luxury malls have begun to hire Western-style loss prevention teams and secret shoppers as well as to install state-of-the-art camera systems and tags. If the dollar amount of the shoplifted items is high enough, residents are jailed, while nonresidents have their photos posted in stores and are deported. In a throwback to the eighteenth century, when female shoplifters used skirts as props, on Zamzama Boulevard, Karachi's main shopping district, teams of burka-wearing boosters hit jewelry stores. Back in 2005, these thieves, who sewed deep pockets in their garments, were so prevalent that jewelers in one Indian city tried to ban burkas. Officials, fearing ethnic strife, declined to do so.

According to Amnesty International, chopping off a thief's hand endures in parts of the Arab world, including Iran, Saudi Arabia, and Somalia. When the Somalian al-Shabab militia amputated the right hand and the left foot of four alleged thieves in 2009, hundreds of people attended the event. But severing is not always dispensed for shoplifting. Sometimes Sharia courts rule that being turned away from heaven will suffice as a punishment.

How to punish shoplifting will always be in question. There are those who believe that, in our unstable economy, given the large thefts of white-collar thugs and high-profile con artists, and the increasing gap between the superrich and everyone else, shoplifting need only be considered in the category of moral turpitude and disciplined with community service. Others think that harsh punishment is our only chance of deterring shop-lifters. However it is sentenced, shoplifting can flash up anywhere, not just in the headlines but in front of us when we least expect it.

Walking down the street in New York on a hot summer afternoon last year, I passed one of the fruit carts that stand on nearly every corner. The vendor, a slight, bald man in his forties, rested under an umbrella. The cart was piled high with avocados, pineapples, mangoes, bananas, and plastic shell boxes of blueberries, raspberries, and strawberries. The man sold different brands than the grocery store or bodega, but everything cost half the price. There were no antishoplifting devices.

School had just let out for the year. A gang of kids, eight or nine of them, maybe in junior high, jogged up behind me in a loose pack, the smallest one at the back. They passed me, and as they passed the fruit vendor, several of them grabbed fistfuls of bananas and cherries, as if they were sampling fruit in a store. They kept jogging, screaming and laughing, eating the fruit. One of the leaders, a big girl in a white T-shirt, clutched a sprig of cherries above her head in victory. The fruit vendor began screaming. He took a few menacing steps after the kids. He would call the police. He raised his fist. He would file a police report. The gang didn't seem to hear him. Or maybe they knew his threats were empty. And when the vendor closed the distance—it didn't take more than a few large steps—instead of continuing down the block, they stopped, turned around, and began throwing chunks of the half-eaten bananas and the cherries at him. A woman walking by got caught in the fruit volley, smacked in the cheek with some cherry flesh. She only muttered a curse of disapproval and, wiping it off, kept walking.

Suddenly tiring of their game, the kids stopped throwing the fruit. They started jogging down the street again. I passed them a half block down. They were gathered around a fire hydrant, eating what fruit they had not thrown at the vendor, spitting out the pits, tossing the brown-yellow peels on the sidewalk, and laughing.

There is no single reason for shoplifting's rise. In our world, where greed and consumerism are encouraged, where social and economic inequality are swelling, and where rogues like Robin Hood are admired, the crime will continue to grow. But a serious study of shoplifting should not be content to bemoan the crime's ubiquity; it should observe that every time you walk into a store, the cost of the crime is reflected in the artillery of antishoplifting devices around you as well as the elevated prices of the items you're buying. Consumers are now suspects. And, indeed, a looming issue for the retail industry is transparency. Maybe in the future stores will make public the details of how they deal with shoplifters just as governments are publishing their secrets. But thus far, no Julian Assange has appeared to reveal the secrets of Bergdorf's, Loehmann's, and everything in between. That is not even taking into account the cost of shoplifting in human and social terms. To accept the crime as an immutable part of the global landscape means to accept that we can't always predict who is shoplifting. It is to accept that trying to get something for nothing is considered by many people the best way to survive—even flourish. Yet if we know we can never eradicate the crime, we can try to take a hard look at the costs. An investigation of where shoplifting came from and why people do it exposes important truths about our markets, our courtrooms, and our identities. It reminds us of the secrets that shoplifters and stores want to hide.

ACKNOWLEDGMENTS

I would like to thank my admirable agent, Lynn Nesbit, for taking a chance on this project and for her enduring support. Ann Godoff offered encouragement, tough-minded notes, and terrific lunches; I am especially grateful to Jack Beatty for his wisdom and patience, his thoughtful, rigorous editing, and his sense of humor. At Penguin, Lindsay Whalen was always on point. Jeanette Gingold brilliantly copyedited. Karen Abbott, Dick Babcock, Sebastian Currier, Gioia Diliberto, David Hirshey, Mary Beth Hughes, Dennis Hutchinson, Brendan McNally, Carlos Murillo, Jonathan Santlofer, Philip Weiss, Rishona Zimring, and Thad Ziolkowski were among those who kindly read drafts, sections of drafts, and provided hand-holding, ears, and other types of advice and sustenance that one needs while writing a book. In New York, Tarik O'Regan and Suki Kim, David Nasaw and Dinitia Smith, and Rob Bourne helped me with housing over the years, and Una Chaudhuri made available access to the Bobst Library, contact information of Sharia scholars, and anecdotes about the UAE. James Piecowye, the host of *Nightline DubaiEye*, sent me a podcast of a show that ran about shoplifting there. Simona Levi answered questions in Barcelona. Elise Slobodin and Catherine Scheinman made contacts in their fields available, and Michael Kinghorn translated the story of one Brazilian shoplifter in Minneapolis. Thanks to

Terence Dixon. Thanks to David Margolick for advising with legal and journalistic issues and agreeing to help on a number of occasions. Celia Lowenstein opened her Rolodex. Lee Froehlich offered various contacts and eyewitness accounts. Stephen Hacker and Michelle Turner supplied local history and gourmet dinners in Louisville. All of my assistants deserve Purple Hearts for helping me tackle obscure research problems and for facing down the mountain of papers involved in writing this book. But Liza Lichtenfeld stands out. Also thanks to Bonnie Litowitz for helping the project along from the beginning.

I owe an unpayback-able debt to Elaina Richardson, the corporation of Yaddo, and the people who make it work for their generosity during the writing of this book. David Plotz and Meghan O'Rourke at *Slate*, Toby Manhire at the *Guardian*, and Nick Goldberg at the *Los Angeles Times* published my earliest writings about shoplifting. Thanks to KGB Literary Reading Series and Suzanne Schneider for letting me read from the manuscript. Many librarians helped me track down obscure sources, including Lyonette Louis-Jacques, Allen Fisher at the National Archives, and the staff at the University of Chicago interlibrary loan department. But no one was as cheerful and responsive as Heather Jagman at DePaul University. Joe LaRocca, King Rogers, David Hill, Gail Caputo, the staff at the FMI, the staff at the National Association for Shoplifting Prevention, Jeanine Arnold at the Uniform Crime Research division of the FBI, Evan Schuman and his blog, StorefrontBacktalk, the people at Theft Talk in Portland, Richard Hollinger, and the other criminologists and scholars, loss prevention agents, physicians, and employees of antishoplifting technology organizations too numerous to name here who generously answered my questions. There are many people I interviewed whose stories in the end did not appear in this book. I would like to thank them. I would also like to thank the people whose stories I did use, especially those who allowed their real names to be used. Finally, Dean Corrin and John Culbert, the associate dean and dean of the Theatre School of DePaul University, gave me academic leaves and other forms of assistance in 2005–6, 2008–9, and 2010.

A word on how I wrote this book: People remained anonymous who wished to. Anyone whose first name I use without a surname is a pseudonym. The names of the people I describe in the groups are pseudonyms. I did not alter details, conflate scenes, or use composites, and I fact-checked everything I could, doing multiple interviews, using police reports, court documents, and the Freedom of Information Act. This book describes shoplifting's past, so historical and court records, scholarly articles, newspaper clippings, transcripts of TV shows, and rare books and manuscripts archives such as the Wellcome Library in London, the British Library, and the Hampshire Archives were part of my research as well. Loss prevention agents at the National Retail Federation, theft addicts at their conferences, and engineers at Sensormatic explained how antitheft devices operate. I went to stores and saw how things worked behind the scenes. I listened.

NOTES

INTRODUCTION

p. 5 *over a million shoplifting offenses:* United States Department of Justice, Federal Bureau of Investigation (September 2009). *Crime in the United States, 2008,* table 7.

p. 5 *more than "the losses . . . ":* quoted in Richard C. Hollinger and Amanda Adams, *2009 National Retail Security Survey,* Security Research Project (NRSS), Department of Sociology and Criminology & Law, University of Florida, Gainesville, 2009, 9.

p. 5 *800,000 people were arrested:* Ibid., table 30. This is a commonly cited figure. See also United States Department of Justice, Federal Bureau of Investigation, *Crime in the United States,* 2008.

p. 6 *Stores do not always keep good records:* To cite just one example of the complexities of record-keeping, in 2006, in a widely publicized shift from its well-known zero-tolerance position on shoplifting, Walmart decided it would only detain adults (not kids or senior citizens) who stole items valued at more than $25.

p. 6 *more than 150 percent: New York Times,* March 15, 1970, 234.

p. 6 *Between 2000 and 2004:* Uniform Crime Reports 2004, figure 2.13.

p. 6 *also climbed slightly:* Uniform Crime Reports 2008, table 7.

p. 6 *In 2008, shoplifting rose:* United States Department of Justice, Federal Bureau of Investigation, Uniform Crime Reporting Program, Supplement to Return A Record Cards limited to Group 1 & Group 2 Cities, 2008.

p. 6 *In 2009:* Uniform Crime Reports, table 23.

p. 6 *According to the National:* NASP internal report. Research since the 1970s settles on a similar number.

p. 6 *But a massive study:* C. Blanco, et al., "Prevalence and Correlates of Shoplifting in the United States: Results from the *National Epidemiologic Survey on Alcohol and Related Conditions (NESARC),*" *American Journal of Psychiatry,* 2008, table 1, 906. Thanks to Carlos Blanco for explaining this data.

p. 6 *10 percent:* American Foundation for Suicide Prevention.

p. 6 *one in forty-eight times:* NASP internal report. Other research supports this finding. In a

2009 survey, for example, British retailers estimated that only half of all shoplifting losses are identified.

p. 7 *"More Consumers, Workers Shoplift . . ."* *USA Today*, June 19, 2008, B1.

p. 7 *between 0 and 8 percent:* McElroy, "Kleptomania, A Report of 20 Cases," 652. *DSM IV Text Revision* puts the percentage of kleptomaniacs "at fewer than 5 percent." However, the *DSM IV Sourcebook* admits that where kleptomania was concerned, there is not "a consistent method of documenting phenomenology and diagnostic criteria" (p. 1015). Some forensic psychiatrists, like Will Cupchik, think it's lower. Some psychopharmacologists, like Jon Grant, suggest that it could be higher. Since the *DSM* definition of kleptomania has changed over time, and many physicians believe it is fuzzy *and* the disease is underrepresented, it is hard to say how many kleptomaniacs exist. Harvey Roy Greenberg—a psychiatrist to whom the American Psychiatric Association refers journalists who have questions about kleptomania—"does not count" himself an expert in the subject and could only say that the kleptomaniacs he had treated were "horribly troubled" (December 6, 2007).

p. 8 *$11.69 billion:* NRSS, 2009, 8, 9.

p. 8 *"crime tax":* Richard Hollinger provided me with this statistic, which appeared in *Consumer Reports*. A 2010 study by the Centre for Retail Research found that the "crime tax" in the UK is 180 pounds per family per year.

p. 8 *1.44 percent:* NRSS, 5.

p. 8 *"There has been . . .":* *Global Retail Theft Barometer*, op. cit, 41.

1. THEFT AND PUNISHMENT

p. 13 *"we're the only [species] . . .":* Author interview with John Marzluff, December 6, 2007.

p. 14 *"Then he who is a good keeper . . .":* Plato, *The Republic*, 8.

p. 15 *"Yet I lusted to thieve . . .":* Saint Augustine, *Confessions*, 32.

p. 15 *"It is not theft . . .":* Aquinas, *Summa Theologica*, 101.

p. 16 *"Be we then so hasty . . .":* More, *Utopia*, 21.

p. 16 *"thieves and robbers range abroad . . .":* Shakespeare, *Richard II*, act 3, scene 2.

p. 16 *"Attired in the form . . .":* Greene, *The Second Part of Cony Catching*, 19.

p. 17 *"Women are more subtile . . .":* Quoted in Barrère, *Dictionary of Jargon*, vol. 2, 16.

p. 17 *"Towards Night these Houses . . .":* Head, *The English Rogue*, 140.

p. 17 *"go into a mercer's shop . . .":* N. H., *The Ladies Dictionary*, 579.

p. 17 *"commonly well clad":* Head, *The Canting Academy*, 106.

p. 17 *"being born under Mercury":* This was a common belief in the sixteenth and seventeenth centuries. It is cited by Autolycus as explanation for his character in Shakespeare's *The Winter's Tale*.

p. 17 *"was so ugly . . .":* Knapp and Baldwin, *The Newgate Calendar*, Mary Frith.

p. 19 *the majority of all crimes:* The numbers are debatable, since before 1800, there were no centralized records of crime. But most historians of eighteenth-century London agree that petty theft was the most popular crime committed and that it skyrocketed in the second decade of the eighteenth century. In his magisterial *Policing and Punishment in London*, the great scholar J. M. Beattie asserts that in 1670, there were 150 people tried for property crimes in London and by the second decade of the eighteenth century, that number had shot up to around 500–600 (pp. 17–19).

p. 19 ***the third most prevalent:*** Oxley, *Convict Maids*, 45.

p. 19 ***two-thirds of all executions:*** This works out to about thirty hangings a year. The frequency of property crime and hanging for it in seventeenth-century England is well known. Gattrell estimates that 35,000 people were condemned to death between 1770 and 1830. But not all of these people were hanged. After 1660, many were transported. Most historians of crime agree that after a dip in hangings for theft in the seventeenth century, hangings rose again in the eighteenth century. J. M. Beattie, for example, surveys a sample drawn from the Old Bailey (308–9).

p. 19 ***By the 1720s:*** Like all statistics on crime prior to the nineteenth century, this is impossible to nail down; still, 10,000 is a commonly cited figure in contemporary literature. Other estimates are higher. Some recent scholars think that the number is lower. There is no doubt that the perception was of London as a city of thieves.

p. 20 ***"the devil . . .":*** Defoe, *The Fortunes and Misfortunes of Moll Flanders*, 164.

p. 20 ***"I pass'd by an apothecary's . . .":*** Ibid., 203.

p. 20 ***"I ventured into a house . . .":*** Ibid., 229.

p. 21 ***"I grew as impudent a thief . . .":*** Ibid., 201.

p. 22 ***"the increase in luxury":*** Rude, *Hanoverian London*, 96.

p. 22 ***"Indeed, could not the Thief . . .":*** Fielding, *An Enquiry*, 125.

p. 24 ***"We, who are thieves . . .":*** Godwin, *Caleb Williams*, 204.

p. 25 ***"I do not believe a fouler murder . . .":*** Sir William Meredith, quoted in Rumbelow, *The Triple Tree*, 113.

p. 25 ***"I was convinced . . .":*** Rousseau, *Confessions*, 34.

p. 25 ***"I accuse her . . .":*** Ibid., 77.

p. 26 ***"Thus I learned . . .":*** Ibid., 27.

p. 26 ***After the French Revolution:*** Early on in my research, I stumbled upon a story about shoplifting, pregnant women, and Napoleon. The story, which I first read in James D. Watson and Andrew Berry's *The Secret Life of DNA*, tells how, before Gregor Mendel discovered the science of modern genetics in the 1850s, scientists explained hereditary disease as arising from a pregnant woman's "wicked thoughts." Berry and Watson write, "On the premise that fetal malformation can result when a pregnant mother's desires are thwarted, leaving her feeling stressed and frustrated," Napoleon passed a law allowing pregnant women to do whatever they wanted, including shoplifting. Asked about his story, Berry had no idea where it came from. "I hope I haven't started an urban legend," he said.

When I posted a query on the discussion forum of the Napoleon Series, a website devoted to Napoleon, only a few scholars had heard the story. One e-sleuth found a reference to it in Bergen Evans's 1946 book, *The Natural History of Nonsense*. In this version of the story, Napoleon repealed a law passed in revolutionary France allowing pregnant women to shoplift. Evans left no notes on his sources. Lyonette Louis-Jacques, a University of Chicago law librarian, helped me track down sources describing a law passed by a revolutionary tribunal in 1795. The law, which was repealed in 1811, forgave pregnant women for committing crimes, including shoplifting, although whether it did so because of genetics, as Berry and Watson suggest, or because of ideas about the sanctity of motherhood, is not clear. And, Louis-Jacques added, Napoleon himself would not have decreed it. The myth anticipates much of our confusion about shoplifting today—is it revolutionary or apolitical? Impulsive or premeditated? A sign of strength or a symptom of women's mental frailty? Shameful because of the act itself or because it echoes greater injustices and reminds us of them?

p. 26 *"If we glance . . .":* de Sade, *Philosophy in the Bedroom*, 313.

p. 27 *"shift from a criminality . . .":* Foucault, *Discipline and Punish*, 77.

p. 27 *"Since then . . .":* Tocqueville, *Journey to America*, 242.

p. 28 *"as much Bristol . . .":* Greenberg, *Crime and Enforcement in the Colony of New York*, 61. There are scant records of punishment before the American Revolution, but Alabama, Florida, and South Carolina may have executed thieves. Since slaves were considered property, to run away was itself a form of theft.

p. 28 *"Crimes against property . . .":* Jefferson, *Memoirs, Correspondence and Miscellany*, vol. 3, 167.

p. 28 *"Nothing was valued . . .":* Wyman, *The Life and Adventures of Seth Wyman*, 7.

p. 29 *"capacious enough . . .":* Ibid., 19.

2. KLEPTOS AND REFORMERS

p. 30 *"trembled very much . . .":* Pinchard, *The Trial of Jane Leigh Perrot*, 8.

p. 31 *"lamented their being obliged . . .":* MacKinnon, *Grand Larceny*, 8.

p. 31 *"pressed to death":* Ibid., 70.

p. 31 *"pale and emaciated":* Quoted in Le Faye, *Jane Austen: A Family Record*, 125.

p. 32 *"Placed in a situation . . .":* Quoted in Austen-Leigh, *Jane Austen, Her Life and Letters*, 136.

p. 32 *"That these wretches . . .":* Le Faye, op. cit., 124

p. 32 *Not so fast:* Today there is a veritable cottage industry on Jane Leigh Perrot, her klepto-mania, and the trial's influence on Jane Austen and her oeuvre. *Jane Austen and Crime, Jane Austen in Context*, and *Women Writing About Money* are some of the titles dealing with it all.

p. 32 *new material concluding that Leigh Perrot:* Galperin, *The Historical Austen*, 38.

p. 32 *"considered Mrs. L.P. . . .":* Quoted in Honan, *Jane Austen: Her Life*, 427, n. 30.

p. 33 *"Had not the French Revolution. . .":* Quoted in Hansard, *The Parliamentary Debates from the Year 1803 to the Present Time*, 267.

p. 33 *"I trust . . .":* Quoted in Follett, *Evangelicalism*, 42.

p. 33 *"a summer airing . . .":* Romilly, *Memoirs of the Life of Sir Samuel Romilly*, 327.

p. 35 *"that morning secreted in her . . .":* De Quincey, *The Household Wreck*, 24.

p. 35 *"By that time . . .":* Ibid., 34.

p. 35 *"organ of the propensity to covet":* Gall and Spurzheim, *Physiognomical System*, 320.

p. 36 *"pilfered everywhere . . .":* Gall, *On the Function of the Brain and Each of Its Parts*, 308. Geoffrey Symcox, the leading scholar on Victor Amadeus II, never heard of the king's shoplifting but speculated that the accusation might refer to his propensity for taking over other countries.

p. 36 *"Petty larcenies . . .":* Gall, op. cit., 323.

p. 36 *klopemania:* Matthey is the originator of this term, according to many nineteenth-century cultural historians, including O'Brien, Abelson, and Whitlock.

p. 37 *"permanent but . . .":* Matthey, also quoted in Fullerton, "Kleptomania: A Brief Intellectual History," 201.

p. 37 *"instinctive, irresistible propensity to steal . . .":* quoted in Miller, *Bon Marche*, 198. Actually both Marc and Matthey use this phrase.

p. 38 *"moral insanity"*: O'Brien, "The Kleptomania Diagnosis," 70, describes this phenomenon.

p. 38 *"reign of libidinous pleasure"*: Proudhon, *What Is Property?*, 247.

p. 39 *"honest thief"*: Letulle, *"Voleuses honnêtes,"* 469.

p. 39 *"flounces of Alençon lace . . ."*: Zola, *The Ladies' Paradise*, 431.

p. 40 *"the father of her children"*: Quoted in O'Brien, op. cit., 67.

p. 40 *"The personal appearance of . . ."*: Allen, "Prize Essay on Kleptomania," 20.

pp. 40–41 *"In the slang of the day . . ."*: Bucknill, quoted in Whitlock, *Crime, Gender, and Consumer Culture,* 203.

p. 41 *"In these days . . ."*: Twain, *Essays and Sketches of Mark Twain*, 74.

p. 41 *"Moses, when he came down . . ."*: Emma Goldman, *Made for America*, 244.

p. 42 *"Negroes are sent . . ."*: Wells, *Southern Horrors and Other Writings*, 126.

p. 42 *Elaine Abelson:* There was also a play called *Kleptomania*, a "Kleptomania Rag," and other cultural artifacts.

p. 43 *"are the subjects of a . . ."*: Krafft-Ebing, *Psychopathia Sexualis*, 543.

p. 43 *"Shoplifting, which . . ."*: Lombroso, *The Female Offender*, 206.

p. 44 *"take hold of something . . ."*: Gross, quoted in Fullerton, op. cit., 202.

p. 44 *"This broad motive . . ."*: Gross, quoted in Stekel, *Peculiarities of Behavior,* 168.

p. 44 *"So-called kleptomania . . ."*: Abraham, *Selected Papers of Karl Abraham*, 355.

p. 44 *"wayward"*: Quoted in Gay, *Freud: A Life for Our Time*, 214.

p. 44 *"amazing and voluptuous spasm"*: Quoted in Shera, "Selfish Passions and Artificial Desire," 162.

pp. 44–45 *"Doubtless . . ."*: Crane, "Criminal Psychology," 451.

p. 45 *"It is not enough . . ."*: Stekel, op. cit., 267. There were several Freudians, including Sabina Spielrein and Franz Wittels, who believed that kleptomania was a type of masturbation for women, or sexual repression.

3. ABBIE HOFFMAN MEETS THE CHINESE HANDCUFFS

p. 46 *"nation's fastest-growing . . ."*: *New York Times*, December 2, 1965, 37; *Uniform Crime Reports 1965*.

p. 46 *"get marbles and erasers . . ."*: *Washington Post*, August 6, 1991, E1.

pp. 46–49 *Minasy details:* Author interviews with Minasy family and with Lillian Curry, the late Mr. Minasy's secretary, February 2006, March 2008, October 2008. Special thanks to Lillian for assisting with press clippings and scrapbooks.

p. 49 *"mixed" neighborhood:* Author interviews with Ronald Assaf, June 2006, June 2008.

p. 49 *"Jack, if we can . . ."*: Ronald Assaf, 2006.

p. 50 *"Even more than today . . ."*: Ibid.

p. 50 *Gradually stores began:* Ibid.

p. 51 *"Strengthened security . . ."*: *Kiplinger's Personal Finance*, November 1970, 5.

p. 52 *"Money Is Shit . . ."*: Rubin, *Do It*, 117.

p. 52 *"All money represents theft . . ."* Ibid., 43.

p. 52 *"The revolutionary will steal . . ."*: Powell, *The Anarchist Cookbook*, 75.

p. 53 *"If you read a New York Times . . ."*: *Rat*, February 6–23, 1970, 9.

p. 53 *"We chained . . ."*: Letter from Barney Rosset, December 29, 2008.

p. 53 *"Ripping off . . . is an act of . . .":* Hoffman, *Steal This Book*, 75.

p. 53 *"We have been shoplifting . . .":* Ibid., 7.

p. 53 *"the food tastes better":* Ibid., 10.

pp. 53–54 *"Sew a plastic bag . . .":* Ibid., 3.

p. 54 *"Specialized uniforms . . .":* Ibid., 2.

p. 54 *upward of 100,000 copies:* Figure mentioned in Jezer, *Abbie Hoffman: American Rebel*, 229. Hoffman himself claimed it sold 300,000 (*Life*, October 22, 1971, 77). In an interview with Barney Rosset on February 3, 2009, he told me the book sold "200,000 if not more" copies. But Rosset has no records.

p. 54 *"second aisle on the left . . .":* *Ramparts*, May 1971, 61.

p. 54 *"foisted on the reading public . . .":* Memo, 6/22/71, folder 4: 136; 4, Hoffman Family Papers.

p. 54 *"where a ten-year-old . . .":* Local news clipping.

p. 55 *"hip Boy Scout . . .":* *New York Times Book Review*, July 18, 1971, 19.

p. 55 *"Where the f—. . .":* *Boston Globe*, July 31, 1971. Also described in Jack Hoffman, *Run, Run, Run*, 172.

p. 55 *"Ripping Off: The New Lifestyle":* *New York Times Magazine*, August 8, 1971, 12.

p. 55 *"Stealing is stealing . . .":* Ibid., 52.

p. 55 *"Saying that shoplifting . . .":* Ibid., 52.

p. 56 *"took pictures as a hobby":* Author interviews with Eddie Davis, July 2007, August 2009; *Louisville-Courier,* June 16, 2006.

p. 56 *"I don't remember what happened":* Author interview with Edward Davis, July 2007.

p. 57 *"subjects known . . .":* Police leaflet from *Paul v. Davis*, 424 U.S. 693 file, the National Archives, Chicago.

p. 57 *"my supervisor . . .":* Edward Davis, op. cit.

p. 57 *"civil liberties, civil rights activists . . .":* Daniel T. Taylor III et al., *Plaintiffs-appellants, v. Kentucky State Bar Association et al., Defendants-appellees*, United States Court of Appeals, Sixth Circuit, 424 F.2d 478, March 26, 1970.

p. 57 *"the great William Kunstler":* Author interviews with Dan Taylor, September 2009.

p. 57 *"it was possible":* Ibid.

p. 58 *"We try harder":* Ibid.

p. 58 *"star performer in the center ring . . .":* Kentucky Court of Appeals in the Narvel Tinsley case, 494 S.W.2d, at 740.

p. 58 *"The case made it difficult . . .":* Edward Davis, August 2009.

p. 58 *"[T]he facts alleged . . .":* Quotes from the Supreme Court hearing of *Paul v. Davis*, 424 U.S. 693 aural transcript of summary and oral arguments at the Oyez Project.

p. 58 *"indiscriminate lumping . . .":* *Paul v. Davis*.

p. 59 *"(a) deprivation . . .":* Ibid.

p. 59 *"proof of any type . . .":* Ibid.

p. 59 *"These fellows . . .":* Ibid.

p. 60 *"Our photographers . . .":* Ibid.

p. 60 *"As for* **Constantineau** *. . .":* Ibid.

p. 60 *"characterized him as active . . .":* Ibid.

p. 60 *"While we have in a number . . .":* Ibid.

pp. 60–61 *"the potential . . .":* Ibid.

p. 61 *"government officials. . . .": New York Times*, November 18, 1979, 19. This case is still mentioned as one of the most important rulings from the Rehnquist court in its narrow definition of civil rights and the Constitution. Linda Greenhouse mentions it in Rehnquist's obituary, *New York Times*, September 4, 2005, 11. It is also mentioned that day in an article about the court in transition. Additionally, there has been much legal scholarship about it. Thanks to Dennis Hutchinson for putting me on to the scholarship.

p. 61 *"our so-called shoplifting case"*: Conference notes, Harry A. Blackmun Papers, Manuscript Division, Library of Congress. Special thanks to Dennis Hutchinson and his daughter, Katy, for collecting these notes.

p. 61 *"struggling"*: Connections with Rene Shaw, *Louisville Courier-Journal*, June 15, 2006, April 7, 2007.

p. 61 *"I just wish things had . . ."*: Edward Davis, op. cit., September 2009.

p. 62 *"In advocating stealing . . ."*: Rubin, *Growing (Up) at 37*, 107.

4. ROBIN HOODS 2.0

p. 63 *"'Becoming autonomous' . . ."*: The Invisible Committee, *The Coming Insurrection*, 42. This is a book that Glenn Beck called "the most evil" he ever read, a commendation that Semiotext(e) pasted on the book jacket as a blurb. Beck, along with other related publicity, drove the book into its sixth printing in 2010, when it also reached number 54 on Amazon.com and appeared on the expanded version of the *New York Times Book Review* best-seller list.

p. 63 *"People secretly . . ."*: Author interview with Stephen Mihm, January 2008.

p. 64 *"They are little more . . ."* Hobsbawm, *Bandits*, 171.

p. 64 *"Bank robbery . . ."*: Ibid., 178.

p. 64 *"I don't think shoplifters . . ."*: Author interview with Eric Hobsbawm, June 2009.

p. 64 *"Those lacy panties . . ."*: Quoted on CBS TV report, October 23, 2006.

p. 64 *"air of a Latin American . . ."* *New York Times*, June 21, 2007, F1.

p. 65 *"some Freegans . . ."*: Author correspondence with Warren Oakes, June 2008, July 2008.

p. 65 *When I called Weissman*: Author interviews with Adam Weissman, May–July 2008.

p. 67 *"Is shoplifting a Freegan issue?"*: Author interview with Madeline Nelson, July 2008.

pp. 68–69 *"Nothing compares . . ."* The Crimethink Workers Collective, *Days of War, Nights of Love*, 235.

p. 70 *"I am not taking a side . . ."*: James Trimarco (Cookie Orlando), December 2008, May 2008.

p. 70 *"My concern . . ."* **and all quotes:** E-mail exchange among Freegans about shoplifting, May–June 2008 and January 2009, kindly provided by Adam Weissman.

p. 71 *"One doesn't destroy . . ."*: E-mail correspondence with David Graeber, June 16, 2008; November 2008.

p. 72 *"the individual's rights . . ."* Author interview with Ryan Watkins-Hughes, May 16, 2006.

p. 72 *"Gen Y . . ."*: Author interview with Zoë Sheehan Saldaña, July 12, 2006.

p. 72 *"a silent protest of . . ."*: Author interview with Andrew Lynn, June 2006.

p. 73 *"It's not worth anything . . ."*: Sheehan Saldaña, op. cit.

p. 74 *"is not far off"*: Author interview with "technical anarchist," September 2009. Author interviews with Simona Levi, November 11, 2006; September 2009.

p. 75 *"our security . . .":* Author interview with A (Yomango member), October 2009.

p. 75 *the "liberated" dress:* A, op. cit.

p. 75 *"Yomango accuses . . .":* *El País*, July 5, 2002; July 6, 2002.

p. 76 *"We realized that . . .":* All quotes are from author interview with "Leo de Cerca," May 2006.

p. 78 *"changed the space":* Interviews with Bani Brufadino, Jeff Stark, Oriana, and Vince Carducci (all February and March 2008).

5. AMONG SHOPLIFTERS

p. 81 **Centre for Retail Research gender report:** Cited in the *Guardian*, July 14, 2005; "The Gender Offenders," data compiled by the Centre for Retail Research, 2010.

pp. 81–82 **Author interviews with Joshua Bamfield:** December 2007, August 2008, May 2009, July 2010.

p. 83 *"is a response to the social order . . .":* Kaplan, *Female Perversions*, 514.

p. 83 *"Very rich women . . .":* Ibid., 304.

p. 84 *"Men tend to be . . .":* Author interview with Jon Grant, November 2005.

p. 84 *"There's an immense . . .":* Author interview with Walter Vandereycken, January 2008. There is a small body of work on this subject.

p. 85 *"[Shoplifting] is less . . .":* Author interviews with Gail Caputo, October 5, 2006; November 2007; May 2008.

p. 85 *"Where are the lines . . ."* Caroline Knapp, *Appetites*, 13.

p. 85 *"Some of 'em . . .":* Author interview with Ellen Chandler, March 14, 2007.

p. 86 *40 percent:* NASP website. Some estimates are higher. Klemke, "Exploring Juvenile Shoplifting," for example, claims that 50–60 percent of young people have shoplifted.

p. 86 *"Where would we be . . ."* Author interviews with Richard Hollinger, April 24, 2006; June 2006.

p. 86 *"the next Kenneth Lay":* Ibid.

p. 87 *"It's considered . . .":* Author interview with Bill O. Hing, July 12, 2006.

p. 87 *"Every day . . ."* *Washington Post*, December 29, 2002, B7.

p. 87 *Marlene Jaggernauth:* Author interviews December 2009, July 2010.

p. 88 *"Every few months . . .":* Bamfield, op. cit.

p. 88 *"primary household shopper":* Dabney, Hollinger, and Dugan, "Who Actually Steals," 710. This phrase was invented by Read Hayes.

p. 88 *$70,000:* C. Blanco et al., "Prevalence and Correlates of Shoplifting in the United States: Results from the National Epidemiologic Survey on Alcohol and Related Conditions (NESARC)," *American Journal of Psychiatry*, 2008, table 1, 906.

p. 88 *"considerable differences . . .":* JoAnn Ray and Katherine H. Briar, "Every Twelfth Shopper: Who Shoplifts and Why?" 1987.

p. 89 *$600,000:* New York State Office of the Attorney General Civil Rights Bureau New York City Office. Macy's Security Monitor Report, November 30, 2005, 3; *New York Times*, January 14, 2005, B1.

p. 89 *"Maybe he has two wives":* Author interview with detective, February 20, 2006.

p. 90 **List of items stolen:** *State of Maryland v. Claude Allen*, Claude Alexander, Arrest Warrant on Charging Document, March 9, 2006. Interview with sources, assorted dates, 2006. Plea memorandum, *State of Maryland v. Claude Allen*, July 7, 2006. The exact items that

Allen allegedly shoplifted vary. At the District of Columbia Court of Appeals Board on Professional Responsibility Hearing before Committee Number Four, April 28, 2008, his defense counsel insisted that he was guilty of shoplifting three items. The arrest warrant on the charging document and the lp reports contend that he shoplifted many items, some of which were reported in the media.

p. 90   *"spend more time with . . .":* New York Times, February 11, 2006, A12.

p. 91   *"Why would . . .":* Washington Post, March 24, 2006, A30.

p. 91   *"For Bush's Ex-Aide . . .":* New York Times, March 13, 2006, 1, 30.

p. 91   *"Close friends . . .":* Washington Post reporter Michael Fletcher on NPR, March 13, 2006. This rumor, which was disseminated in the national media, turned out to be "nothing," as Fletcher put it in a phone conversation in 2010.

p. 92   *"I would go . . .":* Quoted in District of Columbia Court of Appeals Board on Professional Responsibility District of Columbia Court of Appeals Committee Number Four Report on Claude Allen, November 2008, 11–12.

p. 92   *"He was outraged . . .":* Quoted in the April 28, 2008, hearing. Author interviews with Thomas Goldman, December 10, 2008; December 14, 2008.

p. 92   *"We especially . . .":* Quoted in *Legal Times,* March 10, 2010.

6. HOT PRODUCTS

p. 93   *Shoplifting . . . is one of:* Author interview with Ron Clarke, June 2008.

p. 94   *most-shoplifted items:* 2003 Centre for Retail Research report.

p. 95   *"It is difficult to buy . . . ":* Author interview with Bamfield, June 2010.

p. 95   *preferred times of shoplifting: 1999 Retail Theft Trends Report.* Actually, several surveys suggest that most people shoplift on weekends.

p. 95   *"We don't drill that deep":* Author interview with Bill Greer, May 2007.

p. 95   *Steak:* Food Marketing Institute "most-shoplifted" lists 2004–2008. In 2009, the last year this survey was conducted, over-the-counter health and beauty products and pharmaceuticals took back the lead by a tiny number.

p. 96   *"I think it's unlikely . . .":* Author interview with Timothy Jones, July 2006.

p. 96   *I first heard this point of view:* Theft Offenders workshop in Queens, NY, March 25, 2006.

p. 97   *"Where was the beef . . .":* Times and Democrat, January 7, 2010.

p. 97   *"I spent time in jail . . .":* Author interview with Keith McHenry, October 2008.

p. 97   *"electronic shoplifting":* The phrase is first used in reference to Napster in 2001. Before that, "electronic shoplifting" referred to cable TV scams.

p. 97   *"Home Shoplifting Network":* Goodlatte, quoted in *Audio Week,* September 30, 2002.

p. 99   *"But somehow that wasn't the same":* Bellow, *The Adventures of Augie March,* 193.

p. 99   *"It's not a case of . . .":* Author interviews with Alan Edelstein, May, June, July 2008.

p. 99   *"it was very easy to shoplift from . . .":* Sante, quoted in *New York Times,* October 15, 2006; author interview with Sante, April 2007.

p. 99   *"I went to theft as to a liberation . . .":* Sartre, *Saint Genet: Actor and Martyr,* chapter title. The book is full of romantic allusions to thieves.

p. 99   *"a succession of cramped . . .":* Genet, *The Thief's Journal,* 170.

p. 100   *"few critics could do as much":* White, *Genet: A Biography,* 166.

p. 100 *While bibliomania:* Author interview with Nicholas Basbanes, March 2009.

p. 101 *"The moral questions . . .":* Thompson, *Notes on Bibliokleptomania*, 4.

p. 101 *"It is true . . .":* Author interview with Nicholas Basbanes, April 2009.

p. 101 *"drunk, suburban" poseur: New York Observer,* December 23, 2005. *Steal This Book* continues to be one of the most-shoplifted books. A first edition is worth more than $200.

p. 101 *Solano told me:* Author interview with Louisa Solano, March 2008, *Publishers Weekly,* January 26, 2004.

p. 101 *"behind the counter":* Author interviews with editor number 1, September 2009.

p. 102 *"my own conviction . . .":* Author interview with editor number 2, May 2009.

p. 102 *"It's the best-selling book . . .":* Author interviews with Melissa Mitchell, March 25, 2006; July 12, 2007.

pp. 102–3 *"We have no idea . . .":* Author interview with LifeWay store manager, Tennessee, March 2007.

p. 103 *"imbiber[s] . . .":* Merkin, *Dreaming of Hitler*, 239.

p. 104 *"You don't shoplift . . .":* Author interview with Barry Matsuda, summer 2008.

p. 104 *ninety-six cameras:* Author interview with Scott Barefoot, April 2006.

p. 104 *27.1 percent:* Lemire, Beverly, "The Theft of Clothes and Popular Consumerism in Early Modern England," 257.

p. 105 *The most "legendary" thefts:* Author interviews with Terence Dixon, June 2008, June 2009.

p. 106 *"Most of the stores . . .": Washington Post,* April 11, 2006, F1; letters, *Washington Post,* April 18, 206, F2.

p. 107 **Change to Win study:** February 2007.

p. 107 *"In stores where . . .":* CVS press statement about condoms, March 2007.

7. BOOSTERS

p. 109–10 **Data on Woodbury Common:** Woodbury Common website. *New York Times,* December 24, 2005, B4.

p. 110 *"It's like an open-air market . . .":* Author interview with Cliff Weeks, May 7, 2006.

p. 110 *"A center of that size . . .":* Author interview with Michele Rothstein, June 14, 2006.

p. 110 *"West, north, east, south . . .":* Author interview with Chief Robert Kwiatkowski, May 7, 2006.

pp. 110–11 **Statistics:** Kwiatkowski, ibid.; *Times Herald-Record,* February 5, 2005.

p. 110 *"always a lady":* Ibid.

p. 111 *"back to school shoplifting":* Ibid.

p. 112 *626 arrests:* Kwiatkowski. *Times Herald-Record,* December 18, 2004.

p. 112 *70 percent of the town's:* Kwiatkowski, quoted in *Times Herald-Record,* November 14, 2004.

p. 112 *"They [the mall leadership] . . .":* Author interview with Sheila Conroy, May 2006.

p. 113 *"As a major taxpayer . . .":* Michele Rothstein, May 31, 2006.

p. 113 *Boosters:* Author interviews with Tamara, Portland, Oregon.

p. 116 *"'She was so drunk . . .'":* Author interviews with Lisa Paules.

p. 116 **Oregon Department of Corrections statistics:** ODC website.

p. 117 *Theft Talk alum:* Author interviews with John Allen Bradshaw.

p. 119 *"enhancement":* Author interviews with Frank Muscato, May 2008, May 2009.

p. 119 *Now the levels range:* April 2009 legislative spreadsheet, kindly provided by Frank Muscato.

p. 120 *Committee hearing:* The Florida Senate Criminal & Civil Justice Appropriations Committee, April 15, 2009. Regular Session, April 23, 2009.

p. 120 *"My main objective . . .":* Arthenia Joyner, e-mail, October 24, 2009. Bill Analysis and Fiscal Impact Statement prepared by the Criminal and Civil Justice Appropriations Committee, April 15, 2009.

p. 120 *this sort of bill:* Author interview with John Rogers, June 2009.

p. 121 *"a man or a woman . . .": Chicago Tribune,* December 4, 1911, 9.

p. 121 *"manipulation of suckers . . .":* Sutherland, *The Professional Thief,* 3.

8. THE THRILL OF THE STEAL

p. 125 *"It's knowing I'm . . .":* Author interview with shoplifter.

p. 126 *"You begin to . . .":* Author interview with "Donna," December 28, 2006.

p. 126 *"[I shoplifted] . . .":* Author interview with "B," February 2006.

p. 126 *"Sometimes I'll . . .":* Author interview with "Christine," April 9, 2006.

p. 126 *"I was caught . . .":* Author interview with Adam Stein, August 6, 2007.

p. 127 *The self-described "elder of filth":* Author interviews with John Waters, May 2008, June 2008.

p. 128 *Nan, a red-haired:* Author interviews with "Nan," March 2006, 2007.

p. 129 *"I feel like I know . . .":* Author interview with "Doug," November 2005.

p. 129 *"I would get out of . . .":* Author interview with Scott Harris, February 2008, April 2008.

p. 130 *"the neglect of the . . .":* Katz, *Seductions of Crime,* front matter.

p. 130 *"sneaky thrill":* Ibid., table of contents, chapter 2 title.

p. 130 *"seduced and repelled . . .":* Ibid., 5.

p. 130 *"a terrible freedom":* Lesser, "The Shoplifter's Apprentice," 20.

p. 130 *"as much prey . . .":* Ibid., 13.

p. 130 *"benign even pleasurable . . .":* Ibid., 18.

p. 130 *"anything could happen now":* Ibid., 20.

p. 130 *"tingles against her palm":* Goldberg, *Bee Season,* 73.

p. 130 *"luxuriates . . .":* Ibid., 76.

p. 131 *"All she needs . . .":* Harrison, *Exposure,* 164.

p. 131 *I spent a couple:* Author interview with Kathryn Harrison, February 2006.

9. THE RISE AND FALL OF THE SHOPLIFTING CELEBRITY

p. 136 *"Even today . . .": Saturday Evening Post,* April 29, 1961; August 5, 1961.

p. 136 *"Ex-Star Seized as Shoplifter . . .": Los Angeles Times,* January 28, 1966, 1.

p. 136 *"You're under arrest": Los Angeles Times,* April 27, 1966, 1.

p. 136 *"Don't hold my arm so tight . . .":* Ibid.

p. 136 *"mystified": Los Angeles Times,* January 29, 1966, 1; *New York Times,* January 29, 1966, 13.

pp. 136–37 *"For the past thirty years . . .":* Quoted in Lamarr, *Ecstasy and Me,* 240. For more on Anthony Loder's testimony, see *New York Times,* April 23, 1966, 14.

p. 137 *"systematically and methodically": Los Angeles Times,* April 20, 1966, 30.

p. 138 *"Our president was killed . . .": Los Angeles Times,* April 26, 1966, 1.

p. 138 *"Gestapo tactics"*: *Los Angeles Times*, April 27, 1966, 1.

p. 138 *"It was my first . . ."*: Author interview with Ira K. Reiner, July 2008. The jury in the case was initially hung. After the trial, the judge publicly lambasted them about the not-guilty decision. Then Lamarr brought a lawsuit against May's, which was eventually dismissed.

p. 138 *"When poor people . . ."*: Earl Warren, quoted in Cray, *Chief Justice*, 459.

p. 138 *"spoke German"*: Author interview with Hedy Lamarr's lawyer, Joerg Jaeger, July 19, 2010.

p. 138 *"My mother used to . . ."*: *Orlando Sentinel*, August 3, 1991.

p. 139 *"Because of the Jews . . ."*: Dworkin, *Miss America, 1945*, 181.

p. 140 *"Bess Myerson on the Prowl . . ."*: *Life*, July 16, 1971.

p. 140 *"Can't I just pay . . ."*: Quoted in Alexander, *Ms.* magazine, September 1988, 43. According to Alexander, a psychiatrist is "in the news stories," an assertion I could never verify.

p. 141 *"So be it"*: *Philadelphia Daily News*, May 28, 1988.

p. 141 *"I was leaving . . ."*: *New York Times*, May 28, 1988; *New York Times*, July 16, 1988, 31.

p. 141 *"Why Do Aging Women Steal?"*: Headline quoted in the *New York Daily News*, September 2, 2001.

p. 141 *"Midlife Shoplifters . . ."*: Ibid.

p. 141 *"As for the women's movement . . .*: *Ms.* magazine, op. cit.

p. 141 *"would and would not do . . ."*: Alexander, *When She Was Bad*, ix.

p. 142 *"It could be you"*: *Life*, August 1988, 32.

p. 143 *"Anywhere else . . ."*: *New York Times*, November 10, 2002, 12.

p. 143 *"You are a lazy . . ."*: Quote from movie *Girl, Interrupted*.

p. 144 *"The security officers observed . . ."*: *The People of the State of California v. Winona Ryder*, vol. 4, 754.

p. 144 *"the actress was seen . . ."*: Los Angeles County district attorney press release.

p. 145 *"According to . . ."*: Mowbray, *National Review*, September 30, 2002.

p. 145 *"Ms. Ryder was not . . ."*: E-mail correspondence with Sandi Gibbons, press secretary for Los Angeles DA, June 2008.

p. 146 *"Your Honor, may I approach . . ."*: *The People of the State of California v. Winona Ryder*, vol. 2, 3.

p. 146 *"I need . . ."*: Ibid., 12.

p. 146 *"At one point she indicates . . ."*: Ibid., 19.

p. 147 *"I, Winona Ryder, agree . . ."*: Ibid., 21.

p. 147 *"lift up"*: Ibid., 22.

p. 147 *"My client's right . . ."*: Ibid., 123.

p. 148 *"She just appeared to be . . ."*: Ibid., vol. 3, 504.

p. 148 *"Why would they need to . . ."*: Ibid., vol. 4, 798.

p. 149 *"This is not a film performance . . ."*: *Independent* (UK), March 13, 2002.

p. 149 *"Felony Barbie"*: *Slate*, November 13, 2002.

p. 149 *"demure" attire*: *Washington Post*, November 8, 2002.

p. 150 *The full list of the items*: Exhibits listed in summary of *People of the State of California v. Winona Ryder*, obtained from the Superior Court of California, County of Los Angeles, 7, 8.

p. 150 *"We've presented the truth . . ."*: *Los Angeles Times*, November 5, 2002, 3.

p. 151 *"controversial but not in a . . ."*: *London Sun*, December 2, 2002.

p. 152 *"Shoplifting is a serious crime"*: *New York Times*, December 7, 2002, 12.

p. 152 *"She will carry the scarlet . . ."*: BBC, December 6, 2002.

p. 153 *"What's offensive to me . . ."*: CNN.com, December 10, 2002.

p. 153 *"The State can't point to . . ."*: Oral arguments for *Lockyer v. Andrade*, 583 U.S. 63 2003, 13.

p. 154 *"This still remains shoplifting . . ."*: *Ewing v. California*, 538 U.S. 11, 12.

p. 154 *"You say the principal . . ."*: Ibid., 13.

p. 154 *"She may be a double felon . . ."*: *Los Angeles Times*, December 7, 2002, 3.

10. THE SHOPLIFTING ADDICT

p. 155 *"Do you think that . . ."*: Author interviews with theft addicts.

p. 157 *"create public awareness . . ."*: NASP website; author interviews with Peter Berlin, May 16, 2006; July 26, 2006.

p. 159 *"Are we calling it a disease?"*: *The Oprah Winfrey Show*, "Living a Secret Life," November 21, 2004. Also Oprah's follow-up show, February 1, 2005.

p. 160 *"I put out the olive branch . . ."*: Author interview with Terry Shulman, November 2005.

p. 160 *"We don't do theft . . ."*: Author interview with Christine Reilly, July 2, 2006.

p. 161 *"an admitted . . ."*: *National Association for Shoplifting Prevention v. Terrence Shulman*, U.S. CIV 10-360, filed November 2008, 5.

p. 161 *"I am increasingly . . ."*: CASA newsletter, January 2009.

p. 161 *"while I'm certain . . ."*: Ibid.

p. 161 *"limit discussion"*: CASA newsletter, May 2009.

p. 161 *"Likely, we will be filing . . ."*: CASA newsletter, October 2009.

p. 162 *"You choose a target . . ."*: Author interview with Eda Gorbis, August 2, 2007.

p. 162 *"Consistent with the hypo-frontality of addictions . . ."*: J. E., Grant, S. Correia, and T. Brennan-Krohn. "White matter integrity in kleptomania: a pilot study," *Psychiatry Research: Neuroimaging* 147:233–237, Sept. 7, 2006.

p. 162 *"there's actually . . ."*: Author interview with Jon Grant, November 2005.

p. 162 *"altered state[s] . . ."*: Grant, "Dissociative Symptoms in Kleptomania," 77.

p. 162 *"slightly higher than . . ."*: Ibid., 81.

p. 163 *"would report poor quality of life"*: Grant, "Quality of Life in Kleptomania and Pathological Gambling," 34.

p. 163 *"Stealing is an . . ."*: Author interview with Marcus Goldman, February 2006.

p. 164 *"Psychopharmacology . . ."*: Author interviews with Eric Hollander, May and July 2008.

p. 164 *"We believe . . ."*: *Infinite Mind*, November 10, 2005.

p. 164 *"From my experience . . ."*: Author interview with Charlene Alderfer, April 10, 2006.

p. 165 *"We can learn . . ."*: Author interview with Steve Grant, April 2006.

p. 165 *"a set of stories . . ."*: Phillips, *The Beast in the Nursery: On Curiosity and Other Appetites*, 6.

p. 165 *"Psychoanalysis . . ."*: Phillips, *Houdini's Box: The Art of Escape*, 30.

p. 166 *"Patients . . ."*: Author interview with Adam Phillips, December 13, 2006.

p. 167 *"A man who . . ."*: Bollas, *The Shadow of the Object*, 167.

11. TO CATCH A THIEF

p. 171 *"God is a loss prevention agent"*: Author interview with Jerry Biggs, January 2006.

p. 172 *"My first time . . ."*: Author interview with LP agent number 1, February 2006.

p. 173 *"In reality . . .":* Author interview with Gregor Housdon, March 9, 2007.

p. 174 *"a postmodern stage set":* Quoted in Smith and Beaver, *The Architecture of Adrian Smith*, 22.

p. 175 *"one retailer two blocks . . .":* Author interview with Scott Barefoot, April 2006.

p. 175 *six alleged shoplifters:* Statistics about murdered shoplifters, *Houston Press*, January 8, 2004; *Arkansas Democrat-Gazette*, October 21, 2005; *Missourian*, July 27, 2007. Numerous lawsuits such as *Dillard's Department Store v. Hampton* 534 U.S. 1131, *Robinson v. Dillard's*, No. 95-61721 (Harris County, Texas, District Court).

p. 175 *"psychotic":* Quoted in *Houston Press*, op. cit.; *National Law Journal*, Monday, May 28– June 4, 2001. The details of this case make for grim reading.

p. 176 *more than one hundred:* June 8, 2003, Associated Press. Also, "Courting Customers: Assessing Consumer Racial Profiling and Other Marketplace Discrimination," A. M. Harris, G. R. Henderson, J. D. Williams (2005). "Courting Customers: Assessing Consumer Racial Profiling and Other Marketplace Discrimination." *Journal of Public Policy and Marketing, Policy Watch: Commentaries and Viewpoints* 24 (1): 163–171. In this academic paper, the authors analyzed 80 court cases between 1990 and 2002 and found 100 incidences of racial profiling. According to the *National Law Journal* article cited above, the number of false imprisonment suits from 1984 to 2001 is upward of 800.

p. 176 *"There is a persistent . . .":* Author interviews with Jerome Williams, March 14, 2007; July 15, 2010. It's also important to note that, while Dillard's says that it has subsequently provided its loss prevention associates with training in racial profiling, these deaths continue to happen.

p. 176 *"Officers get . . .":* Deposition of Byron Pierce, Dillard's, *Paula Hampton v. Dillard's*, 1997, 30.

p. 176 *"most extensive":* Author interview with Robert McCrie, February 2, 2006.

p. 177 *"not simply ones . . .":* Author interview with Brian Kreiswirth, New York assistant attorney general in the Civil Rights Bureau, June 15, 2007.

p. 177 *more than twelve thousand: New York Times*, June 17, 2003; *New York Times*, January 14, 2005. *New York State Office of the Attorney General Civil Rights Bureau New York City Office, Macy's Security Monitor Report*, November 30, 2005, 3.

p. 177 *"You shouldn't be . . .":* Brian Kreiswirth, op. cit. Some details about Macy's practices and lawsuit were also reported in the national media including, notably, the *New York Times*, January 14, 2005, B3; *New York Times*, January 15, 2005, B3.

p. 177 *thirty-two states:* This number was determined by using a table found on the International Association of Security and Investigative Regulators website and by calling state licensing bureaus.

p. 178 *"Get off me": Detroit Free Press*, August 2, 2000, September 8, 2000. Associated Press, "6 million," October 31, 2002.

p. 179 *"This can happen . . .": Houston Chronicle*, August 8, 2005; *Houston Chronicle*, August 8, 2005, 3; *Houston Chronicle*, November 5, 2005, 3; *Houston Chronicle*, November 16, 2005, 3.

p. 179 *"Today, many of the . . .":* Author interview with Senator Hansen Clarke, July 2008. Thanks to Al Cavasin for background. These events were covered by local media as well as national sources like CNN and the *New York Times*.

p. 180 *"best practice":* Author interviews with Joe LaRocca, February 2006, June 2006.

p. 180 *"there will always be . . .": LPInformation Convention Daily*, June 2005.

p. 181 *"I see what . . .":* LPinformation.com.

p. 181 *"Picking up a piece of . . .": Stores* magazine, May 2006, 24.

p. 182 *"Signaling to others . . .":* Author interview with Read Hayes, May 16, 2006.

p. 182 *"If you walk into Neiman Marcus . . .":* Author interview with Shaun Gabbidon, February 2006.

p. 182 *Along with nineteen:* All quotes from Wicklander-Zulawski seminar, attended July 23, 2006.

12. THE FUTURE OF LP

p. 185 *1 million:* There may be as many as 4 million cameras in the United Kingdom. These statistics are widely debated. However, one thing everyone agrees on is that the number of CCTV cameras in the United Kingdom is far greater than anywhere else in the world. The estimated number of video cameras in the United States is 6 million.

p. 185 *shoplifting rose:* British Retail Consortium, *British Crime Survey 2009.*

p. 185 *5.4 percent: Global Retail Theft Barometer 2009,* table 1.3, 20.

p. 185 *"To CCTV or Not to CCTV":* Armitage, "A Review of Current Research into the Effectiveness of CCTV Systems." Martin Gill and Ron Clarke have also expressed skepticism about CCTV as a shoplifting-prevention tool.

p. 186 *"lead to a Wild West . . .":* Author interview with Jay Stanley, April 2008.

p. 186 *"Which is more . . .":* Author interview with David Riccio, September 2008.

p. 187 *"If you see a young lady . . .":* Quote from Walmart training video, May 2006.

p. 187 *"Senior citizens, they don't . . .":* Author interview with Gregor Housdon, March 9, 2007.

p. 188 *According to the Department . . . :* Quoted in Schor, *The Overspent American,* 40.

p. 188 *"You can tell . . .":* Author interview with LP agent, April 2006.

p. 188 *"A lotta academic . . .":* Author interview with LP agent, April 2006.

p. 191 *"everything I could . . .":* Author interviews with Patrick Sobalvarro, July 3, 2006; August 20, 2006.

p. 192 *"like a velociraptor":* Author interview with Rodney Brooks, January 2008.

13. THE DISEASE IS INCURABLE

p. 196 *"This is not a morality play":* Author interview with the head of the shoplifting program of the National Curriculum Training Institute, a for-profit concern based in the West, March 31, 2006.

p. 196 *"going at it from the . . .":* Author interviews with Lisa Paules, May 2006, February 2007.

p. 197 *"dewy-eyed liberal":* Samenow, *Inside the Criminal Mind,* xviii.

p. 197 *"a person may . . .":* Ibid., 11.

p. 197 *"I am actively working . . .":* E-mail exchange with Steve Houseworth, 2008.

p. 197 *"If you have kleptomania . . .":* Author interview with Steve Houseworth, April 2006.

p. 197 *"People are taught . . .":* Ibid.

p. 198 *"Don't make it complex":* Theft Talk website.

p. 198 *"'You must have eighteen . . .'":* Author interview with Steve Houseworth, op. cit.

p. 198 *"nationally recognized . . .":* These statistics come from NASP's website. A 2007 Washington State study of recidivism and NASP's methods actually showed a slightly higher recidivism rate, in which 7.3 percent were not rearrested for shoplifting or any other crime. By contrast, Theft Talk's recidivism rate hovers at around 13 percent. But it's also worth mentioning that there has not been much scholarly work done on the subject. And what has been done targets young people, who might stop sooner or later or hide their shoplifting more effectively after a time anyway. Further, some criminological studies have concluded that education programs fail to help reduce shoplifting recidivism.

p. 201 *"Kleptomania has no definitive . . .":* Koran, Aboujaoude, et al., "Escitalopram Treatment of Kleptomania," 422.

p. 202 *as "a core . . .":* Hollander, "Brain Function in Impulsive Disorders," 2003.

p. 202 *"There was a decision . . .":* Author interview with Hollander, op. cit.

p. 202 *"None of these suggestions. . .":* *Psychiatric Times* 26 (8), June 26, 2009.

p. 204 *works "like a recipe":* Author interview with counselor, February 2006.

p. 204 *"I confess my heart was . . .":* Dostoevsky, *The Gambler*, 28

pp. 208–9 *"It's then that I need to . . .":* Letter from "Elizabeth."

14. SHAME

p. 211 *"A warrior's self-destruction . . .":* Morris, *The Nobility of Failure*, 15.

p. 211 *"I hate liars . . .":* Author interview with Judge James McKenzie, spring 2006.

p. 211 *"When I was growin' up . . . ":* Ibid.

p. 212 *Memphis's per capita:* Cited in *Memphis Commercial Appeal*, June 31, 2007.

p. 212 *"We had fifteen . . .":* Author interview with Andy Wise, July 2010.

p. 213 *"the principle of the thing":* Author interview with Andy Wise, July 2008.

p. 213 *"If you put . . .":* Author interview with "Sandy," December 2008.

p. 213 *"For me . . .":* Correspondence with Laura McKenzie, 2006.

p. 214 *"they had nothing . . .":* Author interview with Janis Karpinski, June 2008.

p. 214 *"Shame is the . . .":* Author interview with Jonathan Haidt, October 8, 2006.

CONCLUSION

p. 215 *8.8 percent:* 2009 *Global Retail Theft Barometer*, 10. While 2010 studies both in Europe and in the United States showed some declines in shoplifting rates in some countries and attributed them, in some cases, to increased security, it will be many years before we have accurate long-term data or know what these year-to-year rises and falls mean.

p. 215 *"The main crime problem . . .":* summary of 2010 *Global Retail Theft Barometer*. www .retailresearch.org.

p. 216 *"I would ask . . .":* *York Press*, December 21, 2009.

p. 216 *"one psalm short . . .":* *York Press*, December 22, 2009.

p. 216 *"Walmart is . . .":* *York Press*, December 23, 2009.

p. 216 *"it just mimics the theft at the top . . .":* *Times Online*, December 23, 2009.

SELECTED BIBLIOGRAPHY

ARCHIVES

Hoffman Family Papers, Archives and Special Collections at the Thomas R. Dodd Research Center, University of Connecticut at Storrs.

Lyndon Johnson Archives, the National Archives, Houston.

BOOKS AND ARTICLES

Abelson, Elaine. *When Ladies Go A-Thieving: Middle-Class Shoplifters in the Victorian Department Store*. New York: Oxford University Press, 1992.

Abraham, Karl. *Selected Papers of Karl Abraham*. London: Karnac Books, 1988.

Alexander, Shana. *When She Was Bad: The Story of Bess, Hortense, Sukhreet & Nancy*. New York: Random House, 1990.

Allen, Henry. "Prize Essay on Kleptomania, with a View to Determine Whether Kleptomaniacs Should Be Held Disqualified for Employments of Trust and Authority under the Crown." London: H. Balliere, 1869.

Anonymous. *Counterfeit Ladies: The Life and Death of Mary Frith and the Case of Mary Carleton*. Edited and with notes by Janet Todd and Elizabeth Spearling. New York: New York University Press, 1994.

——. *Evasion*. Atlanta, GA: CrimethInc., 2001.

——. *The Life and Death of Mrs. Mary Frith*. Cambridge, UK: Chadwick-Healy, 1997.

Aquinas, Thomas. *Summa Theologica*. New York: Christian Classics, 1981.

Armitage, Rachel. "A Review of Current Research Into the Effectiveness of CCTV Systems in Reducing Crime," Community Safety Practice Briefing. London: Narco Crime and Social Policy Section, 2002.

Augustine. *Confessions of St. Augustine*, vol. 2. New York: Penguin Classics, 1961.

Austen-Leigh, William, and Richard Arthur Austen-Leigh. *Jane Austen: Her Life and Letters, A Family Record*. Middlesex: Echo, 2009.

Balsam, R. H. "Women of the Wednesday Society: The Presentations of Drs. Hilferding, Spielrein, and Hug-Hellmuth." *American Imago* 60: 303–342.

Barrère, Albert Marie Victor. *Dictionary of Jargon, Slang, Cant, Embracing English and American*, vol. 2. Detroit: Gale Research Company, 1889.

Basbanes, Nicholas. *A Gentle Madness: Bibliophiles, Bibliomanes, and the Eternal Passion for Books*. New York: Holt Paperbacks, 1999.

Baumer, Terry, and Dennis P. Rosenbaum. *Combating Retail Theft: Programs and Strategies*. Boston: Butterworth, 1984.

Beattie, J. M. *Policing and Punishment in London 1660–1750: Urban Crime and the Limits of Terror*. New York: Oxford University Press, 2003.

Bellow, Saul. *The Adventures of Augie March*. New York: Penguin, 1996.

Blanco, C., J. Grant, N. M. Petry, H. B. Simpson, A. Alegria , S. M. Liu, and D. Hasin. "Prevalence and Correlates of Shoplifting in the United States: Results from the *National Epidemiologic Survey on Alcohol and Related Conditions (NESARC)*. *American Journal of Psychiatry*, July 2008, 165(7), 905–913.

Bolaño, Roberto. *The Savage Detectives*. Translated by Natasha Wimmer. New York: Farrar, Straus and Giroux, 2008.

Bollas, Christopher. *The Shadow of the Object: Psychoanalysis of the Unknown Thought*. New York: Columbia University Press, 1989.

Cameron, Mary. *The Booster and the Snitch: Department Store Shoplifting*. Glencoe, IL: Free Press of Glencoe, 1964.

Camhi, Leslie. "Stealing Femininity: Department Store Kleptomania as Sexual Disorder." *Differences*, 5, 1, 1993.

Caputo, Gail. *Out in the Storm: Drug-Addicted Women Living as Shoplifters and Sex Workers*. Boston: Northeastern University Series on Crime and the Law, 2008.

Clarke, Ronald V. *Hot Products: Understanding, Anticipating, and Reducing Demand for Stolen Goods*. Policing and Reducing Crime Unit, London: Home Office, 1999.

Colquhoun, Patrick. *A Treatise on the Police of the Metropolis*, 1806 (Patterson Smith Reprint Series in Criminology, Law Enforcement, and Social Problems, Publication No. 42, 1969).

Conner, Lawrence A. *The Shoplifters Are Coming: Don't Steal This Book*. Wilmington, DE: Reports, 1980.

Cooper, David. *The Lessons of the Scaffold: The Public Execution Controversy in Victorian England*. Ohio: Ohio University Press, 1974.

Crane, Harry. "Criminal Psychology." *Psychological Bulletin* 9, 12 (1912), 451–453.

Cray, Ed. *Chief Justice: A Biography of Earl Warren*. New York: Simon & Schuster, 1997.

CrimethInc. Ex-Workers' Collective. *Days of War, Nights of Love: Crimethink for Beginners*. Atlanta, GA: CrimethInc., 2000.

Cupchik, Will. *Why Honest People Shoplift or Commit Other Acts of Theft: Assessment and Treatment of Atypical Theft Offenders—A Comprehensive Resource for Professionals and Laypersons*. Toronto: Will Cupchik, 1997.

Dabney, Dean, Richard C. Hollinger, and Laura Dugan. "Who Actually Steals: A Study of Covertly Observed Shoplifters." *Justice Quarterly* 21:4 (2004), 693–728.

Defoe, Daniel. *The Fortunes and Misfortunes of Moll Flanders*. New York: Penguin Classics, 1989.

"Dillard's Under Scrutiny." *60 Minutes*, March 25, 2001.

Dostoevsky, Fyodor. *The Gambler*. Translated by Andrew R. Macandrew. New York: Norton, 1997.

Durkheim, Émile. *A Moral Education*. New York: Dover, 2002.

Dworkin, Susan. *Miss America, 1945: Bess Myerson's Own Story*. New York: Newmarket Press, 1987.

Esquirol, Jean-Étienne-Dominique. *Mental Maladies: A Treatise on Insanity*. New York: Hafner, 1965.

Fielding, Henry. *An Enquiry into the Causes of the Late Increase of Robbers and Related Writings*. Connecticut: Wesleyan University Press, 1988.

———. *Jonathan Wild*. New York: Oxford World's Classics, 2008.

———. *Tom Jones*. New York: Norton Critical Editions, 1994.

Follett, Richard R. *Evangelicalism, Penal Theory, and the Politics of Criminal Law Reform in England: 1808–30*. New York: Palgrave Macmillan, 2001.

Foucault, Michel. *Discipline and Punish: The Birth of the Prison*. New York: Vintage, 1995.

———. *Madness and Civilization: A History of Insanity in the Age of Reason*. London: Routledge, 1989.

Frank, Robert H. *Luxury Fever: Why Money Fails to Satisfy in an Era of Excess*. New York: Free Press, 1999.

Frank, Robert H., and Philip Cook, *The Winner-Take-All Society: Why the Few at the Top Get So Much More Than the Rest of Us*. New York: Penguin, 1996.

Freud, Anna. *The Writings of Anna Freud*, vol. 4. New York: International Universities Press, 1966.

Friedman, Lawrence M. *Crime and Punishment in American History*. New York: Basic Books, 1994.

Fullerton, R. A. "Psychoanalyzing Kleptomania." *Marketing Theory* (December 2007), 7, 4, 335–352.

Fullerton, R. A., and Girish N. Punj. "Kleptomania: A Brief Intellectual History." *Romance of Marketing*, 11, 2003.

———. "Shoplifting as Moral Insanity, Historical Perspectives on Kleptomania." *Journal of Macromarketing* (June 2004), 24, 1, 8–16.

Gabbidon, Shaun L. "Racial Profiling by Store Clerks and Security Personnel in Retail Establishments: An Exploration of 'Shopping While Black.'" *Journal of Contemporary Criminal Justice* (August 2003), 19, 3, 345–364.

Gall, Franz Joseph. *On the Function of the Brain and Each of Its Parts, with the Possibilities of Determining the Instincts, Propensities, and Talents of the Moral and Intellectual Distinctions of Men and Animals*. Boston: Marsh, Capon, and Lyon, 1835.

Gall, Franz Joseph, and Carl Spurzheim. *The Physiognomical System of Drs. Gall and Spurzheim*. London: Craddock and Joy, 1815.

Galperin, William H. *The Historical Austen*. Philadelphia: University of Pennsylvania Press, 2002.

Gamman, Lorraine P. *"Discourses on Women and Shoplifting: A Critical Analysis of Why Female Crime Mythologies Operate to Legitimate the Incompatibility between Female Gender Roles and the Active Idea of Women as Agents of Crime."* PhD diss., Middlesex University, UK, 1999.

Gattrell, V.A.C. *The Hanging Tree: Execution and the English People 1770–1868*. New York: Oxford University Press, 1996.

Gay, John. *The Beggar's Opera*. London: New Mermaids, 2010.

Gay, Peter. *Freud: A Life for Our Time*. New York: Random House, 1988.

Genet, Jean. *The Thief's Journal*. New York: Grove Press, 1994.

Godwin, William. *Caleb Williams, or Things As They Are*. New York: Penguin Classics. 2003

Goldberg, Myla. *Bee Season: A Novel*. New York: Anchor, 2001.

Goldman, Emma. *Made for America, 1890–1901*, vol. 1. Edited by Candace Falk. Berkeley: University of California Press, 2003.

Goldman, Marcus. *Kleptomania: The Compulsion to Steal—What Can Be Done?* Far Hills, NJ: New Horizon Press, 1998.

Gottlieb, Gabriele. "Theatre of Death: Capital Punishment in Early America 1750–1800." PhD diss., University of Pittsburgh, 2005.

Grant, Jon. "Dissociative Symptoms in Kleptomania." *Psychological Reports* 94 (2004), 77–83.

———. "Quality of Life in Kleptomania and Pathological Gambling." *Comprehensive Psychiatry* 46, 1, (January–February 2005), 34–37.

Grant, Jon, S. W. Kim, and Gregory Fricchione. *Stop Me Because I Can't Stop Myself! Taking Control of Impulsive Behavior*. New York: McGraw-Hill, 2004.

Green, Martin Burgess. *Otto Gross: Freudian Psychoanalyst, 1877–1920*. Lewiston, NY: Edwin Mellen Press, 1999.

Greenberg, Douglas. *Crime and Enforcement in the Colony of New York 1691–1776*. Ithaca, NY: Cornell University Press, 1976.

Greene, Richard. *The Second Part of Cony Catching*. London: Printed by John Wolfe for William Wright, 1591.

Haber, Izak. "An Amerika Dream: A True Yippie's Sentimental Education, or How Abbie Hoffman Won My Heart and Stole 'Steal This Book.'" *Rolling Stone*, September 23–30, 1971, 32–3.

Hansard, T. C., ed. *The Parliamentary Debates from the Year 1803 to the Present Time*. London: 1821.

Harrison, Kathryn. *Exposure*. New York: Warner Books, 1993.

Head, Richard. *The Canting Academy, The Devil's Cabinet Opened*. London: Printed by F. Leach for Mat. Drew, 1673.

———. *The English Rogue Described in the Life of Meriton Latroon*. London: 1666 (2010 reprint Nabu Press).

Hobsbawm, Eric. *Bandits*. New York: New Press, rev. ed., 2000.

Hoffman, Abbie. *Soon to Be a Major Motion Picture*. New York: Putnam, 1980.

———. "Steal This Author, in Which the Master of the Rip-Off Learns That Anything He Can Do, Big Business Can Do Better." *Harper's*, May 1974, 42–49.

———. *Steal This Book*. New York: Four Walls, Eight Windows Press, 2002.

Hoffman, Jack. *Run, Run, Run: The Lives of Abbie Hoffman*. New York: Putnam, 1994.

Hollander, Eric, and Jennifer Greenberg. "Brain Function in Impulsive Disorders." *Psychiatric Times*, March 1, 2003.

Hollinger, R., and A. Adams. *2009 National Retail Survey Final Report*. Gainesville, FL: University of Florida, 2010.

Honan, Park. *Jane Austen: Her Life*. London: Weidenfeld and Nicholson, 1987.

Howson, Gerald. *Thief-Taker General: Jonathan Wild and the Emergence of Crime and Corruption as a Way of Life in Eighteenth-Century England*. London: Transaction Publishers, 1988.

Hyde, Lewis. *The Gift: Imagination and the Life of Property*. New York: Vintage, 2007.

———. *Trickster Makes This World: Mischief, Myth, and Art*. New York: North Point Press, 1999.

Invisible Committee. *The Coming Insurrection*. Cambridge, MA: Semiotext(e), 2009.

Jefferson, Thomas. *Memoirs, Correspondence and Miscellany*, vol. 3. Gutenberg e-book.

Jezer, Marty. *Abbie Hoffman: American Rebel*. New Brunswick, NJ: Rutgers University Press, 1994.

Kaplan, Louise J. *Female Perversions: The Temptations of Emma Bovary*. New York: Anchor, 1991.

Katz, Jack. *Seductions of Crime: Moral and Sensual Attractions in Doing Evil*. New York: Basic Books, 1988.

Keneally, Thomas. *A Commonwealth of Thieves: The Improbable Birth of Australia*. New York: Anchor Books, 2007.

Klemke, Lloyd. "Exploring Juvenile Shoplifting." *Sociology and Social Research* 67(1), 59–66.

———. *The Sociology of Shoplifting: Boosters and Snitches Today*. London: Praeger, 1992.

Knapp, Andrew, and William Baldwin, eds. *The Newgate Calendar: Comprising Interesting Memoirs of the Most Notorious Characters Who Have Been Convicted of Outrages on the Laws of England Since the Commencement of the Eighteenth Century: with Occasional Anecdotes and Observations, Speeches, Confessions, and Last Exclamations of Sufferers*. Electronic resource.

Knapp, Caroline. *Appetites: Why Women Want*. Berkeley: Counterpoint, 2003.

Koestler, Arthur. *Reflections on Hanging*. New York: Macmillan, 1957.

Koran, L., A. Aboujaoude, et al. "Escitalopram Treatment of Kleptomania, an Open-Label Trial Followed by a Double-Blind Discontinuation." *Journal of Clinical Psychiatry* (March 2007), 422–7.

Krafft-Ebing, Richard von. *Psychopathia Sexualis*. Translated and edited by Domino Falls. London: Velvet Publications, 1997.

Lamarr, Hedy. *Ecstasy and Me: My Life as a Woman*. New York: Fawcett Crest, 1968.

Le Faye, Deidre. *Jane Austen, A Family Record*. Cambridge: Cambridge University Press, 2003.

Lasègue, Charles. "Le vol aux étalages." *L'Union médicale* (December 27, 1879), 989–995.

Lemire, Beverly. "The Theft of Clothes and Popular Consumerism in Early Modern England." *Journal of Social History* 24, 2 (Winter 1990), 255–276.

Lesser, Ellen. *The Shoplifter's Apprentice*. New York: Washington Square Press, 1990.

Letulle, M. *"Voleuses honnêtes."* *Gazette médicale de Paris* (October 1, 1887), 469–471.

Lombroso, Cesare. *Criminal Woman, the Prostitute, and the Normal Woman*. Durham, NC: Duke University Press, 2004.

Lombroso, Cesare, and William Ferrero. *The Female Offender*. Introduction by Douglas W. Morison. Colorado: Littleton Press, 1980.

McElroy, S. E., H. G. Pope, and J. I. Hudson. "Kleptomania, A Report of Twenty Cases." *American Journal of Psychiatry* 148 (1991), 652–7.

MacKinnon, Frank Douglas. *Grand Larceny: Being the Trial of Jane Leigh Perrot*. London: Oxford University Press, 1937.

McLynn, Frank. *Crime and Punishment in Eighteenth-Century England*. Oxford: Oxford University Press, 1991.

Makari, George. *Revolution in Mind: The Creation of Psychoanalysis*. New York: Harper, 2008.

Marc, C.C.H. *De la folie, considérée dans ses rapports avec les questions médico-judiciares*. Paris: J. B. Baillère, 1840.

Matthey, André. *Nouvelles recherches sur les maladies de l'esprit*. Paris: Pachoud, 1816.

Mayhew, Henry, et al. *The London Underworld in the Victorian Period: Authentic First-Person Accounts by Beggars, Thieves, and Prostitutes*. Mineola, NY: Dover, 2005.

Merkin, Daphne. *Dreaming of Hitler: Passions and Provocations*. New York: Crown, 1997.

Michaels, Jennifer E. *Anarchy and Eros: Otto Gross' Impact on German Expressionist Writers*. Utah Studies in Literature and Linguistics. New York: Peter Lang, 1983.

Middleton, Thomas. *The Life and Death of Mrs. Mary Frith, Commonly Called Moll Cutpurse*. Edited and with notes and an introduction by Randall S. Nakayama. New York: Garland, 1993.

Mihm, Stephen. *A Nation of Counterfeiters: Capitalists, Con Men, and the Making of the United States*. Cambridge, MA: Harvard University Press, 2008.

Miller, Michael B. *The Bon Marché: Bourgeois Culture and the Department Store, 1869–1920*. Princeton: Princeton University Press, 1988.

Mitchell, Stacy. *Big-Box Swindle: The True Cost of Mega-Retailers and the Fight for America's Independent Businesses*. Boston: Beacon Press, 2006.

Morris, Ivan. *The Nobility of Failure: Tragic Heroes in the History of Japan*. New York: Farrar, Straus and Giroux, 1988.

Murphy, Daniel J. I. *Customers and Thieves: An Ethnography of Shoplifting*. Aldershot, UK: Gower, 1986.

N., H. *The Ladies Dictionary: Being a General Entertainment of the Fair Sex, A Work Never Before Attempted in English*. Eds. John Considine and Sylvia Brown. London: John Dunton, 1694. Reprint, Ashgate, 2010.

O'Brien, Patricia. "The Kleptomania Diagnosis: Bourgeois Women and Theft in Late Nineteenth-Century France." *Journal of Social History* 17 (Fall 1983), 65–7.

Oxley, Deborah. *Convict Maids: The Forced Migration of Women to Australia*. Cambridge: Cambridge University Press, 1997.

People of the State of California v. Winona Ryder. Reporter's transcript, vols. 1–5.

Pepys, Samuel. *Diaries*. New York: Modern Library, 2001.

Phillips, Adam. *The Beast in the Nursery: On Curiosity and Other Appetites*. New York: Vintage, 1999.

Phillips, Adam. *Houdini's Box: The Art of Escape*. New York: Pantheon, 2001.

Pinchard, John. *The Trial of Jane Leigh Perrot, Wife of James Leigh Perrot, Esq, Charged with Stealing a Card of Lace*. Printed by and for Thomas Norris, Bath, England, 1800.

Plato. *The Republic*. New York: Hackett, 1992.

Powell, William. *The Anarchist Cookbook*. New York: Lyle Stuart, 1970.

Preston, Jennifer. *Queen Bess: An Unauthorized Biography of Bess Myerson*. Chicago: Contemporary Books, 1990.

Proudhon, Pierre. *What Is Property? Or an Inquiry into the Principle of Right and of Government*. Edited by Donald R. Kelley and Bonnie G. Smith. Cambridge Texts in the History of Political Thought. Cambridge: Cambridge University Press, 1994.

Ray, JoAnn, and Katherine H. Briar. "Economic Motivators for Shoplifting." *Journal of Sociology and Social Welfare* 15(4), 177–189.

Ray, JoAnn, and Katherine H. Briar. "Every Twelfth Shopper: Who Shoplifts and Why?" *Social Casework* 68 (April), 234–239.

Rees, Sian. *The Floating Brothel: The Extraordinary True Story of an Eighteenth-Century Ship and Its Cargo of Female Convicts.* New York: Hyperion, 2002.

Richardson, Chad, and Rosalva Resendiz. *On The Edge of the Law: Culture, Labor, and Deviance on the South Texas Border.* Austin: University of Texas Press, 2006.

Romilly, Samuel. *Memoirs of the Life of Sir Samuel Romilly,* vol. 2. London: John Murray, 1827.

Rubin, Jerry. *Do It: Scenarios of the Revolution.* New York: Touchstone, 1970.

———. *Growing (Up) at Thirty-Seven.* New York: M. Evans, 1976.

Rudé, George. *Hanoverian London: 1714–1808.* London: Secker & Warburg, 1971.

Rumbelow, Donald. *The Triple Tree: Newgate, Tyburn, and Old Bailey.* Edinburgh: Harrap Publishers, 1982.

Sade, Marquis de. *Justine, Philosophy in the Bedroom, and Other Writings.* New York: Grove Press, 1990.

Samenow, Stanton. *Inside the Criminal Mind.* New York: Crown, 1984.

Sartre, Jean-Paul. *Saint Genet: Actor and Martyr.* New York: Pantheon, 1983.

Saussure, Raymond de. "The Influence of the Concept of Monomania on French Medico-Legal Psychiatry (from 1820 to 1840)." *Journal of the History of Medicine* (1946), 365–97.

Schor, Juliet, B. *The Overspent American: Upscaling, Downshifting, and the New Consumer.* New York: Basic Books, 1998.

Segrave, Kerry. *A Social History of Shoplifting.* Canada: McFarland Press, 2001.

Sennewald, Charles A. *Shoplifters vs. Retailers: The Rights of Both.* Chula Vista, CA: New Century Press, 2000.

Sennewald, Charles A., and John H. Christman. *Shoplifting.* London: Butterworth Heinfeld, 1992.

Shera, Peta Allen. "Selfish Passions and Artificial Desire: Rereading Clérambault's Study of 'Silk Erotomania.'" *Journal of the History of Sexuality* 18, 1 (January 2009), 158–78.

Shulman, Terrence Daryl. *Something for Nothing: Shoplifting Addiction and Recovery.* West Conshohocken, PA: Infinity, 2003.

Sloman, Larry. *Steal This Dream: Abbie Hoffman and the Countercultural Revolution in America.* New York: Doubleday, 1998.

Smith, Adrian, and Robin Beaver. *The Architecture of Adrian Smith, SOM, Towards a Sustainable Future.* Mulgrave, Australia: Images Publishing Group, 2007.

Smith, Eliza. *Memoir of Eliza Smith, Who Was Transported for Shoplifting, Written by Herself, with Some Introductory Remarks, by Mary J. Knott, the Author of "Two Months at Kilkee," Etc.* Dublin: Hardy and Walker; London: Edmund Fry & Son, 1839.

Stekel, Wilhelm. *Peculiarities of Behavior: Wandering Mania, Dipsomania, Kleptomania, Pyromania, and Allied Impulsive Acts.* Translated by James S. Van Teslaar. London: Williams & Norgate, 1925.

Sutherland, Edwin H. *The Professional Thief.* Chicago: University of Chicago Press, 1988.

Thomas, Dana. *Deluxe: How Luxury Lost Its Luster.* New York: Penguin, 2008.

Thompson, Lawrence Sidney. *Notes on Bibliokleptomania.* New York: New York Public Library Edition, 1944.

Tocqueville, Alexis de. *Journey to America.* Translated by George Lawrence; edited by J. P. Mayer. New Haven, CT: Yale University Press, 1960.

Tucker, George Herbert. *Jane Austen, the Woman: Some Biographical Insights.* New York: Palgrave Macmillan, 1995.

Twain, Mark. *Essays and Sketches of Mark Twain*. New York: Barnes & Noble Books, 1995.

Underhill, Paco. *Why We Buy: The Science of Shopping*. New York: Simon & Schuster, 2004.

Wells, Ida B. *Southern Horrors and Other Writings; The Anti-Lynching Campaign of Ida B. Wells, 1892–1900*. Edited by Jacqueline Royster. Boston: Bedford Books, 1996.

White, Edmund. *Genet: A Biography*. New York: Vintage, 1994.

Whitlock, Tammy. *Crime, Gender, and Consumer Culture in Nineteenth-Century England*. Surrey, UK: Ashgate, 2005.

Widiger, Thomas. *DSM IV Sourcebook*, vol. 2. Arlington, VA: American Psychiatric Publishing, 1996.

Williams, Jerome. Expert witness testimony, *Crutchfield v. Dillard's*. November 30, 2005.

Wyman, Seth. *The Life and Adventures of Seth Wyman, Embodying the Principal Events of a Life Spent in Robbery, Theft, Gambling, Passing Counterfeit Money, Etc*. Manchester, NH: J. H. Cate, 1803.

Zola, Emile. *The Ladies' Paradise*. Translated by Brian Nelson. New York: Oxford World Classics, 2008.

INDEX

ABOUT THE AUTHOR

Rachel Shteir is the author of the award-winning *Striptease: The Untold History of the Girlie Show* and *Gypsy: The Art of the Tease*. Her writing has appeared in the *New York Times, Slate, The Guardian, Playboy,* the *Los Angeles Times, Chicago Magazine,* the *Chicago Tribune,* and elsewhere. She is an associate professor and the head of the BFA program in criticism and dramaturgy at the Theatre School at DePaul University.